The *bals publics* at the Paris Opéra

in the Eighteenth Century

LA FOLIE

OU LE GÔUT DU SIÈCLE,

Allemande,

Contredanse Nouvelle.

Dansée pour la 1.re fois au Bal de l'Opera le 14 feb. 1765.

DÉDIÉE

à Madame la Comtesse

DE BEAUMONT D'AUTICHAMPS,

Par son très respectueux serviteur le S.r CAREL,

M.re de Danse Prof. du Roi, auteur de la 1.ere Strasbourgeoise

Prix 4.f la Feuille.

A PARIS

Chez M.elle Castagnery rue des Prouvaires
à la Musique Royale.

Avec Privilege du Roy.

Nous la nommons 1.re tant à cause qu'elle à été la premiere Con-
-tredanse Allemande connue à Paris et nommée telle par M.r Carel,
que pour la distinguer d'une autre faite sur le même air par M.r
Deshayes. Voyez les écrits de ces M.rs dans le Mercure des mois
d'Aoust et Octobre 1764. 2.e Vol. page 197.

Frontispiece: Title page of *La Folie ou le Goût du Siècle* from Sieur de La Cuisse, *Suite du Répertoire des bals, ou 3.e recueil des airs et figures des meilleures et plus nouvelles contredanses* (Paris, 1765), cahier 17, feuille 89.

The *bals publics* at the Paris Opéra

in the Eighteenth Century

*To Marijke —
with cheers and love,
R.O.*

by

Richard Semmens

DANCE & MUSIC SERIES No. 13

PENDRAGON PRESS

HILLSDALE, NY

For Wendy Hilton,

whose artistry, scholarship, and teaching

inspired a generation.

Library of Congress Cataloging-in-Publication Data

Semmens, Richard Templar.
　The *bals publics* at the Paris Opera in the eighteenth century / by Richard Semmens.
　　p. cm. — (Dance & music series ; no. 13)
Includes bibliographical references (p.　) and index.
　1. Balls (Parties)—France—Paris—History—18th century. 2. Opera de Paris—History—18th century. I. Title. II. Dance and music series ; no. 13.
　GV1748 .S46 2003
　793.3'8'094436109033—dc22

　　　　　　　　　　　　2003018442

Table of Contents

List of Illustrations

List of Tables and Charts

ACKNOWLEDGEMENTS

Many have offered me generous advice on this project, and for all of it I am truly grateful. While I cannot possibly acknowledge everyone who has informed my (still growing) understanding of the ideas presented in this book, I am hopeful that most of these individuals will recognize their invaluable contribution, however imperfectly I have grasped and transmitted it. A few deserve special mention. Elizabeth Bartlett has responded to my cries for help with consistent and generous cheerfulness, and has found items in the labyrinth of Parisian archives that simply escaped me. Mary Cyr took time from her own important research to inspect, and to report on a collection of posters at the *Bibliothèque de l'Opéra*. Patricia Rader offered me a detailed description of an important collection of contredanses in the New York Public Library. And Veerle Fack provided me with information on a poster housed in the university library in Ghent. Lisa Philpott, music reference librarian at the University of Western Ontario, has discovered leads, and has offered more support and encouragement than she probably realizes. Finally, I must acknowledge the generous efforts of Diane Winkleby. She read drafts of, and provided me with editorial advice on some of the chapters of this book with exceptional attention to detail. I thank all of you.

Richard Semmens

London, Ontario, 2002

CHAPTER ONE

Context, Genesis, and Overview

On peut assurer que ce Bal forme un des plus beaux Spectacles que l'on puisse voir, tant par le coup d'oeil de la Salle où il se donne, que par la quantité de Masques qu'il attire pendant tout le Carnaval.

Jean-Baptiste Durey de Noinville (1757)[1]

The range of possibilities for what was termed a 'ball' in eighteenth-century France was quite considerable. At one extreme were the carefully regulated *bals parés* that featured designated dancers who performed in a prescribed order, one couple at a time. A detailed account of the idealized conduct of such balls is provided in Pierre Rameau's *Le Maître à danser* of 1725, in the chapters entitled 'Du cerémonial que l'on observe au grand Bal du Roy', and 'De la manière de se conduire avec politesse dans les Bals reglez.'[2] Although Rameau's prescriptions were not always followed to the letter, in most respects his account is confirmed by many descriptions of royal balls of the time.[3] Equally sumptuous, but often less formal than the *bal paré*, were the *bals masqués*. These frequently included elaborately staged *mascarades* that were written, composed, choreographed, and then rehearsed well in advance of the event. Such a ball was given on Saturday, 13 February 1700, in the apartments of Monsieur (the King's brother) at Versailles, and was described in the *Mercure galant* as follows:

> ...He [Monsieur] conceived of seven different little masquerades that interrupted the ball in half-hour intervals. All of these diversions were so well planned, and blended into the ball so naturally, that the instrumentalists [immediately] changed tunes as soon as they saw the arranged masquers entering, and played the airs to which those who were in the masquerade were to dance...[4]

---

[1][Jean-Baptiste Durey de Noinville], *Histoire du théâtre de l'Académie Royale de Musique en France depuis son établissement jusqu'à présent*, 2nd ed. (Paris, 1757), 164. 'Rest assured that this ball represents one of the most beautiful spectacles that can be seen, as much for the sight of the room in which it is held, as for the numerous masquers it attracts throughout all of Carnaval.'

[2]Pierre Rameau, *Le Maître à danser* (Paris, 1725), 49-54, 55-59.

[3]For a useful review of the procedures of the early eighteenth century, see Rebecca Harris-Warrick, 'Ballroom Dancing at the Court of Louis XIV,' *Early Music* 14/1 (1986), passim.

[4]*Mercure galant*, février (1700), 209-10: '...il avoit imaginé sept differentes petites Mascarades qui interrompirent le Bal de demi-heure en demi-heure. Tous ces divertissemens étoient si bien concertez, & se mesloient si naturellement au Bal, que les Violons changeoient d'air dès qu'ils voyoient entrer les Mascarades concertées, & joüoient les airs sur lesquels devoient danser ceux qui composoient ces Mascarades...'

At the other extreme, a 'ball' could also be an entirely impromptu affair, when, for instance, there was a spontaneous decision to dance (to what accompaniment it is not always clear) at a small gathering. Once more, the *Mercure galant* offers a useful example from 20 March 1707: 'Supper finished, *Monseigneur*, the duc de Berry invited one of the Ladies of the company, and danced a menuet with her. There then was formed a kind of little ball that was not long, but most diverting.'[5] The duc de Luynes provides a later example in his *Mémoires*, describing just such an occasion on 19 February 1744, as a 'bal de hasard.'[6] Throughout this colourful range of possibilities, the repertoire of dance styles and types was generally shared: *danses figurés*, new as well as old, for couples; and group dances, among which the *contredanse* reigned supreme.

There was another kind of ball, however, that has not yet been examined systematically by scholars. The *bals publics* held at the opera house in Paris were initiated not long after Louis XIV's death in early September 1715, and they were to remain popular until the collapse of the *ancien régime*. The *bal public* was unlike any other kind of ball, although, as with the *bals masqués*, those in attendance were expected to be masked. It privileged group dances, or those that lent themselves to group performance. And although it seems not to have been susceptible to the careful planning and orderly regulation that obtained at some private balls, the *bal public* began to exert a profound influence on social dancing more generally. I am struck in this regard by another remark by the duc de Luynes, who in 1744 recorded that 'the dancing masters of Versailles have obtained permission from M le comte de Noailles [first Gentleman of Louis XV's bedchamber] to mount a public ball like that of the Opera. It costs a 'petit écu' to enter. The ladies are admitted without paying.'[7] Even though de Luynes goes on to mention that not many attended, his observation still signals a dramatic shift in social modelling, for during Louis XIV's reign it was the royal balls at Versailles (and elsewhere) that had set the standards for all others. By 1744, apparently, the public balls at the Opera had become a model, and they were beginning to affect the courtly routines of Versailles.

[5]*Mercure galant*, mars, 1707, 393: 'Le soupé fini, Monseigneur le Duc de Berry prit une des Dames de la compagnie & dança un Menuet avec elle. Il se forma ensuite une espece de petit Bal qui ne fut pas long, mais qui fut fort divertissant.'

[6]Norbert Dufourcq, ed. *La musique à la cour de Louis XIV et de Louis XV d'après les Mémoires de Sourches et Luynes* (Paris, 1970), 79.

[7]ibid., 78: 'Les maîtres à danser de Versailles ont obtenu permission de M. le comte de Noailles de donner un bal public comme celui de l'Opéra; l'on paye un petit écu pour y entrer. Les femmes y sont reçues sans payer; mais il y en va fort peu.'

It might well be wondered how 'public' a ball could have been in Louis XV's Versailles of 1744. Certainly it must have involved a fairly élite group, suggesting to me that the meaning of 'public' (at least so far as a ball was concerned) must have been quite different from what we might expect today. Just *how* different is highlighted in an account of the dancing prowess of a young Louis XV preserved in the *Mercure galant* of February 1719.[8] The account locates the event in the 'grand Cabinet de Sa Majesté' in the Tuilleries Palace, and describes a sequence of carefully rehearsed dances, relating how only those young courtiers who had become *habitués* of the nine-year old monarch had the honour of dancing along with him. Louis, of course, opened this ball himself, dancing a menuet with the duc de Bouflers, and he also performed a number of what the *Mercure* describes as '*entrées de Balet.*' In total, it is reported, the proceedings lasted about an hour and a half. Before concluding with a listing of those besides the King who had danced, the account notes that 'this ball was public' ('ce Bal fut public'). It was deemed public, perhaps, because without a formal invitation spectators were permitted to look on. Among several meanings of 'public' found in Furetière's *Dictionnaire universel* of 1690 is the following: 'an assembly open to everybody, or to certain selected individuals.'[9] In the case of the 1719 performance at the Tuilleries, the 'public-ness' of this ball seems not to have been a matter of *who danced* but rather of *who looked on.* It is interesting that in the 1727 edition of Furetière's dictionary the definition drops the final clause, 'or to certain selected individuals,' leaving for its entry 'an assembly open to everybody.'[10] I am tempted to infer that the impact the public balls had on evolving social structures may have had a role to play in the modification of this definition of 'public.' For the duc de Luynes in 1744, then, the 'public-ness' of a ball at Versailles may have had something to do with attending as an on-looker, without a formal invitation. But there is more to it than just this.

The idea of a *bal public*—a ball that was neither restricted to a select group of invited participants and observers, nor carefully planned out in advance—was no novelty when the first public balls took place at the Opera in early 1716. Masked balls during carnival in Louis XIV's reign had frequently been 'open' to anyone who wanted to attend. Indeed, in the early years of the eighteenth century the balls hosted by the duc and duchesse du Maine at their chateau in Sceaux are reported to have attracted huge crowds, and to have created unbroken lines of carriages coming and

---

[8]*Mercure galant*, février, 1719, 138-9.

[9]Antoine Furetière, *Dictionnaire universel, contenant generalement tous les mots francois*, (Den Haag, 1690); modern ed. by Pierre Bayle (Paris, 1978).

[10]*Dictionnaire universel, contenant generalement tous les mots francois*, rev. 2nd ed. by Jean-Baptiste Brutel de la Riviere (Den Haag, 1727); reprint ed. (Hildesheim, 1972).

going between the chateau and Paris until the morning hours.[11] Descriptions of these affairs make it clear that they were intended to be public, although because transportation to Sceaux was required, and because those in attendance were typically attired in resplendent costumes, one suspects that only those of some means could afford to go. Sometimes, however, masked balls that were designed to be 'private' became 'public' simply because they attracted large numbers of uninvited guests who, evidently, were nevertheless graciously received. A ball given by the Ambassador of Spain in February 1703 is a case in point, for it is reported that 'to avoid a throng,' he had wished it to be a private ball, but that he 'was obliged to render it public, and open his doors to all the masquers.'[12] Although I cannot document it in any conclusive way, my guess is that in balls that were public (either by accident or design) much of the dancing was performed chiefly by those of high social standing. The account of the Spanish Ambassador's ball just cited, for example, goes on to report that 'people arrived at all hours, and no one departed, and when the musicians had stopped, masquers of the highest standing set themselves to dancing to songs.'[13]

In other respects, however, the *bals publics* at the Paris Opera must have seemed a great novelty. Among the more unusual of their features was the fact that they were not 'hosted.' And because they were not hosted, an important aspect of social interaction became modified: the opportunity to assert rank.[14] Attending a private ball, on the other hand, especially if one were invited as one of the designated dancers, was an honour that had to be undertaken with both care and panache. It offered great opportunities for solidifying or enhancing one's social standing, but, of course, it also presented the potential for losing status. And hosting a private ball, especially one for a prince or princess, was a most impressive way of attracting attention and (hopefully) favour to oneself. Both the invited guest and the host of a private ball were engaging in what many social historians have come to term 'conspicuous consumption,' or they were exchanging what many sociologists since Pierre Bourdieu have called 'cultural capital.'[15] At a

---

[11]Accounts can be found in the *Mercure galant*, février (1700), 154-194, where several carnival balls from this year are described.

[12]*Mercure galant*, février, 1703, 265-6: '...Mr l'Ambassadeur, qui pour éviter la cohuë, n'avoit voulû donner qu'un Bal particulier, fut obligé de le rendre public, & de faire ouvrir ses portes à tous les Masques...'

[13]ibid. '...On y entroit à toute heure & personne n'en sortoit & lorsque les Violons eurent cessé, les Masques du premier rang se mirent à danser aux chansons.'

[14]The social issues surrounding public balls will be explored more fully in chapter four.

[15]See, for example, the influential sociologist, Norbert Elias, *The Court Society*, English trans. by Edmund Jephcott (London, 1983), especially Chapter 5, 'Etiquette and Ceremony.' See further, Sharon Kettering, 'Gift giving and Patronage in Early (cont.)

public ball, however, conspicuous consumption and cultural capital were of no immediate concern, because there was no host and no invited guest. Another novel feature of the *bal public* was also a consequence of the absence of a host: there was an admission charge of six pounds. And yet another novelty was the venue for the public ball—the 'Salle de l'Opéra' in the *Palais-Royal*. To be sure, the *Palais-Royal* had become a familiar location for carnival balls, especially during Monsieur's lifetime (he died in 1701),[16] but they had never been held in the theatre. The principal novelty of this new venue was that it was almost certainly the largest ballroom any of those attending the first public balls had ever seen.[17]

Although new for Parisians, a ball at an opera house was not unprecedented elsewhere. Irene Alm recently has reviewed the circumstances giving rise to the mounting of *feste di ballo* in Venetian opera houses in the final decades of the seventeenth century.[18] As early as 1678 a *festa di ballo*—a type of Venetian ball in which the principal dancing involved a lengthy and elegant promenade—was hosted by the Grimani brothers in their recently opened Teatro S. Giovanni Grisostomo after the final operatic performance of that carnival season. By the 1680s, Alm notes, other Venetian theatres were following suit.[19] Her chief aim in this study is to account for the proliferation of ballroom scenes in Venetian opera of the period (through the early years of the eighteenth century), and to examine how the routines of Venetian balls became modified under the influence of French dancing practices. She argues not only that evolving ballroom procedures can be traced accurately through the operas of the time, but also that holding *feste di ballo* immediately after an operatic performance served to 'dissolve the boundaries'[20] between the world of the theatre and that of Venetian

---

Modern France,' *French History* 2 (1988), 131-51. For a recent reassessment of the Elias 'model,' see Jeroen Duindam, *Myths of Power. Nobert Elias and the Early Modern European Court*, English trans. by Lorri S. Granger and Gerald T. Moran (Amsterdam, n.d. [c1994]). For a useful introduction to Bourdieu's sociology, see David Swartz, *Culture & Power. The Sociology of Pierre Bourdieu* (Chicago, 1997), especially chapter 5, 'Habitus: A Cultural Theory of Action,' 95-116.

[16]The *Mercure galant* gives numerous accounts of balls hosted by Monsieur. See for example February, 1694, 329: 'Le Carnaval s'est passé à l'ordinaire. Monsieur a donné le bal cinq ou six fois au Palais Royal avec la magnificence qui est naturelle à ce grand Prince...'

[17]The venue will be described in detail in chapter two .

[18]Irene Alm, 'Operatic Ballroom Scenes and the Arrival of French Social Dance in Venice,' *Studi musicali* 25 (1996), 345-371.

[19]ibid., 350, 352.

[20]ibid., 357.

carnival festivities. It is a convincing argument, and, because these Venetian opera balls would have been known to at least some Parisians of the early eighteenth century,[21] the *festa di ballo* might have served as a model for the *bal public* at the Paris opera house.[22] If it did serve as a model, however, it did so only in limited respects. For one thing, opera balls in Paris were not restricted to a single evening at the conclusion of carnival season, but rather were mounted several times between November and the beginning of Lent each year. Perhaps more significantly, the practice in Paris, at least in the formative years of the public ball, does not seem to have been linked in any way to operatic performances. As we shall see, moreover, the opera stage in Paris was not just transformed figuratively from an operatic scene into a 'real life' ball; it was physically altered in striking ways.

A kind of public ball, sometimes held in an opera house, that seems more closely related to the *bal public* is the English masquerade. In their article on Johan Jacob Heidegger in *The New Grove Dictionary of Opera*, Elizabeth Gibson and Winton Dean note that masquerades were mounted by the Swiss born impresario at the Haymarket Theatre (Handel's opera house until 1735) 'as early as 1711.'[23] I have been unable to corroborate the claim. Certainly the vogue for masquerades in London seems to have been sufficiently well established by 1711 to provoke a satiric outburst from John Addison in *The Spectator*.[24] Addison has his correspondent decry 'the Midnight Masque, which has of late been very frequently held in one of the most conspicuous Parts of the Town,' but the precise location is not revealed. However, an advertisement in an issue of *The Spectator* from late April, 1711 (No. 53), announces a Masquerade to be held on the first of May at the 'Old Spring Garden' in Charing Cross.[25] Another popular establishment offering masquerades about this time was at Lambeth-Wells.[26] If there were also masquerades at the Haymarket in 1711, they were mounted

---

[21]Alm notes that there are numerous reports preserved in the *Mercure galant* from the 1670s, 80s and 90s that offer detailed descriptions of the Venetian opera ball. ibid., 348.

[22]Another possible Venetian model is the *festino*, a ball (not at the theatre) for which there was an admission charge. See ibid., 348, n8.

[23]*The New Grove Dictionary of Opera*, ed. by Stanley Sadie, 4 vols. (London, 1992), s.v. 'Heidegger, Johan Jacob' by Elizabeth Gibson and Winton Dean. Winton Dean has recently become even more emphatic about Haymarket masquerades mounted 'by at least 1711 (if not earlier).' See Stanley Sadie, ed., *The New Grove Dictionary of Music and Musicians*, 2nd ed. (London, 2001), s.v. 'Heidegger, Johan Jacob' by Winton Dean.

[24]See No. 8, Friday, March 9, 1711 in *The Spectator*, 5 vols., ed. with an Introduction by Donald F. Bond, (Oxford, 1965), I, 35-38.

[25]Cited in ibid., 36.

[26]ibid.

without recourse to even a single advertisement in *The Daily Courant*. This seems an unlikely (but not impossible) proposition, given that the managers of that theatre regularly placed notices in the newspaper for their other offerings throughout the year, and, indeed, they did so for many years to come.[27] Judith Milhous and Robert D. Hume, moreover, have been unable to find any documentary evidence of masquerades at the Haymarket before early March 1717 in their recent study of Heidegger's management of the theatre.[28] The evidence they have uncovered, while quite convincing, is in need of modest revision. Referring to part 2 of *The London Stage*,[29] they write: 'on 2 March opera-goers were advised that they would find the stage "in the same Magnificent Form as it was in the Ball."'[30]

The notice, in fact, is from *The Daily Courant* (No. 4794) of Saturday, 2 March 1717. It informed the public that the performance of Alessandro Scarlatti's *Pyrrhus and Demetrius* on that evening was to be 'without Scenes, the stage being in the same Magnificent Form as it was in the Ball.' It is not the earliest notice of this kind from 1717. On Monday, 18 February *The Daily Courant* gave notice of a ball to be held at the Haymarket the following Thursday (21 February).[31] The day after this ball, the newspaper reported that the performance of Handel's *Amadis* [that is, *Amadigi di Gaula*] on Saturday, 23 February was also to be presented without sets, because the Haymarket stage was still laid out for a ball: 'This Opera will be performed without Scenes, The Stage being in the same Form as it was Yesterday in the Ball.'[32] Indeed, it is possible to conjecture a 'miniature season' of public balls at the Haymarket in the nearly two-week period of 21 February to 4 March. I can only say for certain, however, that there was a ball on Thursday, 21 February 1717 (the one just mentioned), and on Monday, 4 March 1717. A notice from the latter date reads 'NB The doors will be open'd this Evening for the Ball at 8 a Clock, the Coaches are desired to come to the Hay-Market, and the Chairs up Market Lane from the Pall Mall.'[33] Although I cannot document it, it seems quite possible

[27]In a slightly later period, for example, a ball held at the Haymarket on 23 January 1729 was advertised every day (except Sunday) for a week in *The Daily Courant* (Nos. 8508-8514), including the day of the ball.

[28]Judith Milhous and Robert D. Hume, 'Heidegger and the Management of the Haymarket Opera, 1713-17,' *Early Music*, 27/1 (1999), 65-84. See especially, 66-67.

[29]*The London Stage. Part 2: 1700-1729*, ed. by Emmett L. Avery, 2. vols. (Carbondale, Illinois, 1960).

[30]ibid, 67.

[31]The same notice was printed the following day. See *The Daily Courant*, No. 4784, Tuesday, 19 February 1717.

[32]*The Daily Courant*, No. 4787, Friday, 22 February 1717.

[33]*The Daily Courant*, No. 4795, Monday, 4 March 1717.

that there were two additional balls, one on Monday, 25 February (a week before the last ball of the 'season'), and a second on Thursday, 28 February (a week after the first). I believe this is a real possibility because the only two operatic performances during this period (both on Saturdays) were mounted without sets. The following calendar of events at the Haymarket during the period lays out the only known activities in the theatre, drawn from *The London Stage* and *The Daily Courant*, and conjectures the possible timing of two additional balls.

Date	Event	Remarks
Thursday, February 21	Ball 1	announced in *Daily Courant* on February 18 and 19
Friday, February 22	_____	
Saturday, February 23	*Amadis*	no sets
Sunday, February 24	_____	
Monday, February 25	[Ball 2]	conjectural
Tuesday, February 26	_____	
Wednesday, February 27	_____	
Thursday, February 28	[Ball 3]	conjectural
Friday, March 1	_____	
Saturday, March 2	*Pyrrhus and Demetrius*	no sets
Sunday, March 3	_____	
Monday, March 4	Ball 4	announced in *Daily Courant* on March 4

It does not seem likely that a ball held on 21 February would still be cause for a performance of *Pyrrhus and Demetrius* to be given without sets on 2 March, nine days later. (It will be recalled that the Scarlatti opera was offered without sets, not in anticipation of the ball on 4 March, but rather because the stage was 'in the same Magnificent Form as it *was* [my italics] in the Ball.') Intervening balls on the 25th and 28th, on the other hand, could easily have made a compromise to operatic productions a practical necessity. This all suggests to me that some elaborate ballroom décor was set up in the theatre by 21 February,[34]

---

[34]An idea of what the Haymarket Theatre looked like, c1724, when decked out for one of Heidegger's balls is presented in a painting attributed to Giusseppe Grisoni in the collection of the Victoria and Albert Museum in London. It is reproduced in plate 24b of *Survey of London*, vol. xxx, *The Parish of St. James Westminster, South of Piccadilly*, part 1 (London, 1960).

and left in place until after 4 March to accommodate a short-lived masquerade ball season.

Even if there were only two of them, it is certain that public balls were mounted in the London opera house by February 1717. But what were they like? The earliest account that I have been able to locate is from late 1717. In the so-called *Portland Manuscripts*, the following is found in a letter, dated 5 December 1717:

> This night Mr. Hydiker's ball was at the Haymarket, which though in mask, is not now to be called masquerade. The Archbishop and Bishop of London are said to concern themselves in the reconciliation. Mr. Petkum began his ball with the Duchess of Kingston, and after dancing, carried them down to a great apartment, where were several shops with signs...[35]

Because these masquerades attracted derelicts and prostitutes, as well as fashionable society,[36] they became the object of intense and protracted criticism by the clergy and the press. There were endeavours to have them suppressed that proved unsuccessful, in part because their organisers started to call them 'balls' (hence the reference in the above passage to a 'reconciliation'), and in part because they enjoyed royal favour.[37] George I was evidently a regular and enthusiastic participant.[38]

If Gibson and Dean are correct in their dating of masquerades at the Haymarket Theatre as early as 1711, then it seems very likely that an English precedent had a direct influence on the establishment of *bals publics* in Paris. My researches, however, suggest that the success of public balls at the opera house in Paris (and perhaps Venice) provided the model for Heidegger, who only after 1716 saw good financial potential in moving the very popular masquerades into his theatre. As

---

[35]*Report on the Manuscripts of his Grace the Duke of Portland, preserved at Welbeck Abbey*, vol. 5 (Norwich, 1899), 545.

[36]In an advertisement for the ball mentioned in n27 the following is given: 'If any Subscriber or others have any tickets to spare, they are desired not to give them to their servants, but to send them to the Office in the Hay-Market, where the money they cost shall be returned, to prevent their falling into bad hands.' *The Daily Courant*, No. 8513, Wednesday, 22 January 1729.

[37]For a review of this evidence, see the critical notes in Antoine-François [l'Abbé] Prévost, *Mémoires et aventures d'un homme de qualité qui s'est retiré du monde*, Tome V, 'Séjour en Angleterre,' ed. by Mysie E. I. Robertson (Paris, 1934), 158.

[38]In *Manuscripts of the Duke of Portland*, vol. 7, 419-27, is given a piecemeal account of a masquerade held in February, 1726, that is described variously as 'infamous' and 'fruitful of quarrels.' The writer notes that 'great patrons of that diversion were scandalized at it,' but also that 'His Majesty is said to have stayed at the masquerade until five in the morning, and had a hot supper for him in one of the little rooms.'

it turned out, he became very wealthy from their profits.[39] Yet more important than the issue of priority is the fact that the masquerade and the *bal public* shared many features.

•   •   •   •   •

The Establishment of the *bal public*

Some sources claim that original permission to mount public balls was accorded to the syndics of the Paris Opera in the new Letters Patent for the *Académie Royale de Musique* of 1713.[40] The copies of this document that I have examined contain no such reference.[41] Nevertheless, the earliest permission I have located—one dated 30 December 1715—also claims that the Letters Patent of 1713 did, in fact, include a provision for public balls at the Opera. It reads in part:

> Regulation concerning permission accorded to the Académie Royale de Musique to give public balls. Paris, 30 December 1715. His Majesty, having found it good that the Académie Royale de Musique should give a public ball, in consequence of the Privilege accorded to it by Letters Patent of 8 January 1713, and confirmed by those of 2 December 1715, on the advice of the Duc d'Orléans, his uncle, Regent of the Kingdom, orders the following...[42]

The document goes on to present six articles governing the general conduct of the public balls at the Opera, including the requirement that everyone must pay, even for re-admission to the spectacle. There

---

[39]The Abbé Prévost reports that 'une seule Masquerade rapporte à M. Heydegger plus de deux milles guinées.' *Mémoires*, 73.

[40]The claim is made, for example, in Mulsane (pseud.), 'Les bals de l'Opéra,' *La Chronique Musicale. Revue bi-mensuelle de l'art ancien et moderne* 2/10 (1873), 198.

[41]Among others, see the copy preserved in the *Archives nationales*, Paris, reproduced in Marcelle Benoit, *Musiques de Cour. Chapelle, Chambre, Écurie, 1661-1733* (Paris, 1971), 248-52; and that given in [Durey de Noinville], *Histoire de l'Académie Royale de Musique*, 108-117.

[42]Reproduced in [Durey de Noinville], *Histoire de l'Académie Royale de Musique*, 148: 'Concernant la Permission accordée à l'Académie Royale de Musique, de donner des Bals publics. A Paris, le 30 Décembre 1715. Sa Majesté ayant trouvé bon que l'Académie Royale de Musique donnât un Bal public, en conséquence du Privilège à elle accordé par Lettres Patentes du 8 janvier 1713 & confirmées par celles du 2 Décembre 1715 de l'avis de Monsieur le Duc d'Orléans son oncle, Régent du Royaume, a ordonné & ordonee ce qui suit.'

are also regulations concerning attire: everyone is to be masked, and no swords or other arms are permitted. Personal conduct is addressed as well—violence, insult or indecency are strictly prohibited at the doors, and in the ballroom.[43] A complete transcription of this *Règlement* as transmitted by Durey de Noinville in 1757 is given in Appendix 1.

The inaugural public ball took place on 2 January 1716, just three days after the *Règlement* was proclaimed, but there had already been some discussion of the approaching event among diarists of the time. In the autumn of 1715 Saint-Simon wrote:

> Le Chevalier de Bouillon... proposed to the Regent that there be a public ball at the Opera three times a week, to be entered by paying, either masked or unmasked, and where the loges would give a convenient view of the ball to those who did not wish to enter the room. It is believed that a public ball, protected as is the Opera on the days of performances, would be safe from mishaps, and would reduce the number of those disreputable little balls scattered around Paris, where such mishaps so often occur.[44]

And on the 14th of November the marquis de Dangeau commented:

> M Le duc d'Orléans has given M d'Antin permission to put on balls at the Opera three times a week this winter. One will attend only in a mask, and by paying. The chevalier de Bouillon will get a pension of two thousand 'écus' for this affair, on which he has offered advice.[45]

On the one hand, then, the establishment of public balls can be seen as the creation of a kind of institution to be administered and regulated by the Opera, and on the other (but to a lesser extent) as a response to some perceived public 'need,' championed, it seems, by the chevalier de Bouillon, and sanctioned by the Regent. I will argue in chapter three that the financial situation of the Opera also played a critical role in the decision to institute the *bal public*.

---

[43]ibid., 148-50.

[44]A. de Boislisle, ed. *Mémoires de Saint-Simon* (Paris, 1879-1928), vol. 29, 296-7: 'Le chevalier de Bouillon... proposa au Régent qu'il y eût trois fois la semaine un bal public dans la salle de l'Opéra, pour y entrer en payant, masqué et non masqué, et où les loges donneroient la commodité de voir le bal à qui ne voudroit pas entrer dans la salle. On crut qu'un bal public, gardé comme l'est l'Opéra aux jours qu'on le représente, seroit sûr contre les aventures, et tariroit ces petits bals borgnes épars dans Paris, où il en arrivoit si souvent.'

[45]E. Soulié *et al*, eds. *Journal du Marquis de Dangeau* (Paris, 1854), vol. 16, 235: 'M. Le duc d'Orléans a donné à M. d'Antin la permission d'assembler cet hiver des bals trois fois la semaine dans la salle de l'Opéra; on n'y entrera qu'en masque et en payant. Le chevalier de Bouillon... aura deux mille écus de pension sur cette affaire-là, dont il a donné l'avis.'

Whatever the initial impetus may have been, the product enjoyed some immediate success. Dangeau noted in his entry for Thursday, 2 January 1716:

> The balls began tonight in the Opera house. The spectacle, it is said, is very beautiful. There is great order, and the house is magnificently lit. Only those with masks enter, without sword or staff.[46]

And while it seems he did not attend this inaugural event, he nevertheless continued his commentary in his entry for the next day:

> The ball, which began yesterday before midnight, lasted until four in the morning. And everyone who went returned very content. The only shortcoming that was found was that there was not a sufficient crowd for such a large room. But the spectacle was found to be so beautiful that there is no doubt that many more will attend in the future.[47]

The second ball, on Saturday, 4 January, was even 'more beautiful than the last time,' and was attended by the Regent, the duc d'Orléans, who accompanied his daughter, the duchesse de Berry, and several princesses.[48] On the dancing that took place in these early balls the sources are disappointingly silent. I get the impression from them that simply being in attendance was an important concern. The duc de Richelieu, for example, offered the following recollections about the early years of public balls at the Opera in his *Mémoires*:

> Masked balls were given there, and the majority of the ladies, unmasking themselves with the pretext of being inconvenienced by the heat, cared only to have themselves admired and to gossip with all the masquers. The Regent descended into the room with one or another of his mistresses, whom he led around the entire night at the ball, enjoying all the women who found themselves there.[49]

[46]ibid., vol. 16, 291-2: 'Les bals commencèrent le soir dans la salle de l'Opéra. Le spectacle, à ce qu'on dit, est fort beau; il y a un fort grand ordre, et la salle est éclairée magnifiquement: on n'y entre que masqué, et sans épée et sans bâton.'

[47]ibid.: 'Le bal, qui commença hier avant minuit, finit à quatre heures du matin; et tous les gens qui y ont été en sont revenus très-content: le seul défaut qu'on y a trouvé, c'est qu'il n'y avoit pas assez de monde pour une si grande salle; mais le spectacle a été trouvé si beau, qu'on ne doute pas qu'il n'y en vienne beaucoup dans la suite.'

[48]ibid.

[49]Cited in Emile Raunie, ed. *Chansonnier historique du XVIIIe siècle. Recueil de chansons, vaudevilles, sonnets, épigrammes, épitaphes, et autres vers satiriques et historiques* (Osnabrück, 1972), 3, n1: 'on y donnait des bals masqués, et le plus grand nombre des dames, se découvrant sous prétexte d'être incommodées de la chaleur, ne songeaient qu'à se faire admirer et à jaser avec tous les masques. Le Régent descendait dans cette salle avec quelqu'une de ses maîtresses, qu'il promenait toute la nuit dans le bal, s'amusant de toutes les femmes qui s'y trouvaient.'

Compelling evidence of the success that the first season of public balls enjoyed was the introduction of a rival operation the following Carnival season. The *Comédiens* apparently had become envious of the popularity (and the profitability) of the Opera's balls, and by 26 December 1716 had received permission to mount them in their own theatre in the rue des Fossés, Saint-Germain des Prés.[50] According to one source, their case was championed by 'Madame de Berry' (presumably the duchesse, the Regent's daughter).[51] The frères Parfaict—probably not wholly objective observers in the matter—quote a contemporary pamphlet that claims that the decorations for the balls at Saint-Germain des Prés were superior to those at the Opera and, moreover, that there was a great fireplace in the foyer of the theatre, no small consideration for a public building in Paris during the winter.[52] The balls at Saint-Germain des Prés proved to be more popular than those of the Opera in the 1717 season. In fact, Dangeau even reported that the Opera cancelled its final three balls,[53] a claim I can neither confirm nor refute. There is clear evidence, however, that in this second season of public balls there were fewer offered at the Opera than in the previous year (17 compared to 27), and that their receipts declined from 77,877 pounds at the end of the Carnival of 1716, to 14,225 pounds in 1717.[54]

The syndics of the Opera, naturally, protested the new privilege held by the *Comédiens*. A document preserved in the Bibliothèque de l'Opéra,[55] reveals that their case was argued to the Regent along three lines. First, they pointed out that the Paris market was not sufficient to support (profitably, at any rate) two public ball institutions. Second, they argued that the Opera was more needy of supplemental income from public balls than were the *Comédiens*, because the expenses of their productions were far greater. The third argument was rather more

[50]A useful review of these events can be found in Henri LaGrave, *Le Théâtre et le public à Paris de 1715 à 1750* (Paris, 1972), 502-4.

[51]*Anecdotes historiques de l'Opéra de Paris depuis 1672 jusqu'en 1749*, Paris, *Bibliothèque-Musée de l'Opéra*, Ms., fr. C.989, 66: 'Le credit de la protection qu'ils avoient de Madame de Berry leur en fourny l'occasion.'

[52]Etienne Ganeau, *Histoire Journalière de Paris* (Paris, 1716), article 2, 2-4. Cited in Claude Parfaict, *Histoire du théâtre françois* (Paris, 1734-1749), vol. 15, 243-5.

[53]*Mémoires*, vol. xvii, 218: 'les trois derniers jours du Carnaval, l'Académie royale de musique supprima ses bals.'

[54]The data are drawn from three different nineteenth century sources which transmit nearly identical figures: a collection of newspaper clippings preserved in the *Bibilothèque de l'Arsenal*, 'Collection Rondel' R°13033, f.3r-4v, [an article by 'E.M. deLyden' dated '1862']; Muslane [pseud.], 'Les Bals de l'Opéra,' 199; and Albert de Lasalle, *Les treize salles de l'Opéra* (Paris, 1875), 58.

[55]*Anecdotes historiques de l'Opéra de Paris depuis 1672 jusqu'en 1749*, Paris, *Bibliothèque-Musée de l'Opéra*, Ms. fr. C.989, 66-70.

legalistic. The syndics drew attention to the clause in the Opera's *privilège* that limited the number of instrumentalists in productions by any other company to six, a restriction that had been in place since the directorship of Lully, and subsequently reconfirmed numerous times.[56] This, they argued, meant that the Opera was the only institution with the instrumental resources to properly mount a public ball. The arguments evidently were successful. A 'Brevet,' dated 10 December 1717, gave the Directors of the Opera permission to mount balls in their theatre for a period of ten years. It reads, in part:

> His majesty wishes that during the period of ten consecutive years, beginning 1 January 1718, only the holders of the privilege of the said Academy, and to the exclusion of all others in the city of Paris, may mount public balls, for whatever remuneration they deem appropriate.[57]

By the beginning of their third season, then, public balls were an enterprise belonging solely to the Opera.

There is good consistency among the sources that in the first five years of the *bals publics* they typically were mounted three times a week, beginning on, or just before, the *fête des rois* (Epiphany, 6 January), and ending on *mardi gras*. Disregarding the rival season with the *Comédiens*, there were apparently from twenty-five to twenty-seven balls each year.[58] In the case of the 1716 season, in which the first two balls took place slightly earlier (on 2 and 4 January), there would indeed have had to be at least three balls a week in order for the seasonal total of twenty-seven to have been achieved by *mardi gras*, which occurred on 25 February that year. The second season yielded only seventeen balls, likely because, as I have already indicated, there was a rival operation. But there may have been an additional contributing factor: *mardi gras* was rather early that year—9 February. On the other hand, the 1718 season, in which there were once more twenty-seven balls, was not concluded until a comparatively late *mardi gras*, on 1 March. In these early years there does not seem to have been a fixed weekly schedule for the public ball. The marquis de Dangeau observed that

[56]For example in the Letters Patent of 1713, where the following appears: 'Deffondons aussy a nos Comediens de se servir d'aucune voix externe pour chanter aux Comedies, ny de plus de Deux voix d'entre eux, d'avoir plus de six violons ou Joüeurs d'instrumens et de se servir d'aucun Danseur dans leurs representations.' See Benoit, *Musiques de cour*, 249.

[57]Cited in Benoit, *Musiques de cour*, 283-4: 'Sa Majesté veut que pendant l'espace de dix années consecutives, a commencer du premier Janvier 1718, les cessionnaires du privilege de lad. academie puissent seuls dans la ville de Paris, et a l'exclusion de tous autres, donner un Bal public moyennant telle retribution qu'il[s] jugeront a propos...'

[58]Statistics drawn from the nineteenth century sources given in n54.

in 1716 they took place on Mondays, Wednesdays and Saturdays, while in January of 1718 he indicated that they were to be on Sundays, Tuesdays and Fridays.[59]

In the sixth year, however, both the number of balls and the timing of their season were modified. They were mounted only nineteen times that year,[60] yet they began much earlier, on St Martin's Day, 11 November.[61] These modifications may have been a consequence of a change in directorship and management at the Opera in its 1720-21 season. By February 24, 1721 an 'Arrêt du Conseil d'État' was issued that placed the general directorship in the sole control of 'sieur de Francine' [Jean-Nicolas de Francine (1662-1735), Lully's son-in-law], who since 1712 had shared the position with Hyacinthe de Gauréault Dumont.[62] The 'Arrêt' also stipulated that Francine was to prepare a complete accounting of the current state of affairs at the Opera, an order which no doubt resulted in the preparation of the 'Memoire concernant la Regie de l'Opera, & sa situation au premier avril 1721,' cited in note 60.[63] The revised season for public balls first encountered this year was to become the norm. In 1757 Durey de Noinville still described the season as follows: 'This ball begins on St Martin's day, 11 November, and continues every Sunday up to Advent. It resumes on the *fête des rois*, and is given during Carnival two or three times a week until Lent.'[64] This schedule typically permitted between fourteen and nineteen balls each year, depending on the start of Lent. In the 1760-61 season, however, when *mardi gras* was exceptionally early—3 February—only twelve balls took place.[65]

A compilation of financial documents for the Opera, spanning the seasons 1757-58 to 1769-70, and offering details of daily receipts and expenses for its operations, has been preserved in the *Archives Nationales*

[59]See Dufourcq, *La musique à la cour de Louis XIV et Louis XV*, 221. The more normal opera ball schedule of later years is discussed in chapter three.

[60] See the 'Memoire concernant la Regie de l'Opera, & sa situation au premier avril 1721,' Paris, *Archives Nationales*, AJ[13]-3, pièce 6.

[61]See M. de Lescure, ed., *Journal et Mémoires de Mathieu Marais, avocat au parlement de Paris, sur la Régence et le règne de Louis XV (1715-1737)*, 4 vols. (Paris,1863), I, 481: 'Il y a été beaucoup de monde la nuit de Saint-Martin...' [entry from November 1721].

[62]See Durey de Noinville, *Histoire de l'Académie Royale de Musique*, 98.

[63]The 'Memoire' is the earliest surviving complete set of financial 'books' of the Académie Royale de Musique.

[64]*Histoire de l'Académie Royale de Musique*, 164: 'Ce Bal commence le jour de Saint Martin 11 Novembre, & continue tous les Dimanches jusques aux Avents. On le reprend à la Fête des Rois, & on le donne pendant le Carnaval, deux ou trois fois la semaine jusquau Carême.'

[65]Paris, *Archives Nationales*, AJ[13]-9, pièce 141.

in Paris.[66] These documents both confirm Durey de Noinville's observations about the public ball season, and provide additional precision on its annual rhythm. For example, if St Martin's Day happened to fall on Friday or Saturday, the first ball was evidently moved to the Sunday immediately following. Such was the case in the 1757-58 season, which began on Sunday, 13 November, and in 1758-59, which began on Sunday, 12 November. (The practice of shifting the opening of the season in these circumstances seems to have been firmly established: it also occurred, for instance, in the 1775-76 season, which opened on Sunday, 12 November.[67]) The 'November-end' of the season usually made room for just three balls, there being only three Sundays between 11 November and the beginning of Advent. Very occasionally, however, it seems a fourth was 'squeezed in' on a weeknight at the end of the month.[68] When the season resumed in January, the normal practice seems to have been to offer balls principally on Sundays, not counting that of the *fête des rois* which could occur on any day of the week. But sometimes, as Durey de Noinville suggested, they were offered twice a week (on Thursdays, as well), especially if *mardi gras* were to be early.[69] In February, the pace of the offerings quickened: always two every week, on Thursday and Sunday. And in the six days immediately preceding *mardi gras* four balls were scheduled: Thursday, Sunday, Monday, and Tuesday.

There were also rare instances of an extraordinary public ball, offered outside the normal season. One of the better documented of these was occasioned by the arrival of the Turkish ambassador in the spring of 1721. The *Mercure galant* describes a number of performances attended by him. On the evening of 21 June there was a gala *bal public* that opened with a performance of the prologue to Lully's *Bellérophon*.[70] Since this performance involved professionals from the *Académie Royale de Musique*, it might be wondered if a practice in imitation of that of Venice was being attempted. It is certainly possible that Francine, who

---

[66]ibid. The various documents are presented in chronological sequence, and are bound together in leather, but not paginated. References to this source will therefore always cite the season involved.

[67]Paris, *Archives Nationales*, AJ[13]-2.

[68]In 1758 a fourth ball was mounted on Thursday, November 30; and in 1764 a fourth occurred on Friday, November 30. *Archives Nationales*, AJ[13]-9, pièce 141.

[69]ibid. In 1757-58, for example, when *mardi gras* fell on February 7, eight balls were given in January, all of them (except that on Friday, January 6, the season's re-opening) on Sundays or Thursdays.

[70]*Mercure galant*, juin-juillet (1721), Pt. 2, 4-5. In this account the event is said to have taken place over the evening of June 22-23. Other sources, however, claim that it was June 21-22. See, for example, Mathieu Marais, *Journal et Mémoires*, II, 167.

presided over this affair,[71] modelled the proceedings of this particular night on the carnival balls of Venetian opera houses, but this was an exceptional occurrence in Paris. It seems, moreover, that presenting the prologue to *Bellérophon* was not Francine's first choice. The *Mercure* reports that it was offered 'in place of a concert fashioned on Turkish verses that had been proposed.'[72] Mathieu Marais, who was in attendance, confirms that this was indeed the plan, for he noted specifically in his journal that 'there was a concert that was not at all Turkish.'[73] Evidently there were some two thousand paying customers that evening, and as many others turned away at the door. The *Mercure* notes, further, that 'it was impossible to dance in any comfort until after four in the morning, when people began to depart.'[74]

Another exceptional ball occurred over the evening of 24-25 August 1724. On this occasion there was 'a little entertainment, entitled *le Bal des Dieux*, that was followed by a normal ball, at which there was a very attractive and very substantial gathering.'[75] As we shall see in chapter five, public balls were occasionally mounted in the late 1750s and early 1760s as benefits for the singers and dancers of the Académie Royale de Musique after the theatre reopened, following the Easter closure.[76] And in one season from a still later period, in 1781-82, the Opera offered an additional three balls in the month of June.[77] But customarily the Opera's public balls were restricted to the winter months, and the overall season was structured in the way described above.

The typical schedule of a season, of course, could be upset by unforeseen circumstances. Even in the case of a death in the royal family, however, the disruption was short-lived. When, for example, Madame, duchesse d'Orléans (Augusta Maria of Baden, wife to Louis, the Regent's only son) died on Friday, 9 February 1759, the Sunday

[71]ibid. '…M. de Francine fit presenter à l'Ambassadeur & à toute sa retinue une collation delicate avec toute sorte de rafraichissemens.'

[72]ibid. 'On chantá à minuit le Prologue de l'Opera de Bellerophon, au lieu d'un concert travaillé sur des vers Turcs, qu'on s'étoit proposé de faire executer.'

[73]*Journal et Mémoires*, II, 167: 'Il y a eu un concert, qui n'a point été turc, et grand bal masqué au Palais-Royal, la nuit de 21 au 22.'

[74]*Mercure galant*, juin-juillet (1721), Pt.2, 5: '…mais la foule des masques étoit si grande, qu'on ne put danser un peu à l'aise qu'à quatre heures du matin, lors qu'on commença à se retirer.'

[75]*Mercure galant*, aoust (1724), 1811: 'La nuit du 24. au 25. Aoust il y eut sur le Theatre de l'Opera un petit divertissement, intitulé *le Bal des Dieux*, qui fut suivi d'un Bal ordinaire, où il y eut une très-belle & très-nombreuse assemblée.'

[76]See chapter five, n108, n109, and n110.

[77]In a payment record for that season preserved in *Archives Nationales*, AJ[13]-24, dossier IV, pièce 5, the following is found: 'Etat du Payemant aux Musiciens Symphonistes qui ont été Employés aux trois Bals qui ont été donnés par l'Académie Royale de Musique, depuis le 2, 9 et 16 Juin 1782.'

ball (11 February) at the Opera was cancelled. The balls resumed the following Thursday (15 February), although attendance that night was not great.[78] By comparison, the Opera cancelled all of its performances (four in total) for a week.[79] Perhaps the most catastrophic disruption to a public ball season was precipitated by the fire that destroyed the theatre of the *Palais-Royal* on 6 April 1763. Although the *Académie Royale de Musique* was given permission to move its operations—including its *bal public*—to the 'Salle des Machines' in the *Palais des Tuilleries*, there was not sufficient time to prepare the new venue for either operas or balls until February 1764. Instead, a weekly concert series was mounted during the fall, held each Friday in the 'Salle du *Concert spirituel*' (also located in the *Palais des Tuilleries*), except during the month of October, when members of the orchestra were called off to duties at Fontainebleau.[80] Nevertheless, between 2 February 1764 and *mardi gras*, 6 March the Opera managed to mount twelve public balls, a figure not far removed from the normal seasonal total.[81]

The admission charge to the public balls was initially set at 6 *livres tournois* (pounds), a fee that remained utterly stable throughout the century.[82] In addition to the price of admission, loges could be rented at a seasonal rate of 48 *livres tournois* or, on a one-time basis, of five pounds, according to Durey de Noinville.[83] His claim, though, is not consistent with the (admittedly few) surviving financial documents, which indicate three tiers of loge rental. Eight-seat loges could be rented for 60 pounds for an evening, ten-seat loges for 75, and twelve-seat loges for 90.[84] From these details I surmise that a one-time loge rental incorporated the normal 6-pound admission price per person, plus an additional pound and 10 *sols* (or what amounts to 1.5 pounds) per

---

[78]*Archives Nationales*, AJ[13]-9, pièce 141. Based on the gate receipts, I estimate that only 204 people attended.

[79]ibid.

[80]ibid. See further, Paris, *Archives Nationales*, O[1]624-pièce 203.

[81]ibid.

[82]Surviving cashier 'chits' from as late as 1787 still list ticket prices of 6 pounds. See Paris, *Archives Nationales*, O[1]624-pièce 209. Unusually, according to the *Mercure galant*, juin-juillet (1721), Pt. 2, 5, the admission charge to the special ball given for the Turkish Ambassador was just 5 pounds.

[83]Durey de Noinville, *Histoire de l'Académie Royale de Musique*, 164.

[84]*Bibliothèque-Musée de l'Opéra*, CO 5, 'Registre Journal de la Recette à la Porte de l'Opera'. This is a collection of daily accounting 'chits' for the opera balls during the 1756-57 season. A similar set of chits from 1770-71 (the first season in the new theatre of the *Palais-Royal*) reveals additional variety in loge sizes: six-seat loges could be rented for 45 pounds, and four-seat loges for 30. See *Bibliothèque-Musée de l'Opéra*, CO 10.

place in the loge.[85] An entitlement to a loge for the Opera (the 'entitlement' was for a fee, of course, but it was chronically disregarded[86]) was not transferable to the *bal public*.

It is difficult to determine with any certainty how frequently loges for the public ball were actually rented, because normally the Opera's bookkeeping gives statistics on loge rentals overall, including those for performances of ballets and operas. Surviving records from two public ball seasons (those of 1756-57 and 1770-71), however, allow me to make the following observations. It was not very common for loges to be rented before the final five balls of a year. On the Thursday ball and the Monday ball just before *mardi gras*, on the other hand, renting a loge was quite popular among ball-goers, no doubt because those evenings attracted very sizable crowds (almost invariably the largest of the season, as we shall see in chapter three). Ticket sales and loge rentals for these two seasons are summarized in the following table.[87]

	1756-57		1770-71	
	Ticket Sales	Loge Rentals	Ticket Sales	Loge Rentals
Ball 1 (Nov 11)	data lacking		711	0
Ball 2	133	0	470	1
Ball 3	279	0	568	1
Ball 4	98	0	537	2
Ball 5	189	0	470	0
Ball 6	326	0	376	0
Ball 7	492	0	174	0
Ball 8	98	0	514	0
Ball 9	579	1	295	0
Ball 10	210	0	771	0
Ball 11	920	9	533	1
Ball 12	1282 (Thu)	22	1091	3
Ball 13	505	8	1790 (Thu)	17
Ball 14	1273 (Mon)	25	680	5
Ball 15	771 (mardi gras)	5	1545 (Mon)	32
Ball 16	n/a	n/a	969 (mardi gras)	7

[85]An eight-seat loge, for example, cost 8 x 6 [= 48] pounds plus 8 x 1.5 [= 12] for a total of 60 pounds.

[86]In the 'Memoire concernant la Regie de l'Opera, & sa situation au premier avril 1721', (Paris, *Archives Nationales*, AJ[13]-3, pièce 7), for example, one budget item is as follows: 'Il étoit dû pour les Loges ou Places occupées à l'Opera par les Princes ou autres Seigneurs de la Cour: 62,000 [livres]'.

[87]The data is drawn from *Bibliothèque-Musée de l'Opéra*, CO 05, and CO 10.

If the comparatively brisk trade in loge rentals at the final five balls
of a season is disregarded, it does not appear that loges were the coveted
commodity they were for opera-goers. And they seem to have become
even less popular in the closing years of the century. Financial records
from two later seasons (1785-87), for example, report that in the thirty-
one balls accounted for in the documents, loges were rented only seven
times.[88] Rented or not, the loges were far from empty. They were
intended, in fact, as a principal retreat (in reality the *only* retreat) from
the crowded ballroom floor, as Saint-Simon made clear when he
observed that they 'give a convenient view of the ball to those who did
not wish to enter the room.'[89] Renting a loge for a public ball, then,
merely reserved a particular area for one's exclusive use. While I will
address the economic and financial situation of the *bals publics* in greater
detail later in this investigation, I think it is important to point out
here that the admission fee structures of the public ball were in fact
rather steep, effectively restricting attendance to those of considerable
means.

The *bals publics* began late—not before eleven at night—and lasted
well into the small hours of the following day. Durey de Noinville
reports that for a half hour before the ball started, the orchestra,
'with trumpets and tympani, presents a concert of grand symphonic
works by the best masters.'[90] There was good reason for a late start,
since the balls were an enterprise of the Opera, and had to share
space with its other operations. It was common for opera balls (the
beginnings of them, at any rate) to be mounted on the same day as
a performance in the theatre. Of the fourteen balls put on in the
1757-58 season, for example, thirteen began just three or four hours
after the conclusion of an operatic performance.[91] Whether or not
it was thought desirable to start them late (masked balls, after all,
often were late night affairs), at the Opera it was a requirement.
According to the *Reglement* for the *Academie Royale de Musique* of
1714, operas and ballets were to begin at quarter past five in the
afternoon. Singers, instrumentalists and dancers implicated in
the Prologue were to be in place on the theatre stage or in the
orchestra by 'five o'clock sharp, immediately after the ringing of

---

[88]The documents are the series of chits referred to in n82.

[89]See above, n44.

[90]Durey de Noinville, *Histoire de l'Académie Royale de Musique*, 164: '...pendant une
demi-heure avant qu'il commence, ces Instrumens s'assemblent... avec des Tymballes
& des Trompettes, & donnent un Concert composé de grands morceaux de
Symphonie des meilleurs Maîtres.'

[91]See *Archives Nationales*, AJ[13]-9, pièce 141.

the bell.'[92] Ariane Ducrot has calculated that performances must have concluded by about eight-thirty in the evening, but her argument is probably in need of some revision. She suggests that 'after eight-thirty it was better if genteel people were no longer moving about: the dark streets, through which the feeble glimmer of candle-lanterns could barely penetrate, were ripe for ambushes.'[93] The danger was probably not as extreme as Ducrot colourfully proposes, although, as the century progressed, the neighbourhood of the *Palais-Royal* gained notoriety as a haven for prostitutes.[94] Nevertheless, there were frequently large crowds until near daybreak in and around the *Palais-Royal* on the nights of a well-attended *bal public*. Concluding theatrical performances at about eight-thirty provided sufficient time, it seems, to clear the house and stage, and to prepare the 'Salle de l'Opéra' for a ball. How this could have been accomplished in three and a half to four hours will be addressed in chapter two.

•   •   •   •   •

The *bal public* did not (nor was it intended to) supplant other kinds of balls, which remained a centrepiece of courtly etiquette in noble gatherings. It did, however, expand the range of possibilities for attending and participating in one of the more venerable and conspicuous social activities of the *ancien régime*. The Opera's public balls were attended by the highest strata of the nobility and fashionable Parisian society. The duc d'Orléans was a regular participant during the Regency,[95] and even the somewhat reclusive Louis XV is known to have made an occasional appearance. A nicely detailed account of one of these is provided by Edmond-Jean-François Barbier (1689-1771) in his *Journal*. The passage, from March 1737, is worth quoting in full:

[92]Cited in Durey de Noinville, *Histoire de l'Académie Royale de Musique*, 139: 'Article XXXII. Attendu que l'Opera doit commencer à cinq heures un quart, ceux qui représenteront ou danseront dans le Prologue, ainsi que les Symphonistes, seront tenus de se trouver sur le Théâtre & dans l'Orquestre pour y faire leurs fonctions à cinq heures precises, immédiatement après le son de la cloche.'

[93]Ariane Ducrot, 'Les représentations de l'Académie Royale de Musique a Paris au temps de Louis XIV (1671-1715)', *Recherches sur la musique française classique* 10 (1970), 25:'La soirée s'achevait ainsi sur le coup de 8 heures 1/2, heure après laquelle il valait mieux pour les honnêtes gens ne plus circuler: l'obscurité des rues, que trouait à peine la faible lueur des lanternes à chandelle suspendues le long des façades, était propice aux guets-apens.'

[94]See, for example, Valérie Van Crugten-André, '*Que la fête commence...*' in Roland Mortier, and Hervé Hasquin, eds. *Topographie du plaisir sous la Régence. Études sur le XVIIIe siècle*, 24 (Bruxelles, 1998), 13-26.

[95]The passage from the journal of the duc de Richelieu cited in n49, for example, is just one of a host of accounts—many of them unfavourable—that report on the Regent's frequent attendance.

On *lundi gras* [in 1737 it fell on 4 March] the King came to the opera ball *incognito*, one of [a party of] nine. He had dined at Versailles with several noblemen, one of whom had bought nine dominos [that is, half-masks]. The King had a blue cloak with a domino the colour of pink [as his costume]. They emerged from a great carriage in the rue Saint-Nicaise, where there were but three or four men in frock coats on horseback. The King and the others went on foot from the rue Saint-Nicaise to the Opera, and, because they inadvertently had brought only seven tickets, while they numbered nine, they were stopped at the door. They then paid two six pound coins so they could all enter together. The King spent more than an hour and a half without being recognized by anyone. Mademoiselle de Charolais [eventually] recognized him because, apparently, some gallant young nobleman had taken her into his confidence. The King enjoyed himself greatly, and was jostled about. He returned on foot to the dwelling of the [King's] First [Gentleman], where there was transportation [waiting], and where he changed in the light of torches held by one of those little chimney sweeps who stand at the doorway. He even had himself brushed tidy by him at the gate of the First [Gentleman's house], and [in return] gave him a six pound coin. At the ball, it only became known at six in the morning that the King had been there, more than two hours after he had left.[96]

Yet the *bals publics* were also attended by wealthy bourgeois, such as Mathieu Marais who, while certainly well connected (as a lawyer at the *Parlement*), was not of noble birth. His journal makes it clear, however, that he sometimes went.[97] Because they were masked balls, they permitted a more fluid interaction among social ranks, and a less formal protocol in one's conduct.

Since the Opera had an exclusive monopoly in Paris to put on public balls, it is not surprising that they became more widely known as *bals*

---

[96]A. de la Villegille, ed., *Journal historique et anecdotique du règne de Louis XV par E. J. F. Barbier*, 4 vols. (Paris, 1849), II, 142-43: 'Le lundi gras, le roi est venu au bal de l'Opéra incognito, lui neuvième. Il avait soupé, à Versailles, avec plusieurs seigneurs dont l'un avait acheté neuf dominos. Le roi avait une robe bleue avec un domino coleur de rose. Il descendirent de la grande calèche dans la rue Saint-Nicaise; il n'y avait que trois ou quatre hommes à cheval, en redingotte. Le roi et les autres vinrent à pied depuis la rue Saint-Nicaise jusqu'à l'Opéra, et, comme ils n'avaient pris, par inadvertance, que sept billets et qu'ils étaient neuf, on les arrêta à la porte. Ils donnèrent donc deux écus de six livres pour entrer tous ensemble. Le roi fut plus d'une heure et demie sans être reconnu de personne. Mademoiselle de Charolais le reconnut parce que quelque jeune seigneur lui en fit apparemment la confidence, par galanterie. Il se divertit beaucoup, et fut bien poussé. Il s'en retourna à pied chez M. le Premier, où étaient les équipages et où il se déshabilla, et fut éclairé par un de ces Savoyards qui sont à la porte avec des bouts de flambeaux. Il se fit même décrotter par lui, à la porte de M. le Premier, et il lui donna un écu de six livres. On ne sut, dans le bal, que le roi y était venu que sur les six heures du matin, plus de deux heures après qu'il en fut sorti.'

[97]See, for example, the entry cited in n73.

de l'Opéra.[98] Notwithstanding the monopoly, however, other balls of a similar kind (though apparently less reputable) were in evidence sporadically about the city. Perhaps it was these to which Saint-Simon referred when he wrote in 1715 of those 'disreputable little balls scattered around Paris, where mishaps so often occur.'[99] Carl Gustav Tessin, Swedish emissary to the French Court between 1739 and 1742, commented on an up-coming public ball in a letter of July 1741 in the following way:

> Tonight Mons.[r] de Senan, Gentleman from I know not where, will give—I know not how or why—a great banquet at Passy, followed by a masked public ball, to which all of Paris will go, and since I fear staying alone in obscurity, I, too, will attend.[100]

Such a ball, of course, would not have offered direct competition to those of the Opera, because it took place in the summertime. But balls such as this also occurred in the winter months. Indeed, by the 1730s and 40s there were apparently sufficient numbers of them that the Opera began to regard them as a threat, and 'Sr [Jean-François] Berger,' director of the *Académie* from 1744 until November 1747, prepared a request to have them suppressed in January of 1746.[101] He described a proliferation of 'associations particulières vulgairement appellées Pic-nic' that, in the winter months, sponsored comedies, concerts, 'assemblés bourgeoises,' and balls. But because the 'Pic-nics' were mounted in private residences there was little, officially, the Opera could do. In their edition of Louis-Sébastien Mercier's *Parallèle de Paris et de Londres*,[102] Bruneteau and Cottret report that in 1749 an organizer of one of these contested *bals payants* was imprisoned, but they offer

---

[98]This observation has already been made by Henri Le Grave, *Le Théâtre et le public à Paris*, 501. Le Grave's brief sketch of the *bal public* (pp.500-506) in this excellent study is still the most detailed in recent literature.

[99]See n44, above.

[100]Gunnar von Proschwitz, ed., *Tableaux de Paris et de la Cour de France, 1739-1742. Lettres inédites de Carl Gustaf, comte de Tessin*, (Paris, 1983), 172: 'Ce soir Monsr de Senan Gentilhomme de je ne sai d'ou, donnera je ne sai ni comment ni pourquoy un grand souper a Passy suivi d'un Bal public masqué, ou tout Paris ira, et comme je crains de rester seul dans l'obscurité j'iray aussi.'

[101]Reported in *Memoires pour servir a l'histoire de l'Academie Royale de Musique, vulgairement l'Opéra, depuis son établissement en 1669 jusqu'en l'année 1758*, Paris, *Bibliothèque-Musée de l'Opéra*, Rés. 516, 144-46. This is a nineteenth century copy of a study prepared (perhaps as early as 1761) by Amelot, a senior administrator of the Opera in the early 1780s.

[102]A manuscript preserved in Paris, *Bibliothèque de l'Arsenal*, fonds Mercier 15 079 (3), dating from 1781.

no source for the claim, nor do they indicate if it was a result of formal action taken by the *Académie*.[103]

Additional inroads on the Opera's exclusive rights emerged by the late 1760s with the introduction in Paris of 'pleasure gardens,' frequently modelled in both their offerings and their names on those of London. The earliest of these was a large, open air structure designed by an Italian machinist and pyrotechnician, 'Sieur Torré' (d1780), located in the Boulevarde Saint-Martin, and opened as early as 1764.[104] Although Torré's typical fare was pantomimes adorned with elaborate fireworks, in 1768 he received permission to offer *bals publics*.[105] No doubt because it was considered as a sort of Frenchified Vauxhall Gardens in London, by 1773 his establishment became known as the 'Waux-hall d'été' to distinguish it from the 'Waux-hall d'hiver' that had opened in the Foire Saint-Germain in 1769. The latter was also managed by Italian machinists, the Ruggieri brothers, and was an elaborate, oval-shaped building, designed and constructed at considerable expense by LeNoir.[106] It, too, offered masked balls, and was presumably the establishment Charles Burney visited in June 1770, describing it as 'A new Vauxhall':

> ...it is illuminated, and has galleries, that are continued to another room, which is square, and still larger than the first, with two rows of Corinthian pillars ornamented with festoons and illuminations. This is a very elegant room, in which the company dance *minuets, alle-mandes, cotillions,* and *contre danses*...[107]

And by 1774 yet another establishment, the 'Ranelagh' opened (located in the present-day 'jardins de Ranelagh' in la Muette). Its balls became very fashionable, and were frequented regularly by Marie-Antoinette and the comte d'Artois.[108]

No doubt in response to the steady increase in the number of operations such as the Waux-halls and Ranelagh, by the 1770s the Opera had begun to collect annual fees for 'Permissions' it sold for 'les

---

[103]Louis-Sébastien Mercier, *Parallèle de Paris et de Londres*, ed. by Claude Bruneteau, and Bernard Cottret, (Paris, 1982), 194, n51.

[104]See J.A. Dulaure, *Histoire physique, civile et morale de Paris depuis les premiers temps historiques jusqu'à nos jours*, 2nd ed., 10 vols. (Paris, 1824), VIII, 134-36.

[105]ibid.

[106]ibid., 137-38. A useful account of the winter Waux-hall is given in Robert M. Isherwood, *Farce and Fantasy. Popular Entertainment in Eighteenth-Century Paris*, (Oxford, 1986), 56-59.

[107]Charles Burney, *The Present State of Music in France and Italy*, (London, 1773), ed. by Percy A. Scholes as *An Eighteenth-Century Musical Tour in France and Italy* (Oxford, 1959), 13.

[108]*Parallèle de Paris et de Londres*, 195, n56.

bals payants particuliers.' Between 1770 and 1779 the fees for such permissions ranged from a low of 198 pounds (in 1771-72) to a high of 452 pounds (in 1778-79),[109] suggesting that the competition from other 'paying balls' was significant, if not entirely steady. At the conclusion of the opera ball season of 1778-79 a document was prepared by the *Académie Royale de Musique* that presents a lengthy 'Liste des Personnes qui donnent des Bals.'[110] It seems to have been drawn up, in the first instance, to keep a running tally of establishments that offered public balls, so that a fee to be paid to the Opera, based on admission charges and annual income, could be calculated. But the document provides a wealth of other information, as well. It notes the name, and often the qualifications of the proprietor, and the location of the venue. Many of the establishments were run by a 'maître de danse,' but many others were run simply by a 'M[aît]re Vin Traiteur' in a venue that amounted to nothing more than a public house. In a column headed 'Prix de leur Bal' the document sets down the admission charge in some cases, and in others gives either a brief notation about the kind of offering featured at a particular establishment, such as 'Pour Contredanse,' or about the clientele it typically attracted, such as 'Société.' And in a column headed 'Observation' the document offers a number of interesting bits of information in just a word or two: 'tous les jours,' 'médiocre,' 'tres bon,' 'toute l'année bon,' '2 salles,' 'assemblé bourgeoise,' 'société cachée.' Quite surprisingly, the listing runs over nine pages, with well over one hundred and thirty separate establishments that included some kind of public ball among their offerings. It may be that the *bals de l'Opéra* were still regarded in the 1770s as the most resplendent of all *bals payants*; their dominance, nevertheless, was being eroded increasingly.

The opera balls lost some of what remained of their special cachet when a second fire at the *Palais-Royal* destroyed its new theatre (opened in 1770) on 8 June 1781. Although a facility at the Porte Saint-Martin was ready for operatic productions by the following October, no special provisions in its design had been made to accommodate balls, and because attendance began to suffer, the opera balls were sometimes (but not always) mounted at the Panthéon instead.[111] By 1784 plans were made to renovate the new theatre so that balls could be put on more conveniently. The plans evidently were never realized. A printed document criticising the project survives, however, and it paints a rather

[109]Paris, *Archives Nationales*, AJ[13]-9, pièce 156. This is a summary ledger of receipts and expenses at the Opera from 1770 to 1780.

[110]*Archives Nationales*, AJ[13]-10, pièce 7, dossier 1.

[111]Paris, *Archives Nationales*, O[1]624-pièce 209.

gloomy picture of the future prospects of the *bal de l'Opéra*.[112] The document carries with it some authority, for it was prepared by a 'M. de la Ferté', no doubt Papillon de la Ferté (1725-1794), who was director of the Opera from 1776-77, and then again from 1780-90. It is dated 25 February 1784, so it was written during his second watch at the *Académie*. Papillon's view was that there was little point in going to the trouble and expense of constructing a new venue for the opera ball, because receipts from this entertainment had already been in decline, even after the Opera had returned to the *Palais-Royal* in 1770. His observation is only partially supported by surviving financial records, which show reasonably steady (though modest) increases in gate receipts for balls from 1770-71 (73,110 pounds) through 1777-78 (82,314 pounds). This was followed, however, by a sharp decline: 68,659 pounds in 1778-79, and only 54,492 pounds in 1779-80.[113]

More telling than his financial arguments, perhaps, was Papillon's observation that 'the opera balls have passed out of fashion.'[114] He tried to account for the 'peu de goût actuel' for opera balls by remarking:

> There is the proliferation of all the private balls that are virtually innumerable, not only at the homes of persons of distinguished rank, but also among the bourgeoisie. But what detracts even more considerably from the Opera balls are those numerous private balls at which one pays upon entering, even though those who give them announce them simply as social gatherings.[115]

Indeed, Papillon's observations seem to have held true in other European centres as well, where *bals payants* had become a commonplace by the second half of the eighteenth century, often in imitation of Parisian practices. In Stockholm, for example, a French troupe of actors, singers, and dancers that had been assembled through the efforts of Carl Gustav Tessin (the same Swedish diplomat who attended a public ball in Paris in the summer of 1741) sought permission to mount *bals*

[112]Paris, *Archives Nationales*, O¹624-pièce 203. The document is a single, folded oblong folio, printed on both sides.

[113]Paris, *Archives Nationales*, AJ¹³-9, pièce 156.

[114]Paris, *Archives Nationales*, O¹624-pièce 203: 'les Bals de l'Opéra sont passés de mode.'

[115]ibid.: 'Ce peu de goût actuel pour le Bal de l'Opéra peut avoir plusieurs causes, entr'autres celle de la multiplicité de tous les Bals particuliers, qui sont presque sans nombre, tant chez les personnes d'un rang distingué, que parmi la bourgeoisie; mais ce qui nuit encore considérablement aux Bals de l'Opéra, ce sont plusieurs Bals particuliers où l'on paye en entrant, quoique ceux qui les donnent ne les annoncent que comme des assemblées de Société.'

publics in their tennis court theatre sometime after their arrival in Sweden in 1753. According to Mary Skeaping, who has written one the more exhaustive English language studies of ballet in baroque Sweden, the permission was denied.[116] (If the refusal to allow public balls was based in concerns about safety, then the initial decision taken by the Stockholm government was sadly prophetic: King Gustav III was assassinated at an opera ball in 1792.) In Ghent, a series of eight 'redoutes' (to be held in an unspecified 'theatre'), beginning Monday, 13 January 1783, is announced in a surviving poster from that city.[117] The poster, which is printed in French, and uses phrases such as 'elles [the 'redoutes'] commenceront comme d'ordinaire à quatre heures,' and 'l'on païera comme de coûtume 20 escalins,' suggests that this was a series of public balls that had been offered previously.

In Paris it was only during the Revolution and subsequent Terror that the long tradition of annual *bals de l'Opéra* was finally broken, in part because masked assemblies were prohibited for a time.[118] In the Napoleonic era of post-revolutionary Paris, however, the institution of opera balls was restored by at least 'An VIII' (22 September 1799 through 21 September 21 1800).[119] One commentator has claimed that the balls were restored by consular decree and, quite astonishingly, that no dancing was permitted,[120] but I have been unable to verify the source that is cited. It is clear, however, that after their restoration, the *bals de l'Opéra* were offered less frequently, and they continued to face competition from other establishments.[121] In fact, it was not until the inauguration of the famous *Bals Musard* in 1837 that a masked public ball began once more to dominate all others in Paris. That was a different era, however, one as deserving of close examination as the period to be considered in this study. In the chapters that follow, my primary focus will be on the years between 1716, the start of the *bal public* at the Opera, and 1763, when the first fire at the theatre in the

[116]Mary Skeaping, 'Ballet under the Three Crowns,' *Dance Perspectives* 32 (1967), 1-62. Skeaping makes the claim on p. 47.

[117]Universiteit Gent, Centrale Bibliotheek, FVB I R 7. I am indebted to Veerle Fack, a doctoral candidate at the university, for hunting down the shelf number of this document for me. Because this poster reveals much about the conduct of a public ball, it will be revisited later in this study. It is reproduced in Appendix 2.

[118]According to the *Calendrier historique* cited in Muslane [pseud.], 'Les Bals de l'Opéra,' 200.

[119]To my knowledge, the earliest financial records that report on opera ball activities after the revolution date from that year. See *Archives Nationales*, AJ[13]-44, pièce XIII.

[120]*Calendrier historique* cited in Muslane [pseud.], 'Les Bals de l'Opéra,' 200.

[121]See *Archives Nationales*, AJ[13]-67, pièce III, which accounts for balls offered over two months only, and which provides a listing of competing public balls in 1802.

Palais-Royal forced the public ball from its original venue, but I will make frequent references to opera balls as late as the 1780s. It was in these years that the *bal public* seems to have been at its most characteristic.

CHAPTER TWO

The Venue: The Politics of Place

Tout ce que je voy dans cette salle me réjouit, m'éblouït, m'étonne; cette confusion me plaît...

Mercure galant, février (1716)[1]

The newly-instituted *bals publics* were mounted in the 'Salle de l'Opéra'—already one of the hubs of cultural and social life in Paris— and the *Palais-Royal*, in which the 'Salle de l'Opéra' was located, was also the principal residence of the Regent. The *Palais-Royal* with its original theatre had been built as a state residence for Cardinal Richelieu in the 1630s and was completed in 1641. In 1692 Louis XIV made a gift of it to his brother, Monsieur (Philippe I, duc d'Orléans), father of the future Regent. When Monsieur died in 1701 his son, the duc de Chartres, assumed the title Philippe II, duc d'Orléans, and the *Palais-Royal* became his possession.

At the time few would have predicted that d'Orléans was destined to become Regent. Louis XIV's only surviving legitimate son, Louis, 'le Grand Dauphin' was just forty years old, and the Dauphin's three sons were in their youthful prime; in fact one of them (the duc d'Anjou) had ascended to the Spanish throne as Philip V in 1700. In other words, the queue for succession to the French crown must have seemed amply filled, and the prospects of the Orléans branch of the Bourbon dynasty moving to the front of that queue very remote. It was this very remoteness from the succession that has prompted J. H. Shennan to argue that d'Orléans deliberately distanced himself from the Court at Versailles, preferring instead the less closely scrutinized lifestyle that residence in Paris permitted him.[2] Although d'Orléans was a well-educated and highly cultured individual, and although he served his country well as a remarkably gifted military tactician and statesman,

---

[1]*Mercure galant*, février (1716), 199: 'Everything I see in this room cheers me, dazzles me, astonishes me; this confusion pleases me.'

[2]J. H. Shennan, *Philippe, Duke of Orléans, Regent of France, 1715-1723* (London, 1979), 11-12.

his apartments at Versailles were nearly always vacant, and in Paris he acquired the reputation of a hedonist and undiscriminating womanizer.[3]

D'Orléans's journey to the front of the queue of succession was as rapid as it was dramatic. In 1711 the Dauphin died, and within three years two of his sons—the duc de Bourgogne (d1712) and the duc de Berry (d1714)—were dead as well, leaving only the duc d'Anjou (Philip V of Spain), who had been forced to renounce any claim to the French crown as a condition of the Treaty of Utrecht of 1713. Only the duc de Bourgogne's two children were in direct line to succeed Louis XIV, but one of these, the duc de Bretagne, had died in 1712, a victim of the same outbreak of smallpox that had killed his mother and would shortly thereafter kill his father in the same year. By the summer of 1715 Louis XIV, who was nearly seventy-seven years old, and whose health was failing, knew that he likely would not survive until his great-grandson, the future Louis XV, reached the age of majority. According to French laws of succession that was thirteen years of age, still eight years away. Before his death on 1 September 1715, then, the old king named the duc d'Orléans to the office of Regent in his will.

On 2 September the *Parlement* of Paris confirmed that part of the will and proclaimed d'Orléans Regent.[4] Much has been written about the precarious political situation in France at the start of the Regency.[5] The young Louis XV, while not sickly, was not robust with good health. He had become seriously ill in the smallpox outbreak of 1712, and his sometimes fragile health was to cause concern among his subjects more than once during the Regency. Were he not to survive, the possibility of a protracted power struggle, as various claims to the throne were sorted out, was great. But even though Louis XV did survive, the problems facing d'Orléans were still varied and complex. The country's finances, principally owing to the War of the Spanish Succession, were in a ruinous state: contemporary estimates placed France's indebtedness at between 2000 and 2200 *million* livres.[6] As well, Jansenist support among the clergy, engendered in part by the issue of Clement XI's papal bull, *Unigenitus dei filius*, in September 1713, had precipitated

[3]ibid., 14-17.

[4]A useful summary of this session of parliament, and how d'Orléans successfully navigated it can be found in ibid. 29-32. For a contemporaneous account, including the text of some of the speeches made, see M de Lescure, ed., *Journal et mémoires de Mathieu Marais*, I, 157-184.

[5]Among several other studies see J. D. Hardy Jr., *Judicial Politics in the Old Regime: The Parlement of Paris during the Regency* (Baton Rouge, La., 1967); and M. Antoine, *Le conseil du roi sous le règne de Louis XV* (Geneva, 1970).

[6]See Shennan, *Philippe, Duke of Orléans*, 25.

parliamentary crises throughout the realm, and even threatened civil war. And d'Orléans's position as Regent was far from uncontested. The duc du Maine (1670-1736), bastard son of Louis XIV and Madame de Montespan, was a formidable rival with a potent network of support.

I give this very brief sketch of the political situation because, I believe, the establishment of the *bals publics*—within the first four months of the Regency—signals a conspicuous intersection of social, cultural, and political forces. It has often been argued that Louis XIV's elaborate court at Versailles was calculated to occupy the nobility in ultimately harmless pursuits, leaving little time for political intrigue that might lead to insurrection.[7] Although he is justifiably suspicious of many of the features of this construction of French history, Peter Campbell nevertheless has provided an ironic summary of its broad outlines:

> The argument goes that after having defeated the Fronde, that last attempt by the *grands* to acquire real political power, and having also defeated 'selfish' social groups and provincialism, the monarchy was able to rally support and continue building the modern state. The nobles were drawn to court where they were encouraged to spend their fortunes and finally to rely on the monarch for funds. The elaborate court ritual and etiquette, ever respectful of rank, gave them prestige without real power, as they dissipated their energies in quarrels of precedence and the search for favours.[8]

More recent studies have produced a rather different (but not necessarily contrary) account of the actual workings of court at Versailles, and governance in the *ancien régime* in general. There was, among other things, a complex system of patronage and clientage, the primary currencies for which were the 'cultural capital' and 'conspicuous consumption' mentioned in the last chapter. The system operated across class boundaries.[9]

That system did not stop in September 1715; if anything, it was stimulated, and d'Orléans proved himself to be skilled at working it to his advantage. He maintained his 'territory' and his network of support, refusing to abandon his residence or, to the disdain of many, his lifestyle in the *Palais-Royal*. He was notorious among some diarists for

[7]For example, Geroges Pagès, *La monarchie d'ancien régime en France* (Paris, 1928); and R. Mousnier, 'The Development of Monarchical Institutions and Society in France,' in R. Hatton, ed., *Louis XIV and Absolutism* (London, 1976).

[8]Peter R. Campbell, *Power and Politics in Old Regime France, 1720-1745* (London, 1996), 12.

[9]See especially Sharon Kettering, *Patrons, Brokers and Clients in Seventeenth-century France* (New York, 1986). For refinements to her arguments see, further, 'Gift giving and Patronage in Early Modern France,' *French History* 2 (1988), 131-151; 'The Patronage Power of Early Modern French Noblewomen,' *Historical Journal* 32 (1989), 139-158; and 'Friendship and Clientage in Early Modern France,' *French History* 6 (1992), 139-158.

conducting state business at the Opera. Even Saint-Simon, in many respects one of the Regent's staunchest supporters, observed with some exasperation in 1717 that often 'he was there [in his loge] not so much at the Opera as in an office conducting business.'[10] If only indirectly, d'Orléans gave his consent to the creation of *bals publics* at a time and in a situation that make their establishment seem somehow purposeful. There is no evidence to suggest that the idea of balls at the Opera originated with d'Orléans. The chevalier de Bouillon, however, who was identified by both Saint-Simon and Dangeau as the originator of the idea,[11] had been the Regent's *grand-chambellan* until September 1715 (when Bouillon's son, the duc d'Albret, was named to the position).[12] Moreover, the Regent's ruling in the dispute with the *Comédiens* in 1717, which granted an *exclusive* right for the Opera to mount public balls, suggests to me that he may well have wanted them close to hand. It certainly might be wondered why.

Why would d'Orléans be willing to open up his household overnight to large groups of people whose admission was controlled only by their ability to pay? Moreover, several sources confirm that attendance at the balls was conditional on being masked. And if that were not enough, the *Palais-Royal* was to be much more accessible on the evenings of public balls than it typically was for operatic performances. For the latter, it was customary for opera-goers to enter the Salle de l'Opera through the tiny, dead end alleyway known as the *cul-de-sac de l'Opéra*, there being no direct access to the theatre from the rue Saint-Honoré. Entry through the cul-de-sac led one into a 'small inner courtyard,' a 'narrow hallway,' one flight of six steps that led directly to the parterre of the theatre, or another flight of stairs to the loges.[13] Access to the theatre for *bals publics*, on the other hand, was evidently more spacious and comfortable. Article three of the *Règlement* for the conduct of public balls issued in December, 1715 reads: 'There shall be no door of entry into said ball except that which opens onto the 'Place du Palais Royal,' with prohibitions against anyone to enter through the Cul-de-Sac which, to avoid confusion, will be reserved exclusively for those departing.'[14] It seems likely that the 'Place du

[10]A. de Boislisle, ed. *Mémoires de Saint-Simon*, vol. 31, 151: 'Il y étoit moins à l'Opéra que dans un cabinet en affairs.'

[11]See chapter one, notes 44, 45.

[12]*Journal et mémoires de Mathieu Marais*, I, 198.

[13]See Barbara Coeyman, 'Theatres for Opera and Ballet during the Reigns of Louis XIV and Louis XV,' *Early Music* 18/1 (1990), 34.

[14]Cited in Durey de Noinville, *Histoire du théâtre*, 149: 'III. Il n'y aura de porte d'entrée audit Bal, que celle qui donne sur la Place du Palais Royal; avec défenses à toutes personnes d'entrer par celle du Cul-de-Sac, qui pour éviter la confusion sera uniquement reservée pour la sortie.' (See Appendix 1.)

Palais Royal' referred to here is the 'Cour d'entrée' in a plate from Blondel's *L'architecture française*. (See illustration.) Blondel's plans, of course, were drawn in the 1750s, so they may not offer an entirely accurate idea of the layout of the grounds and buildings during the Regency. There can be little doubt, though, that access to the Salle de l'Opéra for public balls offered considerably greater exposure to parts of the *Palais-Royal* than that offered by entrance through the cul-de-sac. All these circumstances—late night crowds, sometimes large ones, the identities of individuals concealed by masks (if only intermittently), and more liberal exposure to areas of the *Palais-Royal* beyond the theatre—must surely have presented some concerns about security. The desirability of public balls at the Opera seems nevertheless to have outweighed any concerns d'Orléans might have entertained.

It may well be that he viewed the *bal public* as a new instrument of state that was not only diverting, but useful to his immediate purposes, as well. The seat of the Court during the Regency was no longer the cloistered world of Versailles, a world with which d'Orléans had never felt particularly close bonds at any rate. In fact, it might be argued that the Court was without a center or a focus with the passing of Louis XIV. And, as Norbert Elias has proposed, an arena for seeking favours, for accumulating prestige (or losing it), or simply for being noticed had become a characteristic feature, indeed an indispensable requirement, of court society in Louis XIV's reign.[15] Without a venue in which to observe and to display the outward manifestations of rank— without a central space to play out the elaborate system of etiquette that may be viewed as a logical outcome of court society in the *ancien régime*—the court was in need of some alternative, however bizarre it might have turned out to be at times. The public balls at the opera provided just such a center, and they brought the Court into the Regent's territory, as well, making him the new focus of social interaction. The etiquette that was nurtured there, however, was in many respects at odds with the routines of the old Court. As we shall see in chapter four, modes of conduct at the opera ball served to minimize the issue of rank rather than to emphasize it.

[15]Norbert Elias, *The Court Society*, English trans. by Edmund Jephcott (London, 1983), passim., but especially chapter 5, 'Etiquette and ceremony: conduct and sentiment of human beings as functions of the power structure of their society,' and chapter 6, 'The bonding of kings through etiquette and status chances.'

34

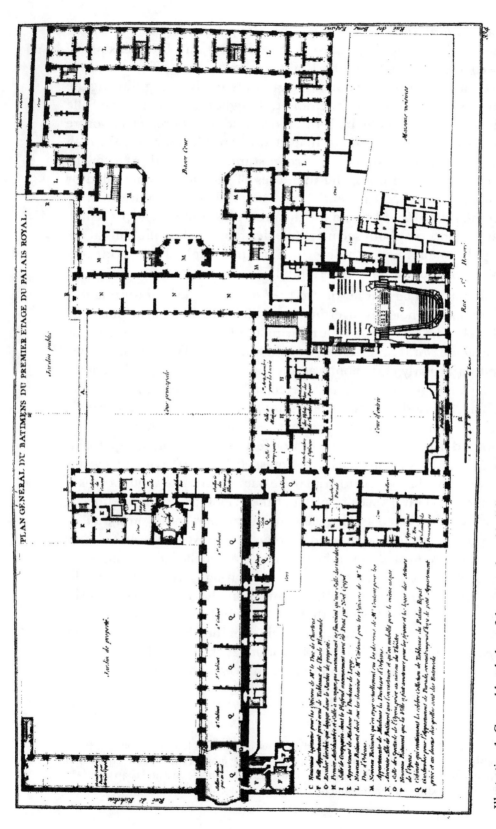

Illustration 1. Ground level plan of the grounds and buildings of the *Palais-Royal* from the *Réimpression de L'architecture françoise de Jacques-François Blondel* [Paris, 1752-6], ed. by Gaudet and Pascal, 4 vols. (Paris, 1904-05) Tome III, Book V, Chapter 9, plate 3. Reproduced with kind permission from the copy owned by the Thomas Fisher Rare Book Library, University of Toronto. The Cour d'entrée is in the lower middle of the plate, to the left of the theatre.

The substitute Court at the *Opéra* must have seemed quite different from the one presided over by Louis XIV at Versailles: it was dazzling, but essentially unstructured, and rather unpredictable. Such qualities, of course, were not uncommon in a masked carnival ball, but they were unusual for what was (in some ways) a quasi-court center. Not very far beneath the glittering surface of the *bals de l'Opéra* were currents that tended to subvert the rigours and formalities that typically had attended court life at Versailles, challenging some of the established patterns of conduct and social behaviour. For one thing, every one who attended an opera ball was, in the first instance, a 'client': there was no privilege of birthright. Even Louis XV and members of his party, as we saw in the last chapter, had to scramble to find two additional admissions to gain access to the ballroom in the Carnival of 1737.

I do not wish to suggest that as early as 1716 d'Orléans was the architect of some new social order. Neither should the *bals publics* be regarded as the product of political (and social) expediency, inextricably linked to the circumstances of the Regency, for the balls remained viable long after Louis XV had re-established Versailles as the seat of royal authority. The social, cultural, and political forces that shaped the Regency, however, also shaped the development of the *bals publics*. Against a backdrop of fragile political stability and economic hardship, the Regency was famous—some would argue even notorious—for its revelries, libertinism, and laissez-faire attitudes.[16] If not the architect of an emergent new etiquette, d'Orléans was certainly a willing participant in it, and at the opera balls mounted adjacent to his household he was an interested, close-range observer.

•   •   •   •   •

[16]See, for example, *Topographie du plaisir sous la Régence*, in *Études sur le XVIIIe Siècle*, 24 (Bruxelles, 1998), passim., but especially 'Que la fête commence...' by Valérie van Crugten-André, 13-26; and 'Écriture et lecture sous la Régence, d'après *Le spectateur français* de Marivaux' by Ling-Ling Sheu, 119-130.

The Theatre Ballroom

Under the protection of the Regent's father, Molière's troupe had been given rent-free use of the theatre in the *Palais-Royal* from January 1661 until the latter's death in February 1673.[17] Lully's *Académie Royale de Musique* was then given use of the theatre, and from 1673 until 1763, when a fire destroyed it, the facility served as principal venue for fully staged musical theatre in Paris. It had been remodeled extensively when Lully took occupancy.[18] Under his supervision, and evidently at the expense of the crown,[19] the famous set designer and machinist, Carlo Vigarini (b1623), converted the theatre into the basic form it would have for the remainder of its existence. This included a 'horseshoe' plan for the auditorium that afforded improved sight lines toward the stage, and an audience capacity of approximately thirteen hundred people: six hundred standing, and seven hundred seated.[20] But the theatre overall was not particularly large, just 35 meters long by 17 meters wide, with the area of the parterre no more than 10 meters at its widest point, adjacent to the orchestra, and just over 6 meters in length. While the stage area was quite deep—17 meters— much of it was devoted to the set area, including several pairs of flats used to produce the effects of deep perspective for which the theatre was well known. So how to mount a ball in such a facility?

Many eighteenth-century accounts of the *bals publics* at the Opera mention a 'machine' that raised the floor of the parterre to the level of the amphitheatre at one end of the room, and the stage at the other, creating an unbroken area for balls far larger than that afforded by either the stage or the auditorium individually. The machine was a novelty in its time, drawing commentary from several observers. Dangeau recorded that 'Madame [the Regent's mother] went to the Opera' on Wednesday, 29 December 1717 'and then saw the machine raising [the floor] that will make the "salle de bal".'[21] She was in her sixty-seventh year at the time, and not one to indulge in balls of any kind, public or private. Indeed, she was an outspoken critic of the opera balls, as we shall see in chapter four, but she was interested, just

[17]See Georges Mongrédien, *Daily Life in the French Theatre at the Time of Molière* (London, 1969), 87-91.

[18]For a review of the history of this theatre see Spire Pitou, *The Paris Opera. An Encyclopedia of Operas Ballets, Composers and Performers*, vol. 1, *Genesis and Glory* (London, 1983), 13-28.

[19]ibid., 13.

[20]This information and subsequent details about the theatre's specifications are drawn from Coeyman, 'Theatres for Opera and Ballet,' 33-34.

[21]*Journal*, vol. xvii, 220: 'Madame alla à l'Opéra dans sa loge et vit ensuitte remonter la machine qui fera la salle de bal…'

the same, in observing the 'machine' at work. One scholar has suggested it took about half an hour for the machine to complete the process of raising the floor.[22] The *machine pour les bals*, as it came to be known, became a standard feature for the institution of public balls in Paris: the *comédiens* had one built for their theatre in the single season they offered public balls; and when the new opera house at Versailles was finally completed in 1770, it included such a machine (one that still exists, although it is not accessible for public visits). In the same year, the completely rebuilt theatre of the *Palais-Royal* also opened, and it too had a new *machine pour les bals*. The only illustration that I have discovered is of the latter machine, from a plate of 1771.[23]

The design and construction of the Opera's first machine were under the supervision of Louis-Étienne-François Duchêne, one of the 'syndics' of the Academy after 1712, and one of its 'Inspectors' between 1714 and 1721.[24] Among Duchêne's duties were the care of the 'Magasin' (a sort of services facility), the costumes, the scenery, and the decorations of the Opera, so it is not surprising that he also became involved in the development of a machine and décor for the *bals publics*. According to the *Anecdotes historiques*:

Mr Duchêne's idea was that the floor of the ball would be that of the parterre, [which was] to be raised from above by jacks with winches. He proposed this idea to Mr [le Duc] Dantin,[25] [and] recommended to him one Father Sebastien, [who was] very capable in mechanics. The latter was at a house in the country for three weeks where it was impossible to talk with him. This decided Mr Duchêne on consulting Brother Nicolas, an Augustinian [monk], who had rebuilt the drawbridge at Rouën, and who might have some familiarity with the idea Mr Duchêne had conceived. Brother Nicolas thought of another means, based on a machine at Marly; it was the latter plan that was executed.

To put it into practice it was necessary to excavate beneath the parterre to a depth of three feet in order to place a frame around it. Despite the construction work, through the attention and activity of Mr Duchêne, the room was ready in sixteen days to put on the first ball on the Eve of St Genevieve's Day, the second day of the year 1716. What is even more surprising is that the Opera, during the

[22]Charles Bouvet, 'L'Académie royale de musique et les deux salles de spectacle du Palais Royal,' in *La Merveilleuse vie du Palais-Royal* (Paris, 1929-30), 31-44.

[23]The plate faces page 36 in Bouvet, 'Les deux salles de spectacle.'

[24]Information on Duchêne's positions at the Opera may be found in Durey de Noinville, *Histoire du théâtre*, 94-98. See further, Jean Gourret, *Ces hommes qui ont fait l'Opéra*, (Paris, 1984), 34-36.

[25]Attached to the *Maison du Roi*, he served as royal advisor to the Opera between 1715 and 1717. See Gourret, *Ces hommes*, 35-36.

entire time of this construction work, did not cancel a single day of performances for the public.[26]

Although this is a nicely detailed account, it offers little precision about how the machine worked, beyond the suggestion that it likely did not raise the floor from above—Duchêne's original idea. A much more detailed description of Brother Nicolas's invention is presented in the *Histoire du théâtre français* of the Frères Parfaict, who quote a passage from the *Histoire Journalière de Paris* of 1717 in volume fifteen of their work. The description is of the machine designed for the *Comédiens*, but it is still worth quoting at some length.

> Their ballroom was more decorated than that of the Opera, but in the same manner: the parterre [was] raised to the level of the stage and the amphitheatre, both joined together by means of hinged flaps. But the machine was easier [to use than that of the Opera] even though [designed] by the same inventor, *Le Frère Nicolas*, Augustin, known for other inventions (among others that of the turning bridge at the Tuilleries, etc.). Four levers, mounted on four posts placed at its four corners, raised and lowered the floor of the parterre, sometimes holding as many as twenty persons [during the process]. When it is at the desired height, sixteen grooved pegs placed underneath it, between the beams and the floor, hold and support it, along with four iron arms pulled out from the two sides where the hinged flaps are mounted. The process is executed with such ease that, if necessary, six children would suffice [to operate it].[27]

[26]*Bibliothèque-Musée de l'Opéra*, Ms.fr. C.989. *Anecdotes historiques de l'Opéra de Paris de 1672 jusqu'en 1749*, 59-63: 'L'idée du Sr Duchêne étoit que le plancher du bal resta la parterre pour en etre levé par des crics en dessus avec des manivelles; il proposa a Mr Dantin cette idée; il luy commetta le père Sebastien fort habile dans le mecanique; il étoit pour trois semaines dans une maison de compagne, ou il étoit impossible de luy parler,—ce qui determina le Sr Duchêne a consulter le frere Nicolas Augustin qui avoit retabli le Pont de bateau de Rouën qui pouvoit avoir quelques raport a l'idée que led. Sieur Duchêne avait conçüe; Le frere Nicolas en imagina une autre sur l'idée de la machine de Marly; c'est celle qui a été executé. Pour la mettre a éxécution—il fallu creuser le parterre de trois pieds de profondeur pour y mettre une charpente; Malgré ces travaux par les soins et l'activité dud. Sieur Duchêne, il fit mettre cette salle en état en 16 jours de tems pour donner le p^er bal la veille de Ste Genevieve, le 2e de l'année 1716. Ce qui est de plus surprenant c'est que l'opera pendant tout le tems de ces travaux n'a pas cessé un jour sans etre representé au public.'

[27]*Histoire du théâtre françois*, vol. 15, 243-244: 'Leur Salle étoit plus décorée que celle de l'Opéra, mais de la même façon; le Parterre élevé au niveau du Théatre, & de l'Amphithéatre, les joignoit de même par le moyen de deux abatans; mais la machine étoit plus aisée, quoique du même Inventeur, *le Frère Nicolas*, Augustin, connu par d'autres inventions, (entr'autres celle du Pont tournant des Thuilleries, &c.). Quatre leviers enchassés dans quatre poteaux placés aux quatre angles, élevoient & abaissoient le plancher du Parterre, chargé quelquefois de plus de vingt personnes. Quand il est à la hauteur qu'il convient, seize chevillettes fourchées, couchées dessous entre les solives & le plancher, se dressent & le soutiennent, avec quatre branches de fer, attachées au deux côtés, qui reçoivent les abatans; ce qui s'éxécutoit avec tant de facilité, que six enfans, dans un besoin, pouvoient suffire.'

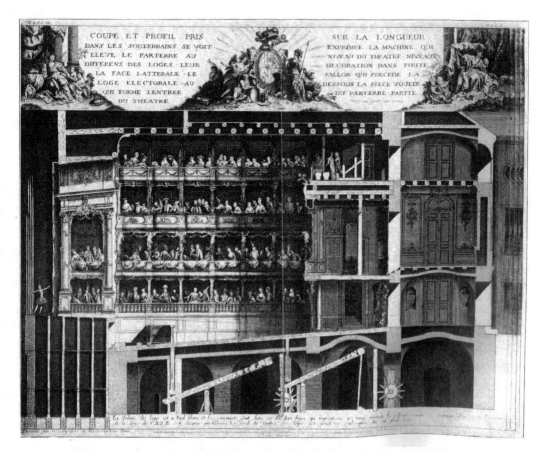

Illustration 2. Cross-section and profile of the second theatre of the *Palais-Royal*, reproduced from *La Merveilleuse vie du Palais-Royale* (Paris, 1929-30). Plate facing p. 35.

The Frères Parfaict go on to report that to construct the machine and prepare the theatre for the public ball season, the *Comédiens* found it necessary to shut down their operation between 20 and 23 October 1716. It is impossible to say whether the machine of the Opera had precisely the design of the one described here. A comment in the *Anecdotes historiques* suggests that the two machines might have been slightly different: 'They [the *Comédiens*] obtained [the services of] Frère Nicolas to build the 'machine du bal.' He did not construct one like that of the Opera, but the one Mr Duchêne had suggested to him.'[28] Since Duchêne's idea was a mechanism that would raise the floor from above, however, I am inclined to mistrust this observation. The machine depicted in the plate of 1771 (see illustration) conforms in some details to the description of the one built by the *Comédiens*: the cross-section shows two large levers mounted on two posts with capstans, beneath

[28]*Anecdotes historiques*, 66-70: 'Ils se servirent de frere Nicolas pour faire la machine du bal; il ne se feroy pas de celle de qu'il avoit fait pour l'opera, mais de celle dont le Sr Duchêne luy avoit donné l'idée.'

the parterre. The level of the stage can be seen here about a third of the way up the left border, where a performer gestures with opened arms.

What did the *salle du bal* look like after the floor had been raised and a new space for the *bal public* had been created? Early accounts, as we have seen briefly in chapter one, remark on both attractive decorations and splendid lighting. But it is not until after a remodeling of the Opera's ballroom facility by the famous scene designer and machinist, Giovanni Niccolò Servandoni (1695-1766) in 1727 that a detailed description survives. This description, from the *Mercure galant* of November, 1727, is exceptionally generous in its detail,[29] but difficult to interpret in many respects, because some of the information seems inconsistent, or even contradictory. So precise is some of the data, in fact, that it most certainly was assembled from something beyond an 'eye witness' account. Portions of the lengthy passage are devoted to a very detailed description of the many arches and arcades that lined the ballroom. In the following translation I have omitted some paragraphs that dwell at great length on these details, as well as the opening few sentences, which offer information only about the typical schedule of the opera ball season. Nevertheless, the account is transcribed in its entirety in Appendix 3.

> [At the ball given on St Martin's Day, November 11, 1727] the room was decked out in a new decoration made by M. Servandoni, [a] talented Florentine painter, [and] designer of the superb [set of the] Palace of Ninus in the opera, *Pirame & Thisbé*, about which a detailed description may be found in the *Mercure* from October of last year. This new decoration is ornamented with mirrors, of which some are most ingeniously deployed for the effect they are to make: and for this they are angled above one's line of sight in order that one can not see one's reflection, and [also] so that one can be fooled, through their placement, into thinking the room is once again larger than it is, by reflecting objects which are duplicated [in the mirrors], by making places, or enclosures and openings appear in all directions, where one expected only to see empty air. But before describing this room, let us say something of the old one.
>
> It is known that the parterre of the Opera is raised to the level of the stage and amphitheatre to form the floor of the ballroom, which was 86 feet long by 23 wide. It terminated in an oval on the loges side [of the room]; it does so now. It formed a square on the stage side, with an alcove in the rear, where the orchestra was placed. Along the sides [of the original stage area] masques and other figures had been painted, to look like [those in] the real loges which are situated along the same plane: this section was without ceiling.

[29]*Mercure galant*, novembre (1727), 2513-19. Much of this description is also given— virtually *verbatim*—in Durey de Noinville, *Histoire du théâtre*, 160-164.

In its new layout, M. Servandoni found a means of gaining 7 feet in [the room's] width and 12 in its length, including the demi-octagonal room which he skillfully positioned in the 24-foot wide space [of the stage] left available to him from the wall at the far end.

The new room forms a kind of gallery [that is] 98 feet in length, including the demi-octagonnal [area], which, through the means of mirrors by which it is bordered, appears to the eyes as a complete octagonal room. All the chandeliers, candelabras, and girandoles are reflected in these mirrors, such that the length of the entire room thereby appears doubled, as does the number of spectators.

The mirrors along the sides [of the demi-octagonal room], viewed in profile, are placed with art and symmetry in a complex pattern, enriched with various kinds of marble, the ornaments of which are all golden bronze.

The room, or gallery, may be divided into three sections: the first comprises the area that the loges border; the second [is] a square room; and the third [is] the demi-octaganal room, of which we have just spoken. The loges are decorated with railings [decked] with covers of the richest fabrics and the most beautiful of colours at the supports, [nevertheless] preserving an appropriate coordination with the original colour of the ceiling which stretches above the loges.

Two buffets, one on each side, separate the lower [level] of the loges end of the room, which measures 30 feet square by 22 feet in elevation, at the top of which is an ingenious [false] ceiling, adorned with golden roses enclosed in lozenges, and encircled by ovals that form a sort of border.

Two columns on pedestals, [carved] in relief, mark the entrance to the ballroom. There a real curtain of rich fabric with golden fringe is seen, hung in festoon. These columns are joined to the corners [of the entry way], just as the other eighteen fluted columns painted onto the walls of the three other sides of the room [are made to appear]. They imitate the colour of breccia marble, as does the baseboard [of each pedestal]. They are 13 and a half feet in height, including the base and the capital. Their pedestals are five feet high, including the socles; the architrave, frieze and cornice [are together] three and a half feet in height. The great cornice that stretches around the room [just below the false ceilings] is [sculpted] in relief. The space between the [two] columns that form the sides of the large arches is 12 feet, and that between those of the smaller arches [is] four and a half feet. On the three sides of the room [where the columns are painted rather than sculpted in relief] there is a large [central] arch and two smaller [flanking] ones. Those that are on the right and the left [that is, the smaller arches] are 14 feet high, including the [top] railing, by 7 and a half feet wide. They are supported by coupled columns. The rear columns that support a cornice are 18 inches [wide]; this cornice serves as an impost to the large arches, and obtains at the same [height for the triple arch groupings] in both the square and [demi-]octagonal rooms. Above [and between the imposts] an archi-

Illustration 3. Interior of the Paris Opéra during a performance of Lully's *Armide*. Drawing with gouache by Gabriel-Jacques Saint-Aubin (1724-1780). Courtesy, Museum of Fine Arts, Boston. Reproduced with permission. ©2002 Museum of Fine Arts, Boston. All Rights Reserved.

volt rises, where two figures are seen holding a wall clock. In the middle of the large arches there is a group of four figures playing different instruments. Where the mirrors begin [in the demi-octagonal room] these arches are bordered by curtains of crimson velour, raised by cords of braided gold which, in hanging, serve to hide the joins between the [panes of the] mirrors, such that they appear to be all of one piece. Festoons of garlands produce the same effect.

The square room and the [demi-]octagonal room are further adorned with 20 [coupled] columns with their rear pilasters [coloured] in mottled blue marble, as are the 4 [rear] pilasters [in the triple arch groups] of the demi-octogonal room. [As well, a grouping of] six statues in antique style depicts Mercury and Momus in the rear, and along the sides [are] four life-size muses, painted in white marble, as are the other figures. These are the work of Charles Vanlo, and are painted in very good taste. . .

The great arch at the rear where the third part of the gallery begins is 16 feet high by 10 wide. There two Heroes [sculpted] in relief hold the King's Arms. This arch serves as the entry into the demi-octagonal room, into which one climbs up three steps, and the layout of which is at the level of the bottom of the railings, so as to indicate the possibility of walking behind the arches along the sides [of the room]. . .

Twenty-two crystal chandeliers, each fitted with twelve candles, hang from the three [false] ceilings from cords with gold and silken tassles. Thirty-two candlesticks holding two candles are placed in the space between the pilasters that support the loges. Ten girandoles, each with five candles, are placed on the coupled columns of the great [i.e., square] room; and in the [demi-] octagonal room there is a girandole of three arms on each of the columns.

Thirty instrumentalists, placed fifteen at each end of the room, make up the orchestra for the *Bal*. But for a half hour before it begins, these instrumentalists gather in the [demi-]octagonal room, with timpani and trumpets, and present a concert of grand symphonic works by the best masters.

In the absence of any surviving eighteenth century illustration of the Opera's ballroom, we are fortunate to have this vivid account, the more so since it provides information about the original layout, as well as the renovated facility. Nevertheless, it has been helpful to my 'mental' reconstruction of the room to refer to the well-known drawing, with watercolour and gouache, by Gabriel-Jacques Saint-Aubin (1724-1780), of a moment captured in a performance of Lully's *Armide* in the Paris opera house of 1747.[30] (See illustration.) This is the only known depiction of the stage and auditorium that includes a view of both parterre and loges during a performance. As Neal Zaslaw has pointed out, Saint-Aubin's perspective is from the left of center in the amphitheatre, looking over the crowd in the parterre toward the stage. Using Saint-Aubin's point of view, and referring to the 1727 description in the *Mercure*, it is not difficult to imagine how the original ballroom was laid out. It terminated, at one end, behind Saint-Aubin in what the *Mercure* called 'the oval on the loges side' of the room. Although new and elaborate decorations were in place after Servandoni's remodeling, this end of the ballroom (the amphitheatre) remained structurally unchanged even after 1727. I am unable to say with certainty whether the benches in the amphitheatre were removed during balls, but it is reasonable to assume that they were.[31] From this end of the room, the floor opened out on a single level, covering the orchestra pit, and eventually reaching the stage, which was originally squared off to form the far end of the space. Here, according to the *Mercure*, an 'alcove' marked the location of the orchestra. In its new disposition, however, the stage end of the room became a separate gallery, bordered by mirrors, and articulated by a front and rear archway. Its shape ('demi-octagonal') was not unlike the horseshoe 'oval' of the loges end of the ballroom (behind Saint-Aubin). The increase to the overall dimensions of the room reported in the *Mercure*'s description was evidently restricted to the new gallery at the stage end, a gallery that was slightly elevated, since one entered it by climbing 'up three steps.'

The largest portion of the facility was an area of 30 square feet (slightly more than 9 meters squared) referred to in the *Mercure* account as the 'square room.' It occupied that part of the amphitheatre borderd by the two, nearly parallel rows of loges (before they curve into each other—behind Saint-Aubin—to form a horseshoe shape). It also included all of the parterre, the area covering the orchestra pit, and the opening of the stage. As we shall see, this represented a principal

[30]See Neal Zaslaw, 'At the Paris Opera in 1747,' *Early Music* 11/4 (1983), 515-17, where a black and white reproduction is given and discussed. The drawing (again, black and white) is also reproduced in Heinrich Besseler, Max Schneider, general eds., *Musikgeschichte in Bildern*, Bd. IV/1: *Oper. Szene und Darstellung von 1600 bis 1900*, Hellmuth Christian Wolff, ed. (Leipzig, n.d.), 'Abbildung 96', 112-13. In his commentary, Wolff claims the drawing represents a performance of 1761. Barbara Coeyman, 'Theatres for Opera and Ballet,' 33, correctly locates the performance in 1747, but says that it was of Lully's *Alceste*, instead of his *Armide*.

[31]Coeyman, 'Theatres for Opera and Ballet,' 34, remarks that various illustrations depict from six to ten benches, suggesting to me that they were not fixed in their placement.

socializing area of the ballroom. At either end of the square room were dancing spaces, adjacent to the new locations for the two orchestras. The numerous archways, pillars, and columns, described in meticulous detail in the passage, lined the perimeter of this central area (as well as that of the demi-octagonal gallery), giving the illusion of arcades beyond. Most of these, as well as much of the other decorations, were painted onto flats. The archway of the principal entry, as well as those at either ends of the demi-octagonal gallery, and a number of pillars, however, were three- dimensional carvings. Presumably they were made of wood and painted.

In fact, such décor drew on a rich heritage of visual imagery that recurs over and over in ballroom settings of the seventeenth and eighteenth centuries.[32] The space for dancing was typically square or rectangular (or occasionally octagonal), although there was no particular reason to favour such a design, since a dancing area was normally created 'within a room,' as distinct from simply using the space 'of a room.' The ballroom area overall was made to appear as graciously large as possible. That it often became hopelessly crowded does not compromise the intent of spaciousness. In the case of the *bal de l'Opéra*, grandeur was a featured attraction. Overall, after the 1727 remodeling, the ballroom was '98 feet (almost 32m) in length, including the demi-octagone,' and nearly 10 meters wide, though not uniformly so: the demi-octagonal portion of the room was just 24 feet wide (close to 8m).[33] Decorations such as those described in the *Mercure* were virtual icons of the ballroom, and they endured for some time. As a case in point, it is useful to revisit the account from 1770 of Charles Burney's evening at the Waux-hall in Paris. It will be recalled that he wrote of it, '...it is illuminated, and has galleries, that are continued to another room, which is square, and still larger than the first, with two rows of Corinthian pillars ornamented with festoons and illuminations. This is a very elegant room, in which the company dance *minuets, allemandes, cotillions,* and *contre danses*.'[34]

[32]This kind of imagery is featured, for example, in an engraving by Jean Le Pautre of a ball given at Versailles in 1668. For an interesting review of this depiction, see Barbara Coeyman, 'Social Dance in the 1668 *Feste de Versailles*: architecture and performance context,' *Early Music* 26/2 (1998), 264-82.

[33]Durey de Noinville, *Histoire du théâtre*, 162. The metric conversions are taken from LeGrave, *Le Théâtre et le public*, 504. They are at odds with the measurements offered by Coeyman, 'Theatres for Opera and Ballet,' 33, who observes that the entire theatre was 35m long by 17m wide.

[34]Charles Burney, *The Present State of Music in France and Italy*, 13.

Another enduring icon of the ballroom was its brilliant illumination. At the *bal public* in its heyday the lighted room must have been something to behold. Durey de Noinville reported that there were 'more than three hundred candles in the room,'[35] but his observation seems vastly understated. From his description, based almost entirely on that provided in the *Mercure,* I estimate that there were well over five hundred candles (if, indeed, they were all lit). Given the mirrors and the rich bronze hues that dominated the décor, the room must have been bathed in a rich, golden light.

What might be concluded from the visual imagery typical of the seventeenth- and eighteenth-century ballroom? Those in attendance— whether dancing or observing—were transported to an idealized world, located in some halcyon time and space of classical antiquity. Crowds notwithstanding, each individual found herself or himself in a larger-than-life situation, confronted by the spectre of gods, muses and heroes of the past (in the form of statues), and illuminated personally by a brilliant light far more intense than that of any other nighttime venue. She or he could not help being on display, nor help noticing those others on display in the assembled company. It is surely not an accident that the layout of the opera house on the evenings of public balls drew heavily on such potent imagery. It replicated, but on a larger scale, the most resplendent of ballroom facilities crafted for some noble households when a ball was to take place. In fact, it may well be that the demi-octagonal room, framed as it was by mirrors that were contrived to appear as a single, continuous piece, was a response to the spectacular *Gallerie des Glaces* at Versailles, in which royal balls had been mounted from time to time. In Louis XIV's reign, its use seems to have been reserved for especially important occasions.[36] But it was also used occasionally for balls during Louis XV's reign, such as the so-called Yew Tree Ball that took place in the *Gallerie des Glaces* at the end of Carnival in 1745.[37] Somewhat unusual for a royal ball at Versailles, this one was an all night affair (over the evening of 25-26 February), just like those held at the opera house.

Since I have been unable to locate any illustration of the opera house ballroom, it is impossible for me to say where the great arched entrance was located. It will be recalled, however, that access to the *bal public* via the *cul-de-sac* was expressly prohibited, so there is no reason to assume that the principal entry was on the 'stage left' side of the auditorium,

[35]*Histoire du théâtre,* 163.

[36]Such as for balls celebrating the marriage of the duc and duchesse de Bourgogne in early December, 1697. See Rebecca Harris-Warrick, 'Ballroom Dancing at the Court of Louis XIV,' *Early Music* 14/1 (1986), 44-45.

[37]ibid.

as it was for operatic performances. In fact, the access into theatre on the evening of a ball through the 'Cour d'entrée' suggests that it was probably on the 'stage right' side of the room (or to Saint-Aubin's left).

At the base of the loges that framed the 'salon quarré' portion of the ballroom, buffets were set up along the two lengthways sides. Here refreshments could be purchased.[38] But because there was no convenient area for consuming them in what was, on many evenings, a rather crowded part of the ballroom, refreshments often were carried up into the loges. A lively account of the social mingling that was characteristic of the *bals publics* clearly alludes to this practice. A gentleman masquer in this description has retreated from the crowded ballroom floor, and has seated himself in the loges beside a costumed lady, with whom he strikes up a conversation.

> 'It would be unproductive and even misleading [of me],' I said to her, 'to offer you some refreshments: you do not seem to me to be so fatigued, attractive masquer, to have such a need.'[39]

If the amphitheatre end of the square room were not so crowded, however, it seems likely that refreshments were also consumed at or near the buffets.

A final unusual feature of the layout of the theatre after Servadoni's renovations had been put into place was the deployment of the orchestra. The *Mercure* reports that it consisted of thirty instrumentalists who performed at 'each end of the room,' fifteen on each side. 'But for half an hour before it begins,' it is explained, 'these instrumentalists gather in the [demi-]octagonal room' to present a concert. Because there is a distinction in locations made here (or so it seems) between the 'two extremities of the room' and the 'salon demi-octagone,' and because the latter was slightly elevated, I have suggested that the principal dancing space at the *bal public* was restricted to the 'square room.' (A square dancing space that projects the illusion of grandeur and spaciousness, moreover, is part of the visual imagery typical of the eighteenth-century French ballroom.) I believe the two instrumental

---

[38]Data on the sale of refreshments is very scarce. In the *Memoire concernant la Regie de l'Opera, & sa situation au premier avril 1721*, a line item in an accounting of receipts from the opera balls of that year reads: 'Produit des Buffets, déduit la remise l'on lui a fait pour les mauvaises nuits de 270, reste 738.' Archives *Nationales*, AJ[13]-3, pièce 6.

[39]*Mercure galant*, février (1716), 199: 'Il seroit inutile & mefféant même, lui dis-je, de vous offrir des rafraîchissemens: vous ne m'avez pas l'air assez echauffée, beau Masque, pour en avoir besoin.' This account seems to have been calculated to satirize the amorous adventures which, in the opinion of its author, were the chief activity of the *bal public*. Indeed, in just under 100 pages of text, adulterous trysts, mistaken identities, and secret sexual encounters are the principal focus.

groups played at the two ends of the square room, and not the two ends of the ballroom overall. This still would have left a distance of 17-18 meters between the two groups, and must have presented logistical problems to both musicians and dancers, an issue that I will address later in this study.

The transformation of the theatre into a *salle de bal*, in summary, relied on resources from the opera house, but drew its 'scenic' materials not from the spectacular array of theatrical props or stage effects available, but from a rich heritage of ballroom imagery that had emerged during Louis XIV's reign. In fact, the opera ball had all the trappings of a luxuriant *bal particulier*, but all on an exceedingly grand scale.

With the exception of the loges, the entire facility—including dance floor, elaborate decorations, and refreshment stands—was laid out in a single, large, and well-lit room, with a separate gallery at the far end. Such a layout did not meet with universal approval. In a fictitious, and humorous, but nevertheless believable anecdote recounted in the *Mercure* of February 1716, a young man is forced into the loges, because there was no place to rest in the ballroom proper:

> 'I went out from my place,' he says, 'eight days ago at midnight, to take myself to the Opera Ball. I was alone, somewhat melancholy, and not without reason. Eventually, masked in an ample costume, I entered into the Ballroom, where I discovered a large and brilliant assembly. I made several rounds without speaking to anyone; bored in the end, and very weary from all the comings and goings, I planted myself in a loge, where I found a useful place to sleep in peace.'[40]

For the same reasons, the Abbé Prévost found Heidegger's design(s) for the Haymarket Theatre's masquerades more amenable. In his *Mémoires* he compared them to his experiences of Parisian public assemblies, but it is not clear if Prévost is referring specifically to an opera ball in Paris (nor, indeed, if he ever attended one). Following his sojourn to London in 1728-30, he nevertheless reported:

> The spectacle appeared enchanting to me. I am not speaking of the multitude of masquers and the galant appearance of their costumes. In that respect our assemblies in Paris compare favourably to those of England. But the layout of the room where this entertainment is given

[40]*Mercure galant*, février (1716), 197: 'Je sortis, dit-il, il y a huit jours à minuit de chez moy, pour me rendre au Bal de l'Opera. J'étois seul, assez mélancolique, & non sans raison. Enfin masqué sous un ample domino, j'entray dans la salle du Bal, où je trouvay une nombreuse & brillante Assemblée. J'y fis plusieurs tours sans parler à personne; ennuyé à la fin, & très las de toutes ces allées & venuës, je fus me camper dans un loge, où je trouvay une place commode pour dormir à mon aise.'

is one of the most beautiful things in the world. Everything is the invention of the famous Mr. Heydegger... There are also revels in the place, [and] there are rooms set aside for this. There are still others to which one can retire to relax when one is fatigued by dancing, or by the noise of the crowd. In short, everything is of an admirable order and taste.[41]

Prévost was also impressed by the fact that the refreshments to be had—'all manner of wines, fruits, preserves'—were included in the admission price.[42] Moreover, as we saw in accounts of Haymarket masquerades documented in the Portland manuscripts, discussed in the last chapter briefly, refreshment stands and booths were also located on a lower level in the theatre. 'Mr Petkum', it will be recalled, 'carried them [his company] down to a great apartment' after he had danced. The passage continues:

> [There] were several shops with signs, a chocolate booth with one [server] in Spanish habit [that is, costume], a coffee house with a master *à la Turc*, a comfiture [that is, 'sweets' booth] with a French habit, a booth for liquors with Italian and strong drinks, with one in a Muscovite habit, a kitchen with cold meat, and every one of these inviting the company as they came into their booths.[43]

It is true that there was a café located directly below the amphitheatre at the Paris Opera, too,[44] but I have found no evidence that it was accessible during a public ball.

Heidegger's conception of a public ball space, then, was one that utilized several rooms. On this count, the London masquerades seem to have conformed more closely to a layout regularly encountered in the private balls of noble households. Formal or masked balls in and around Paris, too, very often made use of several rooms featuring distinct activities. Among numerous examples recorded in the *Mercure galant* the following is part of a description of a ball given for the

---

[41]*Mémoires et avantures d'un homme de qualité*, V, 73-4: 'Le spectacle me parut enchanté. Je ne parle point de la multitude des masques & de l'air galant de leurs habits. Nos Assemblées de Paris valent bien, de ce côté-là, celles d'Angleterre. Mais la disposition de la salle, où se donne ce divertissement, est une des plus belles choses du monde. Tout est de l'invention du fameux M. Heydegger... On joue aussi dans ce lieu de délices; il y a des salles destinées pour cela. Il y en a d'autres, où l'on peut se retirer pour être tranquille, lorsqu'on est las de la danse & du bruit de la multitude. Enfin, tout y est d'un ordre & d'un goût admirable.'

[42]ibid.: 'Il est vrai qu'on donne en abondance, & sans rien paier de plus, toutes sortes de vins, de fruits, de confitures & de rafraîchissemens.'

[43]*Manuscripts of his Grace the Duke of Portland*, V, 545-6.

[44]See Coeyman, 'Theatres for Opera and Ballet', 34.

Duchesse de Bourgogne in February 1700 by the Marquis d'Antin at the Hôtel d'Antin (formerly the Hôtel de Soissons):

> There were seven rooms, all of them large, [and] all brilliantly lit. They were richly furnished. Violins and oboes had been placed in three rooms. The others were used for rest. Those where one danced were not contiguous, so that there was between each dancing room a room in which to relax.[45]

At the *bals de l'Opéra*, however, everything was concentrated in a single large space. While it may not have been intentional, this aspect of the opera balls in Paris served to maximize one's exposure to those in attendance at all times.

The two other venues for opera balls—the facility at the Tuilleries, which served from 1764 through 1769, and the second theatre at the *Palais-Royal*, which was used from 1770 to 1781—were both treated to descriptions in the pages of the *Mercure galant*.[46] The Tuilleries ballroom was larger than the older facility in both length and width, but was still set out as a single, rectangular room. Its décor and general layout were, in other respects, much the same. The buffets, however, were relocated to a 'balcony' situated on the same level as the loges, at one end of the ballroom, directly above the amphitheatre.[47] The new ballroom of the *Palais-Royal* was of a somewhat different design. Perhaps in recognition of one of the features of the original ballroom, the new one was laid out as an octagon—a complete one now—with a diameter of over forty feet (roughly 13 meters).[48] In some respects it must have been much like an expansive indoors gazebo, for it was flanked around its perimeter by 'columns, statues and mirrors,' and was crowned by a spectacular ceiling.[49] Unlike earlier opera ballrooms, which had essentially made use of all the available floor area, this one was set up *within* the theatre, leaving some space beyond the perimeter of the

---

[45]*Mercure galant*, février (1700), 216: 'Il y avoit sept chambres toutes brillantes de lumieres, tout le nombre en estoit grand. Elles estoient richement meublées. On avoit placé des Violons & des Hautsbois dans trois pieces. Les autres servoient à se reposer. Celles où l'on dansoient n'estoient pas de suite, & il y avoit entre chaque salle du Bal, une autre Salle pour se délasser...'

[46]For the former, see *Mercure galant*, février (1764), 195-197, and for the latter, *Mercure galant*, mars (1770), 141-148.

[47]ibid., 195-196: 'les Balcons qui forment la partie du milieu & dans lesquels sont établis des Buffets vis-à-vis de grands trumeaux de glaces... La Salle, en totalité, est plus longue & plus large qu'à l'ancien Opéra.'

[48]The *Mercure galant*, mars (1770), 148, contains a minor printing mishap (at least in the copies I have examined): the moveable piece of type destined to form the second digit of a two-digit number (beginning with a '4') was damaged, leaving a space where the second digit should have printed.

[49]ibid.

octagon unused. As we shall see in the last chapter, even with a more compact and symmetrical design, the orchestra was still divided into two separate groups in this facility.

The *bal public*, in short, was designed with spectacle and lively social intercourse in mind. It was a place to be seen (in the relative anonymity of disguise, to be sure), to mingle, and to observe the interaction of others. The Regent regularly did just that. And he was not the only duc d'Orléans to do so. The Regent's grandson, Louis-Philippe (1725-1785) was also an enthusiastic patron of the opera ball. When the first theatre was destroyed by fire in 1763 he entered into an elaborate and very costly negotiation with the city of Paris, holders of the *Académie*'s privilege since 1749, to retain the location of a new opera house in the *Palais-Royal*. In the end he was successful.[50] Having the opera theatre rebuilt in his residence was important to d'Orléans, not only because of financial commitments—in the arrangements negotiated with the city he had agreed to donate and to develop properties adjacent to the palace[51]—but as an issue of personal interest, as well. The *bals de l'Opéra*, in particular, seem to have been a special concern: in the first full season of balls in the new theatre, 1770-71, he and members his household attended frequently. A receipt from the end of that season reads: 'In addition, from M[on]s[ein]g[eu]r le duc d'Orléans and Mlle la duchesse de Chartres, for fifty-one tickets for them and persons of their court during the course of the ball [season], received the sum of three hundred and six pounds.'[52] At the time, the duchesse de Chartres mentioned here (she was the daughter-in-law of d'Orléans), and her husband the duc de Chartres, even had apartments in the *Palais-Royal* that offered them direct access to the theatre.[53] For the d'Orléans family the institution of opera balls held in their household had become something worth protecting.

---

[50]A brief review of some of these negotiations can be found in Norman Demuth, *French Opera. Its Development to the Revolution* (Sussex, 1963), 222-23.

[51]The *Mercure* reported that city footed the bill for the theatre, but that d'Orléans furnished and oversaw the development of grounds just outside the new theatre. Besides gardens, these developed areas included shops and restaurants. See *Mercure galant*, mars (1770), 141-42.

[52]*Bibliothèque-Musée de l'Opéra*, CO 10, 1770-71.

[53]See Robert M. Isherwood, *Farce and Fantasy*, 217. Isherwood offers an account of the duc de Chartres' many efforts to locate a third opera house in the Palais-Royal after the second theatre burned in 1781. He is mistaken, however, in his claim that Chartres 'eventually won' the battle (see p.221).

CHAPTER THREE

Economics, Finances, and Attendance

Il y a été beaucoup de monde la nuit de Saint-Martin, et on a vendu ses billets à perte presque du tout pour aller danser, pendant qu'on meurt de faim chez soi. Voilà les François et les Parisiens.

Mathieu Marais (1720)[1]

We have already seen that France's finances at the beginning of the Regency were in need of critical attention: the country was a staggering two billion *livres* in debt. Although d'Orléans had inhertied the situation rather than created it, and although he implemented a number of fiscal reforms (some, to be sure, less successful than others) during his tenure as Regent, he is often vilified for leaving the country in worse economic shape than he found it. The failure of some of d'Orléans's fiscal policies is normally attributed to his controller-general of finance, John Law (1671-1729), who held that position officially only for the first four months of 1720, but whose ideas and activities were influential from the very beginning of the Regent's term of office.[2]

Law persuaded d'Orléans of a scheme he believed could quickly reduce the country's debt, re-establish confidence among France's trading partners, and increase domestic productivity. His idea—not an original one—was that of a central bank that would deal in credit and paper currency to stimulate investment. By 1716 d'Orléans gave permission to charter a *Banque générale*, still at this point a private institution with Law at the helm, and authorized it to issue paper money, the first ever used in France. To create an attractive opportunity for investors Law amalgamated the *Compagnie d'Occident* (sometimes referred to as the 'Mississippi Company'), in which he had acquired a controlling interest, with the French East India Company, forming the *Compagnie des Indes*. By 1718 his *Banque générale* had become the royal bank and its paper currency was guaranteed by the crown. When he became controller-general Law merged the assets of his *Compagnie des*

---

[1]M.de Lescure, ed., *Journal et mémoires de Mathieu Marais*, I, 481: 'There was a large crowd there the night of Saint Martin's, and bank notes were sold for next to nothing [so that one could] go to dance, even while at home people were dying of hunger. That's the French and the Parisians for you.'

[2]For a usefully even-handed account of Law and his controversial 'system,' and its impact on the Regency, see Shennan, *Philippe, Duke of Orléans*, 103-125.

Indes with the royal bank and was able to cut the country's debt by nearly half. But his *système* stimulated a flood of investment that artificially raised the value of stocks far beyond the revenue that reasonably could be expected from the holdings of the *Compagnie des Indes*. In 1720 a huge sell-off occurred, to the great profit of a few insiders, and the financial ruin of thousands of others. Law departed France in disgrace, and d'Orléans's reputation suffered considerably.[3]

This volatile economic situation affected the newly instituted *bals publics* both directly and indirectly, but not always in predictable ways. In one of the short-lived periods of relative prosperity under Law's *système*, for example, during the carnival season of 1720, the receipts from the *bals publics* more than doubled those of the previous year: 116,038 pounds in 1720, compared to 51,859 in 1719.[4] Such an outcome is, perhaps, not surprising in prosperous times. In the Spring of 1720, however, in an effort to ward off the spiralling sell-off of central bank stocks, the value of the new paper currency, as well as shares in the *Compagnie des Indes*, was reduced by fifty per cent. By the Fall the larger denominations of the new currency were declared worthless, and by the following Spring all paper money was withdrawn from circulation.[5] The central bank collapsed. And yet, the public ball season of 1720-21 (the first to begin on St Martin's day) does not seem to have been seriously compromised. Mathieu Marais commented wryly about its opening in the passage quoted at the opening of this chapter, noting that there was a large crowd. And he made a similar observation about the 'extraordianary' public ball held the following June (1721), in honour of the visiting Turkish ambassador: 'there was... a grand masked ball at the *Palais-Royal* the night of the 21st and 22nd. All the ladies flocked to it, and the gentlemen followed them. One is ruined, yet one dances. That's the French for you.'[6]

Because Marais was not of noble birth, it may have been impossible for him to countenance people spending money on public balls in the very difficult economic times of late 1720 and 1721. Norbert Elias has suggested, however, that something like the ironic disdain of a Marais, or the seemingly reckless spending of the nobility who attended public

[3]ibid. See further, H. Montgomery Hyde, *John Law: The History of an Honest Adventure*, rev. ed. (London, 1969).

[4]From figures reported in Albert de Lasalle, *Les treize salles de l'Opéra*, 58.

[5]M. de Lescure, ed. *Journal et Mémoires de Mathieu Marais*, vol. 1. The entries from July through December of 1720 are filled with details of the various proclamations of the devaluation of the currency.

[6]ibid., vol. 2, 167: 'Il y a eu un concert, qui n'a point été turc, et grand bal masqué au Palais-Royal, la nuit du 21 au 22. Toutes les femmes y ont couru et les hommes les y ont suivies: ont est ruiné et on danse. Voilà les François.' This ball is discussed in chapter one. See n70-74.

balls at this time, are perfectly consistent with the court society of eighteenth-century France. He argues:

> What appears as extravagance from the standpoint of the bourgeois economic ethic—'if he was running into debt why did he not reduce expenses?'—is in reality the expression of the seignorial ethos of rank. This ethos grows out of the structure and activity of court society, and is at the same time a precondition for the continuance of this activity. It is not freely chosen.[7]

In other words, a social occasion that offered the opportunity for attracting attention to oneself was of overriding importance for the nobility, while for the successful bourgeois financial matters took precedence.[8] Certainly both groups were victimized by the economic hardships of the period, but the nobility was not inclined to 'cut its losses' by becoming more frugal, for its gains and losses were measured more immediately in terms of 'prestige.' And so it is that Edmond-Jean-François Barbier, a younger contemporary of Marais, and also a bourgeois lawyer of *parlement*, remarked about a public ball at the Opera held on 16 November 1721: 'the magnificence of this festivity is of the highest order, for nearly all the *seigneurs* are in attire of golden or silver cloth. That's the current fashion.'[9] Despite a far-from-favourable economic climate, then, the *bals publics* thrived during the Regency.

Although the overall economy of the nation forms an important backdrop to the early history of the *bal public*, it was the fiscal woes of its parent institution—the Opera—that had more immediate impact on its initial development. The Opera's financial troubles originated well before Louis XIV died, and they would never be satisfactorily resolved until after the collapse of the *ancien régime*, but there is no doubt that its difficulties were exacerbated by the economic malaise of the Regency. The Marquis de Dangeau remarked in April of 1717:

> There is loud talk about excusing the Opera from the pensions it owes, without which [recourse] it is thought this spectacle cannot survive. [But] no one wishes to make such a sacrifice, and it is to be hoped that the Opera does not fail, for in a city like Paris many spectacles are necessary.[10]

---

[7]*The Court Society*, 53.

[8]ibid., 92.

[9]A. de la Villegille, ed. *Journal*, I, 111: 'La magnificence pour cette fête est extrême, car les seigneurs sont presque tous en habits de drap d'or ou de drap d'argent. C'est la mode à présent.'

[10]*Journal*, vol. xvii, jeudi, 1er avril: 'On parle fort de retrancher les pensions qui sont sur l'Opéra, sans quoi on ne croit pas que ce spectacle puisse continuer. Personne ne veut se charger de ce détail-là et l'on voudroit bien que l'Opéra ne tombe pas, car dans une ville comme Paris, il faut beaucoup de spectacles.'

The 'pensions' referred to by Dangeau were an onerous financial burden on the Opera that had been accruing for some time. At Lully's death in March, 1687 the directorship of the Opera reverted very briefly—for just three months—to two of his three sons, Louis and Jean-Louis de Lully. A *brevet* of the end of June of that year, however, named Jean-Baptiste Lully's son-in-law, Jean-Nicolas de Francine (1662-1735), the new director for a period of three years.[11] At the time the Opera's operations and finances were in robust good health. But one of the clauses in the *brevet* naming Francine director ordered that Lully's heirs, including his widow and children, continue to receive the annual profits of the Opera, divided among them according to a formula originally stipulated in the composer's will.[12] This represents the earliest layer of 'pensions' that were to play a progressively burdensome role in the Opera's finances in the coming years.

When Francine's first term as director of the Opera was drawing to a close a new *brevet* of 1 March 1689 renewed his appointment for ten years. This contract gave Francine rights to the profits of the Opera, but in other respects would turn out to be most disadvantageous to him. For one thing, it specified a fixed value—10,000 pounds—for the total annual pension Lully's heirs were to receive. Such an arrangement, of course, would suit Francine's purposes well if the profits from the Opera were healthy, but it would cost him dearly if they were not, because the contract required that the pension be paid 'monthly' and with a 'priority over all other expenses.'[13] As it turned out, the *Academie Royale de Musique* became unprofitable for Francine, and bills went unpaid, as did salaries, with the result that musicians, singers, and dancers were often late for rehearsals and performances, or even absent altogether.[14] Francine was forced to borrow heavily in order to keep the operation going.[15] It is hardly to be wondered, then, that when his second term came up for renewal at the end of 1698 the Royal Privilege was significantly modified.

The Privilege, dated 30 December 1698, made Hyacinthe Gauréault Dumont (c1647-1726) co-director with Francine for another period of

[11]See Benoit, *Musiques de cour*, 108-109. See further, Jean Gourret, *Ces hommes qui ont fait l'Opéra*, 30-31.

[12]See Benoit, *Musiques de cour*, 108-109.

[13]The document is reproduced in Durey de Noinville, *Histoire du théâtre*, 89: 'Pensions de dix mille livres, pour la Veuve & enfans du sieur Lully... payée par préférence à toutes autres dépenses, & de mois en mois.'

[14]For a useful summary of the Opera's finances of this period, see Gourret, *Ces hommes qui on fait l'Opéra*, 30-38.

[15]His principal creditors—Thouassin, l'Apotre, and de Montarsy—became associate directors with Francine during the latter part of this term. Gourret, *Ces hommes qui ont fait l'Opéra*, 32, 205.

ten years, the former entitled to one-quarter of the Opera's profits, and the latter three-quarters. But there would be few profits to share. Indeed, the Privilege placed so many new encumbrances on the Opera's budget that it is surprising to me that Francine was willing to agree to continue. Besides the 10,000 pound pension for Lully's heirs, the Privilege established annual pensions for a number of retirees of the Opera, to be paid in monthly instalments.[16] And in addition to these new ongoing expenses, the Opera had an additional 'poor tax' levied against its receipts. The *quart des pauvres*, as it was called, directed one-sixth of gate receipts to the hospital at the *Hôtel Dieu* as well as the *Hôpital générale*. This was no small expense, amounting to over 26,500 pounds in 1702 alone.[17]

By the end of 1704 the Opera was more than 350,000 pounds in debt, and Francine and Dumont actively sought out someone willing to take over the operation.[18] They found such an individual in Pierre Guyenet (d1712), a wealthy financier with whom they were able to strike an agreement, one that received the blessing of the crown in new letters patent issued on 7 October 1704.[19] It is difficult to understand what made Guyenet believe that he could succeed where Francine had failed, especially since he agreed to take on a number of expenses of seemingly crippling proportions. Besides assuming responsibility for all Francine and Dumont's debts—including those dating from Francine's first term—Guyenet agreed to a one-time payment of 75,000 pounds to Francine, and 25,000 to Dumont. Additionally Francine would receive an annual pension, in quarterly installments, of 8,624 pounds 'in times of war' or 11,624 'in times of peace.'[20]

To his credit, Guyenet managed to pay off over 200,000 pounds of the amount due the past creditors of the Opera, but he could not avoid taking on new debts. One of these was for the purchase of a sizeable property where he hoped to build a new 'Magasin' that would serve as a business office for the Opera, as a rehearsal space, and as a

[16]The complete text of the Privilege is given in Benoit, *Musiques de cour*, 157-158. See further, Gourret, *Ces hommes qui ont fait l'Opéra*, 32-33.

[17]According to Jérôme de LaGorce, *L'Opéra à Paris au temps de Louis XIV* (Paris, 1992), 112. LaGorce gives no source for this figure, but he also notes that in the same year the *Comédiens* had to pay 31,576 pounds as their *quart des pauvres*. This work provides a very useful and detailed—if not always fully documented—analysis of the management and finances of the Opera through 1715.

[18]Gourret, *Ces hommes qui ont fait l'Opéra*, 32-33.

[19]Benoit, *Musiques de cour*, 191-192. The complete text of the original agreement, from the *Archives de Maître Albertini, notaire à Fointainebleau*, is given in Gourret, *Ces hommes qui ont fait l'Opéra*, 255-260.

[20]ibid.

large storage area for its stage properties. The *Académie Royale de Musique* had been paying rent for such a facility at a cost of between 3500 and 4000 pounds a year, so when in August 1711 Guyenet spent 5400 pounds for the new property, it probably seemed like a sound, long-term investment.[21] But it was a project he would never see completed, and when it was, three years after his death, it was not the property Guyenet had purchased that was developed, but rather one in the rue Nicaise, adjacent to the rented space that had formerly served as the Opera's services facility. The purchase of property in late 1711 has often led scholars to believe that the new 'Magasin' was built in 1712,[22] but it was not until 1715 that it was opened, and the cost of its construction seems to have been a significant factor in the establishment of the *bal public*.

When Guyenet died a ruined man in 1712, the Opera's overall indebtedness is estimated to have been close to 400,000 pounds, and one source lists his personal indebtedness at an astonishing 1,500,000.[23] Guyenet's creditors, their heirs and trustees would keep a stranglehold on the Opera's finances for many years to come. In the short term, however, it was deemed appropriate to place the management of the Opera in the hands of four syndics, who had been nominated shortly after Guyenet's death by a cabal of his creditors to represent their interests in the operations of the Opera. The four were: Mathurin Besnier, a lawyer in the *parlement*; Pierre de Laval de Saint-Pont, a bourgeois of Paris; Etienne Lambert Chomat, a wealthy merchant; and Duchêne, who, as we saw earlier (see p.37), became the inspector in charge of the new services building, and who oversaw the refurbishing of the theatre in the *Palais-Royal* as it was transformed into the venue for the *bals publics*. The four were confirmed as directors in letters patent of 8 January 1713,[24] and since none was in a position to offer artistic guidance, André Cardinal Destouches was made Inspector General.

When the *bals publics* were inaugurated just three years later, the Opera was in precarious financial straits. It was hoped initially that the balls would yield profits that could alleviate fiscal pressures from the two sources briefly outlined above: pensions, and the new services facility, the 'Magasin.' I have been able to locate at least one source that directly links profits from the early years of the balls to the payment of pensions. It notes that 'His Majesty decided on 27 August 1724 that pensions of 10,000 pounds assigned to the profits of the ball were to

[21]LaGorce, *L'Opéra à Paris*, 147-148.

[22]For example, Gourret, *Ces hommes qui ont fait l'Opéra*, 41.

[23]LaGorce, *L'Opéra à Paris*, 155.

[24]Durey de Noinville, *Histoire du théâtre*, vol. 1, 93-94.

be discontinued.'[25] Most other financial records, however, make such a direct link impossible to trace. On the other hand, a number of sources confirm that the expenses for the construction and the ongoing operations of the services building were to be addressed principally by revenues from the opera balls.[26] Among the more explicit of these is an imprint of 1719, published not long after the facility had opened. It reads in one passage:

> This Magasin is located in the rue Saint Niçaise. It is quite a large building, recently constructed, and cost one hundred and twenty thousand pounds to build. It is rectangular in shape, containing [among other things] four areas for lodgings. At the front is the dwelling of one of the syndics, across from the ateliers of the workers. To the right is the rehearsal hall, and to the left the assembly room. Wardrobes for the costumes are placed around this [latter] room. It was in consideration of this facility that the Opera was accorded an exclusive privilege for balls, their revenue being destined to reimburse the individual who provided the financing, after which this building belongs properly to the crown.[27]

The Magasin remained an important facility for the Opera for many years. In 1752 Durey de Noinville reported that it was the location for both the singing and dance schools of the Academy, and that it housed work areas for the set and costume designers, the machinist, the tailor, for the music copyist, harpsichord tuner, and the chief cashier.[28] I have been unable to discover if profits from the opera balls continued to fund such essential operations. Those financial records that do survive, however, suggest that ball revenues after about 1725 were no longer earmarked for specific budget areas, but rather contributed only in a general way to the Opera's finances overall.

---

[25]*Memoires pour servir a l'histoire de l'Académie Royale de Musique*, 78: 'La majesté decida le 27 août 1724 que les pensions de 10,000 l assignés sur le produit du Bal seroient supprimés...'

[26]See, for example, Albert de Lasalle, *Les treize salles de l'Opéra*, 36.

[27]*Lettres historiques sur tous les spectacles de Paris*, (Paris, 1719), 119-20: 'Ce Magazin est situé dans la rue Saint Nicaise. C'est une assez grande Maison nouvellement bâtie, & qui a coûté á construire cent vingt mille livres. Sa figure est un quarré long qui soûtient quatre corps de logis. Sur le devant est le logement d'un des Syndics, vis-á-vis les atteliers des Ouvriers; à main droite, la sale des repetitions, & à la maine gauche la sale des assemblées. On a pratiqué autour de cette sale des armoires pour les habits. C'est en consideration de ce bâtiment qu'on a accordé à l'Opera le Privilege exclusif des bals; la recette étant destinée à rembourser celuy qui en fait les avances, après quoy ce bâtiment restera en propre au Roy.' [One copy of this comparatively rare imprint may be found at the *Bibliothèque-Musée de l'Opéra*, under the shelf number C.1147.]

[28]*Histoire du théâtre*, I, 143-44.

In all the records I have examined I have not found a single season in which the *bals de l'Opéra* did not turn a profit. Their success, however, was never sufficient to rescue the Academy from an ever-worsening indebtedness.[29] In 1749 the city of Paris took over managerial and financial responsibility for the Opera, which nevertheless remained a 'royal academy.' (It returned to an operation of the 'Maison du Roi' in 1780.[30]) Although this move, too, proved unsuccessful—one source relates that the Opera's indebtedness had grown to 1,132,972 pounds by 1757[31]—it yielded at least one positive result: after 1749 financial record keeping at the Opera became both more complete and more meticulous. Even so, only a comparative handful of records has survived. Enough remains, however, to offer a good idea of the opera ball's finances, and how they contributed to the operations of the Opera more generally. These records also offer a tantalizing glimpse into public ball attendance, documenting just when in the season it seems to have been *de rigueur* to go.

•   •   •   •   •

Compared to the costs of mounting productions of operas and ballets, the expenses incurred to put on *bals publics* were rather modest. The decorations and other fixtures—periodic replacement and renovation notwithstanding—essentially presented a one-time expense. In the *Memoire concernant la Regie de l'Opera, & sa situation au premier avril 1721*,[32] prepared by Francine (or at least assembled under his supervision), an estimate is given for the value of the ball's 'properties': 'Etablissement du Bal, Planches, Decoration, Lustres, Plaques, formes, tapisserie & autres' are appraised at 31,500 pounds. By way of comparison, the same document appraises the value of the Opera's inventory—its costumes, machines, decorations and furnishings—at 160,000 pounds. But in addition to this, other 'equipment' such as a harpsichord and double bass are valued at 2500 pounds, ancillary

---

[29]In addition to its useful assessment of the management and finances of the Opera in the period immediately following Lully's death (as reported above in n14), Jean Gourret also provides comprehensive coverage of later periods. On the eighteenth century records, see *Ces hommes qui ont fait l'Opéra*, 13-91, 216-219, 255-262. A recent English language account (though less detailed, and essentially without commentary) is Caroline Wood, and Graham Sadler, eds., *French Baroque Opera. A Reader* (Aldershot, 2000), Ch. 1, 'The Paris Opéra (1672-1770): management and mismanagement,' 1-21.

[30]The *arrêt du Conseil d'Etat* of 17 March 1780 is given in Gourret, *Ces hommes qui ont fait l'Opéra*, 262. The law was enacted on April 1st.

[31]*Memoires pour servir a l'histoire de l'Académie Royale de Musique*, 205.

[32]*Archives Nationales*, AJ[13]-3.

facilities of the opera house, such as the 'Caffé' and the 'Cul-de-sac' are valued at 25,575 pounds, and the Magasin and its furnishings are valued at 133,422 pounds. Overall, then, the capital invested in the Opera's physical plant amounted to 321,497 pounds, over ten times that of the public ball. Whereas in 1721 alone the net profits from the balls were sufficient to cover the costs of their 'initial' investment, the Opera was destined never to recover the costs of its own.

There were, of course, ongoing operational expenses to mount public balls, including salaries for both musicians and support staff, the cost of candles, fire wood, and that of printing (principally posters and tickets). In the financial documents that survive, however, a detailed breakdown of such costs is rare, and typically yields information only on salaries. For seven seasons of public balls mounted in the original theatre of the *Palais-Royal*, nevertheless, there are surviving financial records that report on the overall yearly expenses to put on public balls. These are summarized in the following table.[33] In this table I have included a calculation for the 'Cost per Ball' not found in the original documents, simply by dividing the 'Seasonal Cost' by the number of balls offered.

Table 3.1 Opera Ball Expenses, 1720-21, 1757-63

Season	Number of Balls	Seasonal Cost	Cost per Ball
1720-21	19	19,586 (pounds)	1030 (pounds)
1757-58	14	11,644.16	831
1758-59	17	12,439.1	731
1759-60	14	10,307.7	736
1760-61	12	8,763.11	730
1761-62	16	11,589.14	724
1762-63	14	10,369.12.6	740

I am unable to account for the higher costs incurred in the 1720-21 season. It may be that since these figures are taken from an exceptional accounting—it was drawn up in response to Francine's once more assuming sole directorship of the Academy (see p.15, n62)—they reported expenses that in subsequent years were not normally included. In the late 1750s and early 60s, at any rate, it cost (roughly) between 700 and 800 pounds to put on a public ball. In the two seasons that followed the first fire at the opera house, however, the *bals publics* were

---

[33]The figures have been compiled from *Archives Nationales*, AJ[13]-3, and AJ[13]-9, pièces 142, 146, 148, 149, 150 and 151.

held at the Tuilleries, and this added to their expense, as the following figures show.[34]

Table 3.2 Opera Ball Expenses, 1763-65

Season	Number of Balls	Seasonal Cost	Cost per Ball
1763-64	12	12,570.2 (pounds)	1,047 (pounds)
1764-65	16	16,450.96	1,028

And after the new theatre in the *Palais-Royal* was opened in 1770, the operating expenses of the *bal public* became still greater.[35] Unfortunately the data for these years is incomplete, yielding only partial information on how many balls were mounted in the years between 1771 and the mid-1780s.

Table 3.3 Opera Ball Expenses, 1770-80

Season	Number of Balls	Seasonal Cost	Cost per Ball
1770-71	16[36]	22,588 (pounds)	1411 (pounds}
1771-72	?	26,948	?
1772-73	?	23,096	?
1773-74	?	18,269	?
1774-75	?	24,737	?
1775-76	16[37]	20,556	1284
1776-77	?	20,445	?
1777-78	?	25,156	?
1778-79	?	21,122	?
1779-80	?	19,198	?

Still, these less complete statistics reveal that, compared to the 1750s, it cost almost twice as much in the 1770s to put on a public ball. It is also true, however, that the gate receipts during the 1770s showed a marked upswing, and, since the price of admission at that time remained unchanged from earlier years, it may be concluded that

---

[34]*Archives Nationales*, AJ[13]-9, pièces 152, 153.

[35]Figures in the following table are drawn from *Archives Nationales*, AJ[13]-9, pièce 156.

[36]This figure is drawn from attendance records preserved at the *Bibliothèque-Musée de l'Opéra*, CO 10.

[37]This figure is drawn from *Archives Nationales*, AJ[13]-9, pièce 2.

attendance must have increased as well.[38] An increase to both costs and revenues can be explained, if only in part, by the larger space overall that the new theatre at the *Palais-Royal* afforded. A larger space, of course, accommodated greater numbers, but it also meant an increase to the costs of lighting and heating. Moreover, the size of the ball orchestra had grown from thirty instrumentalists overall in the 1750s and 1760s to forty by the 1780-81 season[39] (the last season in this new facility before it, too, was destroyed by fire), and this contributed significantly to the expense of salaries (an increase of 33% if the number of balls remained constant).

The most costly of the ongoing expenses of the public balls were salaries, and chief among these were those of the members of the ball orchestra. Unfortunately, although a few, scattered payment records for other employees of the *Academie Royale de Musique* (singers, instrumentalists, dancers) survive from the 1750s, 60s and 70s,[40] I have been unable to locate any for employees of the opera ball before 1780-81.[41] The evidence from that season, however, clarifies a number of practices that might be assumed to have been in place in previous years as well. First, payment was on a 'per service' basis, and second, there was more than one rate of pay. In 1780-81 there were three tiers for salaries: 12 pounds per service, 10 per service, and 8 per service. Four individuals (three string players— violin and/or viola—and one bassist) received the highest rate of pay, fourteen others received 10 pounds per service (string players, oboists, timpanists, and a bassist), and the remainder 8. (The precise make-up of the orchestra and how its members were expected to perform their duties will be addressed in the last chapter.) In the absence of other evidence, it may be presumed that this distinction in salary levels was based primarily on seniority. In total, the 1780-81 salary costs for the opera ball orchestra was 6842 pounds (for a season of seventeen balls). Evidence from the early 1750s, moreover, reveals that an additional modest honorarium (a '*gratification*' of 40 or 50 *sols* per ball in the 1751-52 season) was paid to

[38]As late as 1787, a collection of receipt ledgers still reveals that a single price of admission was 6 pounds. Because at this time the Opera was operating out of the theatre in the Porte Saint-Martin, the number and types of loges were different from earlier venues, the fee structures for their rental at balls were also modified. See *Archives Nationales*, O¹624-pièce 209.

[39]Rosters or payment records for members of the opera ball orchestra survive for a number of seasons, among them 1757-58, 1766-67, and 1780-81. *Archives Nationales*, AJ¹³-1-A21, AJ¹³-23, dossier 8.

[40]For example, *Archives Nationales*, AJ¹³-22, dossier 22, preserves payment ledgers (with the signatures of the musicians and dancers) for opera employees during the 1770s.

[41]*Archives Nationales*, AJ¹³-23-dossier 8.

four non-musicians who were charged with 'monitoring the conduct' of the two orchestras.[42]

The records from 1780-81 also report on salaries earned by various functionaries employed at the opera balls.[43] Their fees were also paid on a per service basis, the majority of them receiving 3 pounds each ball. But there were more of these workers than one might expect: twenty-seven of them, in fact, who served in various capacities. The most generously paid handled money or tickets. The 'receiver-general,' who evidently operated out of the Magasin (he is called the 'Receveur au Bureau'), was paid at a rate of 12 pounds per ball. Four ticket takers (called either 'Controlleur' or 'Receveur') received 6 pounds each ball, while two others received 3. The remaining employees all received 3 pounds per ball as well. These included fourteen individuals who were stationed in the theatre loges—five of them worked at only four balls during this season. Three other employees, called 'Avertisseurs,' were stationed on the ballroom floor, two on the King's side, and one on the Queen's. I am not able say with any certainty what their duties might have been, but it may well be that they were to announce the sequence of dances. (This issue will be considered more fully in the last chapter.) Finally, three other workers were called 'Portiers,' two of them charged with providing services to the public ('service public' and 'service courant'), and one who was to guard the costumes of the orchestra members ('Garde des dominos des Symphonistes'). The total annual cost in salaries for these employees that year was 1,539 pounds.

The records for this season do not supply information about other employees who provided necessary services at each ball: guards, and workers who set up the facility, raising the floor, arranging the décor, and lighting the hundreds of candles. The Amelot manuscript, however, offers estimates (rather precise ones) for the nightly costs of such services. It claims, for example, that there were 60 guards at each ball, at a cost of 106 pounds, 16 *sols* each evening. The workers who raised and lowered the 'Machine des Bals' are reported in this source to have earned 75 pounds in total at each ball.[44] Although these figures are only estimates, I am inclined to trust their accuracy, because the source estimates an annual cost for mounting balls at 12,000 pounds. This

[42]*Archives Nationales*, AJ[13]-1, pièce 4: 'Il est aussy accordé aux Srs Parin et Champion une somme de 50" a chacun et aux Srs Marchand et Joublay chacun une somme de 40 sols de Gratification par chaque Bal pour les peines et soins qu'ils se donnent dans la conduite des deux Orchestres.' See further pp. 133-134.

[43]*Archives Nationales*, AJ[13]-23-dossier 8.

[44]*Bibliothèque-Musée de l'Opéra*, Rés. 516: *Memoires pour servir a l'histoire de l'Académie Royale de Musique, vulgairement l'Opéra, depuis son établissement en 1669 jusqu'en l'année 1758*, 507-8.

total is entirely consistent with those from the later 1750s and early 1760s offered in Table 3.1.

The table on pages 66-67 attempts to give a synopsis of the overall finances of the opera ball—the revenues as well as the expenses— from 1757-1780 for all the complete seasons for which records have survived. [See Table 3.4]

The table includes the day *mardi gras* fell at the end of each season because this information can be helpful when the precise number of balls offered is unknown. In the 1777-78 season, for example, a comparatively late mardi gras (3 March compared to 11 February in the previous year) was likely the primary reason for a healthy increase in expenses: there were more balls that year than in 1776-77. Yet, because the gate receipts remained virtually unchanged in the two seasons, the profits decreased by more than 4,000 pounds (about 8%) in 1777-78. On the other hand, it was a relatively early mardi gras in 1780 (8 February) that no doubt contributed to the sharp decline in profits in that season. (The drop of nearly 2,000 pounds in expenses from the previous season suggests there were probably two fewer balls). The precipitous fall in gate receipts in the final two seasons accounted for in table 3.4 is puzzling. It seems likely that the opera balls experienced stiff competition from other *bals payants*. While I have been unsuccessful in discovering figures for 'permissions fees' collected from these other operations in 1779-80, in 1778-79 they amounted to 452 pounds,[45] some 23% higher than in any previous season for which records survive. Whatever the cause, the decline in profits in these two seasons mirrors a disastrous outcome for the Opera overall. In 1778-79 it lost 210,942 pounds, and in 1779-80 a whopping 585,611 pounds.[46] Seen in this light, the steady profitability of the *bals publics* over the years must have been highly valued by the directors of the Opera.

But even though the *bals publics* consistently turned an annual profit, they were not uniformly successful throughout any given season. Indeed, in some seasons the balls of November and early January were so poorly attended that they almost certainly lost money. For example, only ninety-five people attended (or at least purchased tickets for) the second ball of the 1762-3 season, held on Sunday, 14 November. If my estimation of the costs of mounting a ball that year are correct (740 pounds, see table 3.1 on p.61), then the operation lost 170 pounds that evening.

• • • • •

[45]*Archives Nationales* AJ¹³-9, pièce 156.

[46]Gourret, *Ces hommes*, 79-82, attributes the huge losses in these seasons to the inept directorship of Jacques de Vismes du Valgay, who held the position from April, 1778 until March, 1780.

Table 3.4 Overall Public Ball Finances, 1757 through 1780

Season	Gate Receipts	Overall Expenses	Net Profit	No. of Balls	Mardi gras	Comment
	Venue: Palais-Royal, Theatre 1					
1757-58	52,596 (pounds)	11,644 (pounds)	40,952 (pounds)	14	Feb 7	
1758-59	54,150	12,439	41,711	17	Feb 27	d. Duchesse d'Orléans, Feb 9
1759-60	45,822	10,307	35,515	14	Feb 19	
1760-61[47]	37,650	8,763	28,887	12	Feb 3	
1761-62	41,094	11,589	29,505	16	Feb 23	
1762-63	42,798	10,369	32,429	14	Feb 15	
	Venue: Palais des Tuilleries					
1763-64	56,188	12,570	43,618	12	Mar 6	fire; season begins Fri Feb 2
1764-65	63,447	16,450	46,997	16	Feb 19	
1765-66[48]	44,559	?	?	13	Feb 11	d. M le Dauphin, Jan 6
1766-67	74,545	?	?	17	Mar 3	
1767-68 [lacking]						
1768-69 [lacking]						
1769-70	65,773	?	?	17	Feb 2	
1771-72	77,502	26,948	50,554	?	Mar 3	
1772-73	78,153	23,096	55,057	?	Feb 23	

[47]Because the receipts for the ball held on Sunday, 1 February 1761 (the Sunday before mardi gras) are missing, the figures for this season are slightly skewered.

[48]The incomplete data for 1765-1770 is drawn from *Archives Nationales*, AJ[13]-9, pièce 141.[5]

Table 3.4 (continued)

Season	Gate Receipts	Overall Expenses	Net Profit	No. of Balls	Mardi gras	Comment
		Venue: Palais-Royal, Theatre 2				
1770-71	73,110	22,588	50,522	16	Feb 12	
1771-72	77,502	26,948	50,554	?	Mar 3	
1772-73	78,153	23,096	55,057	?	Feb 23	
1773-74	71,967	18,269	53,698	?	Feb 15	
1774-75	82,200	24,737	57,463	?	Feb 28	
1775-76	80,076[49]	20,556	59,520	16	Feb 20	3,252 at ball of Th Feb 15
1776-77	82,179	20,445	61,734	?	Feb 11	
1777-78	82,314	25,156	57,158	?	Mar 3	
1778-79	68,659	21,122	47,537	?	Feb 16	troubles under deVismes
1779-80	54,492	19,198	35,294	?	Feb 8	opera loses 796,553 in 2 yrs

[49] In *Archives Nationales*, AJ[13]-9, pièce 2 the figure is reported as 80,076 pounds, while in AJ[13]-9, pièce 156 it is 80,280. I believe the former is correct, since it agrees with the sum obtained from the annual gate receipts for the year. The latter, on the other hand, is from a summary table accounting for an entire ten year span.

Attendance

There are two kinds of documents that permit a reconstruction of attendance (ticket purchase) over a season. The first of these are printed or hand-written 'chits' that contain a precise accounting of the number of tickets sold and loges rented for a particular evening, along with the total revenue these sales and rentals generated. Evidently they were compiled to serve as source materials for an annual ledger. Few of these documents dating from before the collapse of the *ancien régime* have survived.[50] The other kind of document, while somewhat more plentiful, only permits a conjecture about attendance. They record the gate receipts for each ball of a season. Because the single admission price remained stable (6 pounds), however, a reasonably accurate idea of the total attendance can be obtained (by dividing the gate receipts of an evening by six). What cannot be certain in such a calculation, of course, is how loge rentals might have contributed to the nightly total. Because they have some impact (although generally not a great one) on an estimate of attendance based on gate receipts, it is useful here to review the fee structures for loge rentals at an opera ball.

In the original theatre of the Palais-Royal three kinds of loges were available:

Size	Cost
8-seat	60 (pounds)
10-seat	75
12-seat	90

In the new theatre there were four:[51]

Size	Cost
4-seat	30 (pounds)
6-seat	45
8-seat	60
10-seat	75

---

[50]I have located and consulted the following: *Bibliothèque-Musée de l'Opéra*, CO 5, CO 10, CO 13, CO 15 (for the seasons 1756-57, 1770-71, 1774-75, and 1775-76); and *Archives Nationales*, O¹624-pièce 209 (for the seasons 1785-86 and 1786-87).

[51]For the six seasons (1764 through 1769-70) during which the balls were held in the Tuilleries Palace, I have been unable to locate any specific information on loge rentals (or indeed if they were even available for rental at balls). The theatre certainly made loges available during operatic performances, however: the *Mercure galant* reported in March 1770 (pp. 190-195), that the loges were laid out as they had been at the *Palais-Royal*, and that they accommodated the same numbers.

In the hypothetical case where the gate receipts for an evening were, say, 15,000 pounds (a very high sum, approached only once in the documents I have seen), it might be estimated that there were twenty-five hundred people in attendance, if loge rentals were not considered. In principle (but only in principle), however, this estimate might be out by a factor of 25% if, for example, only two thousand were in attendance, all of whom, nevertheless, rented 10-seat loges. The latter situation, of course, is an impossibility (because two hundred 10-seat loges were not available), but it illustrates the potential for error such estimates present. A complete set of chits for the ball held on *lundi gras* of 1771 (February 11) has survived. This ball represents an extreme case of loge rentals for a single night (but 'extreme' only within an admittedly small sampling). On that evening seventeen 6-seat loges, nine 8-seat loges, four 4-seat loges, and two 10-seat loges were all rented, and overall the gate receipts were 10,845 pounds.[52] If one did not know about the loge rentals, one could estimate that there were one thousand, eight hundred and seven people (actually one thousand, eight hundred, seven and a half) in attendance. The actual figures reveal that there were one thousand, five hundred and forty-five single ticket holders, one hundred and two in 6-seat loges, seventy-two in 8-seat loges, twenty in 10-seat loges, and sixteen in 4-seat loges, for a total of one thousand, seven hundred and fifty-five paying customers (1545 + 210). Even on this occasion, when thirty-two loges were rented, the calculation is out only by a factor of just under 3%. The fewer the loge rentals, of course, the more accurate this method of calculation becomes. For example, the ball of Sunday, 6 February 1757 took in 3,534 pounds, including a rental for one 8-seat loge (at 60 pounds).[53] I would calculate an attendance of five hundred and eighty-eight based on gate receipts, while the actual figure for single admissions was five hundred and seventy-nine, plus eight others who rented a loge, for a total of five hundred and eighty-seven. In this kind of situation the margin of error is very small, indeed.

Even when precise figures on loge rentals are known, there are still other factors that make a calculation of attendance only an estimate at best. There is the possibility, for example, that some of those who purchased a ticket did not attend, or that fewer people than the notional capacity of a loge rented it for slightly more than the optimal price (when, say, a group of seven rented an 8-seat loge). In general, though, dividing gate receipts by six yields an estimate of attendance that is

[52]*Bibliothèque-Musée de l'Opéra*, CO 10.

[53]*Bibliothèque-Musée de l'Opéra*, CO 5.

fairly reliable, probably accurate to within 3%, as I suggested above. In the discussion that follows, I have relied on this calculation, and, when information on loge rentals is known, I have assumed that the loges were fully occupied.

Records for the following seasons either report precise figures on public ball attendance, or permit a reliable estimate of it: 1756-1767, 1769-1771, 1775-1776, and 1785-1787. Daily attendance figures and the date of each ball in these seasons are presented in Appendix 4. Before considering statistics from these years, it will be helpful simply to reproduce attendance figures from two seasons: one from the 1750s, when the opera balls were held in the original theatre of the *Palais-Royal*, and one from the 1770s, when they were held in the new one. The records from 1758-1759 preserve information about gate receipts only, so I have had to calculate an attendance according to the procedures described above. The records from 1770-1771, on the other hand, preserve precise information on tickets sold and loges rented.

Table 3.5 The 1758-59 Public Ball Season

	Attendance	Receipts
1. Sunday, 12 Nov	288	1,728 (pounds)
2. Sunday, 19 Nov	272	1,632
3. Sunday, 26 Nov	367	2,202
4. Thursday, 30 Nov	300	1,800
5. Sunday, 7 Jan	416	2,496
6. Sunday, 14 Jan	343	2,058
7. Sunday, 21 Jan	337	2,022
8. Thursday, 25 Jan	66	396
9. Sunday, 28 Jan	433	2,598
10. Sunday, 4 Feb	487	2,922
11. Thursday, 8 Feb	147	882
Sunday, 11 Feb	'Mort de Mad. la Duchesse d'Orléans' [no ball]	
12. Thursday, 15 Feb	204	1,224
13. Sunday, 18 Feb	863	5,181
14. Thursday, 22 Feb	1,309	7,854
15. Sunday, 25 Feb	453	2,718
16. Lundi gras, 26 Feb	2,148	12,888
17. Mardi gras, 27 Feb	591	3,549

Since the total gate receipts for the thirteenth and seventeenth balls this season are not divisible by six, loge rentals must have come into play, and the attendance given in table 3.5 for those evenings is only an estimate. The more detailed information about attendance and receipts during the 1770-1771 season is given in table 3.6.

Table 3.6 The 1770-71 Public Ball Season

Attendance		Receipts
1. Sunday, 11 Nov		
711	single entries	4,266 (pounds)
2. Sunday, 18 Nov		
470	single entries	2,820
3. Sunday, 25 Nov		
568	single entries	3,408
1	loge-6 places	45
Total 574		3,453

(cont.)

Table 3.6 (continued)

Attendance			Receipts
4. Friday, 30 Nov			
	537	single entries	3,222
	1	loge-6 places	45
	1	loge-8 places	60
Total	551		3,327
5. Sunday, 6 Jan			
	470	single entries	2,820
6. Sunday, 13 Jan			
	376	single entries	2,256
7. Thursday, 17 Jan			
	174	single entries	1,044
8. Sunday, 20 Jan			
	514	single entries	3,084
9. Thursday, 24 Jan			
	295	single entries	1,770
10. Sunday, 27 Jan			
	771	single entries	4,626
11. Thursday, 31 Jan			
	533	single entries	3,198
	1	loge-8 places	60
Total	541		3,258
12. Sunday, 3 Feb			
	1,091	single entries	6,546
	2	loges-6 places	90
	1	loge-8 places	60
Total	1,111		6,696
13. Thursday 'gras', 7 Feb			
	1,790	single entries	10,740
	13	loges-6 places	585
	3	loges-4 places	90
	1	loge-10 places	75
Total	1,890		11,490
14. Sunday, 10 Feb			
	680	single entries	4,080
	2	loges-8 places	120
	3	loges-6 places	135
Total	714		4,335
15. Monday [gras], 11 Feb			
	1,545	single entries	9,270
	9	loges-8 places	540
	2	loges-10 places	150
	17	loges-6 places	765
	4	loges-4places	120
Total	1,755		10,845
16. Mardi gras, 12 Feb			
	969	single entries	5,814
	4	loges-8 places	240
	3	loges-6 places	135
Total	1,019		6,189

Attendance at the first six balls in the 1770-71 season, it can be seen, was slightly better than that of 1758-59, but this is almost certainly a by-product of the novelty of a first season in the new theatre at the *Palais-Royal*. Overall, the figures reveal similar tendencies: modest and variable attendance until the final five balls of the season, at which point there is a dramatic upswing. As I will show presently, this, in fact, is a normal pattern in almost every season for which I have had an opportunity to examine records.

Table 3.7, next page, summarizes the information concerning attendance contained in all the surviving records from 1756 until 1787 (which accounts for only sixteen complete seasons). I have organized the data, somewhat arbitrarily, by month, even though the single most conspicuous factor in higher or lower attendance at the public ball seems to have been the number of them remaining before the end of the season. I have also incorporated other information into this table. I have indicated the 'low' and the 'high' attendance at any *single* ball during each month, and in the column marked 'Comment' I have noted (among other things) if there were two or more balls in a month that attracted more than a thousand customers. This column also indicates the day (invariably among the last four balls of the season) the highest attendance for the year was achieved. The figures from the 1780s are somewhat anomalous on a number of counts. For one thing, the overall attendance seems to have been dismal, in part because the opera balls were not held in a single venue throughout any one season (see chapter one), and in part because the competition from other *bals payants* was becoming intense. While the normal season in this final decade of the *ancien régime* still accommodated fourteen to seventeen balls, it began in December rather than November. These qualifications about the 1780s notwithstanding, Table 3.7 (next page) reveals that the public ball season normally unfolded with a typical rhythm.

Table 3.7 Overall Attendance by Month, 1756-1787

Year	Month	No. of Balls	Receipts	Attendance	Loges Rented	Low	High	Comment
1756	NOV	2	2472	412	0	133	279	3 balls mounted; data for Nov 11 is lacking
1757	JAN	4	6630	1105	0	98	492	
	FEB	8	38688	6206	70	98	1477	2 balls >1000; high lundi gras
	NOV	2	2730	455	?	219	236	
1758	JAN	8	21702	3647	?	205	1006	
	FEB	4	28164	4694	?	759	1649	2 balls >1000; high lundi gras
	NOV	4	7362	1227	?	272	367	
1759	JAN	5	9570	1595	?	66	433	
	FEB	8	37218	6202	?	147	2148	2 balls >1000; high lundi gras
	NOV	3	3034	505	?	124	191	
1760	JAN	4	6750	1125	?	184	425	
	FEB	7	29442	6006	?	242	1477	3 balls >1000; high lundi gras
	NOV	3	2916	486	?	140	194	
1761	JAN	7	21057	3509	?	155	1215	
	FEB	2	13677	2279	?	890	1389	data for Sun, Feb 1 lacking; high lundi gras (Feb 2)
	NOV	3	3102	517	?	126	208	
1762	JAN	5	10086	1681	?	230	468	
	FEB	8	27906	4650	?	107	1387	high lundi gras
	NOV	3	2208	368	?	95	137	
1763	JAN	5	8688	1448	?	148	496	
	FEB	6	31902	5316	?	285	1576	2 balls >1000; high lundi gras
1764	FEB	8	25663	4277	?	319	861	season starts late because of fire at Palais-Royal
	MAR	4	30525	5087	?	662	2070	2 balls >1000; high lundi gras
	NOV	4	6336	1056	?	211	324	
1765	JAN	5	12066	2011	?	169	702	
	FEB	7	45048	7508	?	352	1973	3 balls >1000; high lundi gras
	NOV	3	4764	794	?	253	287	
1766	JAN	5	6564	1094	?	95	402	Dauphin's death cancels ball of Jan 6
	FEB	5	33231	5538	?	559	2077	2 balls >1000; high lundi gras
	NOV	3	5298	883	?	251	354	
1767	JAN	4	8106	1351	?	215	510	
	FEB	7	36747	11928	?	308	1842	2 balls >1000
	MAR	3	24394	4065	?	938	1944	2 balls >1000; high lundi gras
1769	NOV	4	4653	975	?	202	279	
1770	JAN	4	9942	1657	?	205	625	
	FEB	9	49944	8323	?	208	1913	3 balls >1000; high lundi gras

(cont.)

Table 3.7 (cont.)

Year	Month	No. of Balls	Receipts	Atten-dance	Loges Rented	Low	High	Comment
	NOV	4	13866	2306	3	470	711	
1771	JAN	7	18858	3141	1	174	771	
	FEB	5	40055	6489	64	714	1890	4 balls >1000; high Thu, Feb 7
1775	NOV	4	7776	1294	?	250	375	
1776	JAN	5	8676	1446	?	123	359	
	FEB	7	63624	10603	?	535	3252	4 balls >1000; high Thu, Feb 15
1785	DEC	2	720	120	0	56	64	ball season no longer starts in Nov
1786	JAN	5	4680	780	0	98	202	
	FEB	10	28014	4599	7	78	1294	high mardi gras
	DEC	3	816	136	0	34	61	
1787	JAN	4	1998	333	0	66	94	
	FEB	7	31764	5294	0	97	1588	2 balls >1000; high mardi gras

To facilitate comparisons, the monthly attendance totals recorded in table 3.7 (in the central column) are plotted in the following chart. (See chart 3.1, next page.) The two monochrome shadings in this chart serve merely to distinguish one season from the next. There were only two seasons that were not comprised of three months: 1764, when the fire of April 1673 necessitated a compression of the following season into the months of February and March; and 1766-1767, when a late mardi gras (3 March) allowed the season to spill into a fourth month. Discounting those two, all the other seasons but one present much the same attendance curve: a less than impressive November, a slightly better January, and a healthy February. The one exception is the season of 1760-1761, during which January attendance outstripped that of February by well over thirteen hundred customers. Once more, the timing of mardi gras was a crucial factor. It was on February 3 in 1761, and only three balls could be scheduled in the month (moreover, the data for one of these, is lacking).

Attendance at the opening balls of a season—those mounted in November (or December in the 1780s)—was, at best, sparse. The most conspicuous spike in November attendance shown in chart 3.1 is for 1770, when the inauguration of the new facility for the *bal public* seems to have been an attraction. The highest November total in the original theatre was in 1758, but still just one thousand, two hundred and twenty-seven in all attended the four balls offered. This total falls significantly short of the high for any other month for which statistics are available. Only once, however, did a November ball attract fewer than one hundred: on 14 November 1762, when only ninety-five souls were in attendance (as indicated in table 3.7). In the opening of the two seasons from the 1780s for which records survive, attendance was so poor that

76

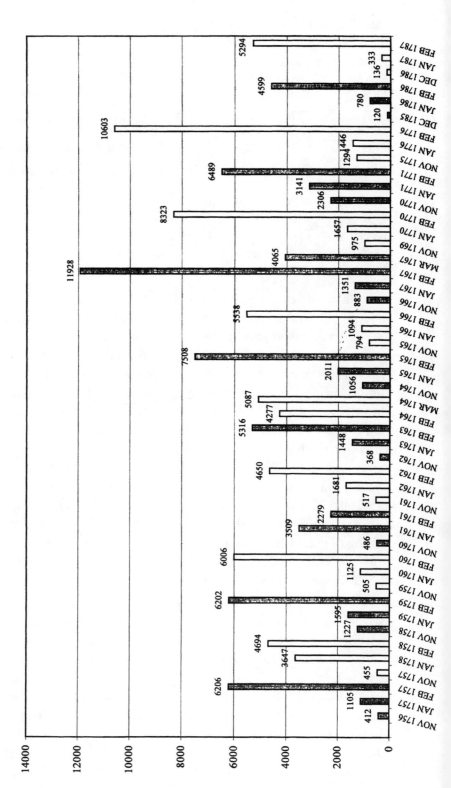

Chart 3.1 Seasonal Attendance by Month
1756-1787

it is difficult to fathom how the few who did go might have behaved. The *high* attendance in December balls of those two years was just sixty-four, and on the evening of 26 December 1786 there were only thirty-four customers!

Because the record is so incomplete, it is dangerous to draw any definitive conclusions about typical attendance at the opening of a public ball season. It will be recalled, though, that Dangeau's remarks about the early balls of the first season, when the *bal public* was a real novelty, paint much the same picture as the one I have just sketched. He wrote that the only shortcoming at the first ball was that 'there was not a sufficient crowd for so large a room.'[54] After the start of the second season he made a similar remark on 28 December 1716 (the *bal public* still opened shortly after Christmas at that time): the balls continue three times a week, 'but it is said that the crowd is much smaller than it was last year.'[55] Mathieu Marais, on the other hand, observed that the first ball of the 1720-21 season was well attended.[56] Still, I think it is a reasonable suggestion that, in general, the opening of the public ball season did not present a big attraction.

Attendance at the balls of January was somewhat volatile, as the totals for that month plotted in chart 3.1 suggest. But part of this volatility is no more than a function of the number of balls mounted. The conspicuous spikes of the chart occur when there were seven or eight balls in the month (as opposed to the more typical four or five). Another contributing factor to the volatility was the proximity of mardi gras to the end of January. Table 3.7 reveals that a January ball could be attended by as many as one thousand, two hundred and fifteen (that of Thursday, 29 January 1761), or as few as sixty-six (that of Thursday, 25 January 1759). The healthy attendance at the late January ball of 1761, however, deserves some qualification. The ball mounted the Thursday before mardi gras was always one of the most popular to attend. In the 1750s and 1760s, in fact, it was consistently the second most popular ball of the entire season, only once attracting fewer than one thousand customers. In the two complete seasons of the 1770s for which records survive, it was *the* most popular ball of the season (see February statistics for 1771 and 1776 in table 3.7). The high total for January 29, 1761, then, can be explained by the fact that mardi gras was very early that year (3 February), and 29 January was the Thursday preceding it. Such a large crowd at a January ball, however, was not

[54]See chapter one, n47.

[55]*Journal*, vol. 16, 512: 'On dit que la foule est bien moins grande aux bals qu'elle n'était l'année passée.'

[56]In the passage cited at the heading of this chapter, and translated in n1.

normal. In only one other instance among the records for seasons I have been able to examine was a January ball attended by more than a thousand people. That occurred in 1758 (also, as it turns out, on January 29), the fifth to last ball of the season. On average, though, January balls drew between two hundred and five hundred customers.

By far the most popular time to attend a *bal public* was during the month of February, and the Opera management took advantage of this fact, when possible, by consistently offering more balls in that month than in any other. On average the monthly attendance for February exceeded that of January by two- or three-fold. It was not uncommon (as the information in table 3.7 reveals) for three of the balls mounted in February to attract well over a one thousand customers (it happened in 1760, 1765, and 1770), and in February of 1771 all four balls were attended by more than a thousand customers. February balls were popular, of course, because it was the month in which the climax of carnival season usually fell. When mardi gras was early, such as in 1761 as we have just seen, strong gate receipts migrated back into January, and when it occasionally fell very late—in early March, such as in 1764—they clustered around a slightly later date.

No matter when mardi gras fell, however, one pattern remained constant: the final four balls of a season, on the final Thursday, Sunday, Monday, and Tuesday of carnival, drew the largest crowds. That of mardi gras itself, interestingly, was almost always just the third most popular of the four, while that of the Sunday before mardi gras sometimes slipped into fifth place in popularity in the season overall.[57] Nevertheless, these four balls played a critical role in the financial success of a season. Table 3.8 shows the percentage of gate receipts of the final four balls to those of the season overall for the same years summarized in Table 3.7.

---

[57]The 1761-1762 season seems exceptional, for only three hundred and ninety attended the ball on the Sunday before mardi gras, placing it ninth in terms of attendance in the sixteen balls offered that season.

Table 3.8 Receipts from last 4 balls related to seasonal total

Season	Total Receipts	Receipts: last 4 Balls	% of last 4 to Total
1756-57	47,790 (pounds)	26,646 (pounds)	55.7%
1757-58	52,596	28,164	53.5%
1758-59	54,150	27,009	49.9%
1759-60	45,822	23,928	52.2%
1760-61	37,650	20,970	55.7%
1761-62	41,094	19,626	47.8%
1762-63	42,798	25,542	59.7%
1764[58]	56,188	30,525	54.3%
1764-65	63,447	31,668	49.9%
1765-66	44,559	29,223	65.6%
1766-67	74,545	35,449	47.5%
1769-70	64,539	30,737	47.6%
1770-71	72,779	33,359	45.8%
1775-76	80,076	48,672	60.1%
1785-86	33,414	18,366	54.92%
1786-87	34,578	27,360	79.1%

As I indicated in the notes to table 3.4, data for the gate receipts from the ball held on the Sunday before mardi gras (Sunday, 1 February) in 1761 has not survived, so the figures given for the 1760-1761 season in table 3.8 are not entirely accurate. Yet, because the missing receipts affect the season total as well as that from the last four balls, the percentage given is quite reliable. The table reveals that the impact the final four balls had on the financial success of a season overall was quite potent. In the 1762-63 season, for example, if the final four balls had taken in just the average receipts from first ten of that year (1605 pounds), then the net profit for the season would tumble from 32,429 pounds (see table 3.4) to 12,107, a drop of nearly 63%. The most extreme case in table 3.8, however, is the final one. More people attended the ball on mardi gras in 1787 (one thousand, five hundred and eighty-eight) than the *total* attendance for the first ten balls of that season (just one thousand, two hundred and three).

Before 1771, the ball held on lundi gras invariably attracted the largest crowd of the season. It would be impossible to gather the necessary statistics, of course, but it may be that attending private masked balls on lundi gras was also more popular than on mardi gras

[58]Season did not start until February.

Chart 3.2 Attendance on Thursday Balls

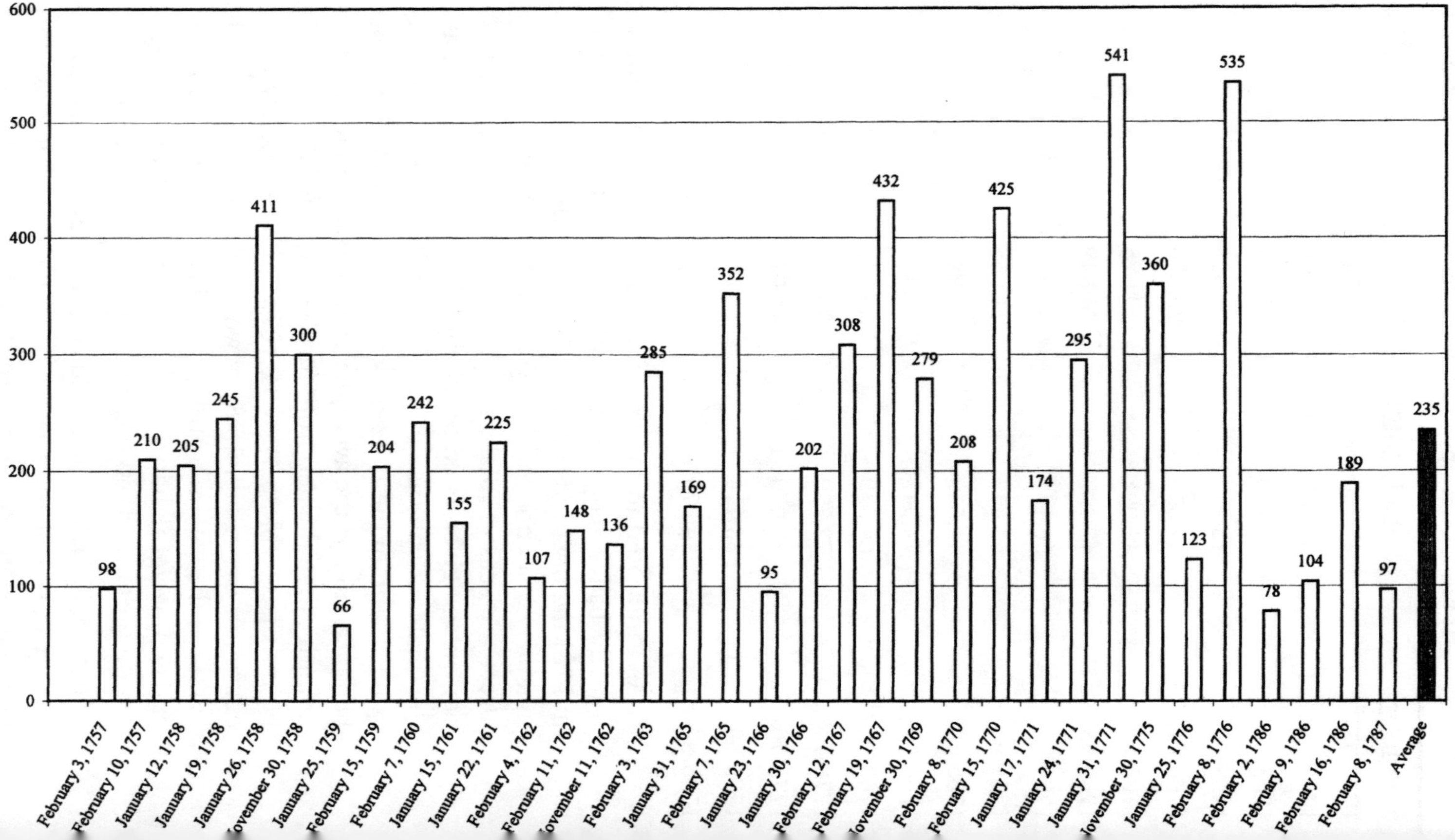

Date	Attendance
February 3, 1757	98
February 10, 1757	210
January 12, 1758	205
January 19, 1758	245
January 26, 1758	411
November 30, 1758	300
January 25, 1759	66
February 15, 1759	204
February 7, 1760	242
January 15, 1761	155
January 22, 1761	225
February 4, 1762	107
February 11, 1762	148
November 11, 1762	136
February 3, 1763	285
January 31, 1765	169
February 7, 1765	352
January 23, 1766	95
January 30, 1766	202
February 12, 1767	308
November 19, 1767	432
November 30, 1769	279
February 8, 1770	208
February 15, 1770	425
January 17, 1771	174
January 24, 1771	295
January 31, 1771	541
November 30, 1775	360
January 25, 1776	123
February 8, 1776	535
February 2, 1786	78
February 9, 1786	104
February 16, 1786	189
February 8, 1787	97
Average	235

in Paris. If that were the case, then the attendance pattern of opera balls simply reflected the trends of local custom. My suspicion, however, is that attendance at the *bal public* was greater on lundi gras principally because it was more fashionable on mardi gras to attend *bals particuliers*. Wherever the truth may lie, it was not uncommon before 1771 for the attendance to drop by at least five hundred between the two final balls of the season, and occasionally the decline was much more dramatic: from two thousand, one hundred and forty-eight to five hundred and ninety-one in 1759, or from two thousand and seventy-seven to nine hundred and eighty-five in 1766. Even in the 1770s, when the ball on the Thursday before mardi gras seems to have become the most popular of the season, or in the 1780s, when that of mardi gras itself drew the largest crowds, the ball of lundi gras remained an attractive event. In the 1770s it came in a close second, and in the 1780s was either a close second or a close third.[59]

A final observation about attendance trends at the *bal public* deserves brief attention. Not counting the balls that were mounted on fixed dates (more or less)—the season opener on St Martin's day (11 November), the final ball of November (typically 30 November), and that of the *fête des rois* (6 January)—the opera balls were affairs of a Sunday or a Thursday evening. Those mounted on Sundays show the same general patterns in attendance characteristic of the season overall. Up to the final four balls of a season, those mounted on Thursdays, on the other hand, more often than not were rather sparsely attended. In chart 3.2 I plot the attendance of all Thursday balls, except those of the Thursday immediately before mardi gras (which, as we have seen, were always well attended). Of the thirty-four balls accounted for in this chart, fourteen were attended by fewer than two hundred customers, and on only two occasions did attendance exceed five hundred (both those comparatively late balls in the season). The average attendance at Thursday balls was just two hundred and thirty-five (the mean attendance was two hundred and eight), even though fully half of them (seventeen) occurred in the month of February, otherwise a very popular time to attend a ball. It seems almost certain that eight of the thirty-four balls in question here—those with an attendance of fewer than one hundred and twenty-five—lost money on those evenings. [Chart 3.2, opposite]

[59]See *Bibliothèque-Musée de l'Opéra*, CO 10, for statistics for 1771, and *Archives Nationales*, AJ[13]-9, pièce 2 for 1776. For 1786 and 1787, see *Archives Nationales*, O[1]624, pièce 209. The sampling from these two decades is so small that it is exceedingly dangerous to claim a new attendance pattern had really established itself.

One possible explanation for the generally weak showing for balls mounted on Thursday is that attending an operatic performance (or, indeed, a play) on that afternoon and early evening was more popular. Or perhaps Thursday night balls suffered because they made attending *Friday* afternoon operas more difficult. By the second half of the century opera performances on Fridays were often reported to have been a most popular attraction,[60] but no statistical study has been undertaken to verify these reports. While it is not impossible that one might have wished to attend the theatre and still have the stamina (or the inclination) to attend an opera ball in the same twenty-four hour period, it seems more likely to me that one chose one or the other of those activities. (Some instrumentalists, as we shall see in chapter five, did not enjoy the luxury of such a choice.) It would be interesting to track attendance at the opera during these years in the way I have done for public balls, to see if there is any correlation between particularly high attendance at one, and low at the other. That, however, must await another study.

•   •   •   •   •

The *bal de l'Opéra* emerged in a very difficult economic climate and yet was immediately successful. While its parent institution fell further into debt, the public ball continued to turn a steady profit, and established itself as one of the most consistently popular attractions of Paris at the height of carnival season. But the price of admission was far from inconsequential. Attending even a single opera ball in a season would simply have been out of reach to any but the reasonably well off: the wealthy bourgeois, or the nobility. As an illustration, I can offer the following. A *very* good annual salary for a member of the opera orchestra in the late 1730s, for example, was 700 pounds.[61] If I were to equate that hypothetically to a decently paid orchestral musician of today who earns $50,000 a year, then in current dollars it would cost that individual about $430 to attend just a single public ball.

The throngs who flocked to the *bal de l'Opéra* on the final evenings of carnival, then, were either not spendthrifts, or they were wealthy. And they *did* attend in throngs. The notional capacity of the original

[60] From 1752 through the 1780s something like the following is regularly included in the theatrical calendars, this one taken from *Spectacles de Paris* (Paris, 1773), p.[iv]: 'mais c'est le Vendredi surt-out, qu'on voit jouer les bons Acteurs.'

[61] According to an inventory of 1738, soloists of the *petit choeur*, not counting the music director, Jean-Féry Rebel (the *batteur de mesure*) who made 1200 pounds, earned in a range of 400 to 800 pounds. See Graham Sadler, 'Rameau's Singers and Players at the Paris Opéra. A little-known Inventory of 1738,' *Early Music* 11/4 (1983), 462.

theatre in the *Palais-Royal* for operatic performances was about thirteen hundred spectators,[62] while that of the new theatre was about two thousand.[63] It is therefore very difficult to fathom what might have transpired in the old theatre on lundi gras in 1759, when two thousand, one hundred and forty-eight customers showed up for the ball, or on the Thursday before mardi gras in 1776, when three thousand, two hundred and fifty-two (!) attended the ball in the new theatre. Until the crowds started to thin, it seems very unlikely that anything approaching organized dancing could have occurred. And even if it did, it must have been undertaken without the benefit of hearing much of the accompanying music. The music and dancing that were a featured attraction at the public ball under more optimal circumstances will be considered in chapter five.

[62]See Coeyman, 'Theatres for Opera and Ballet,' *Early Music* 18/1 (1990), 34.
[63]*The New Grove Dictionary of Opera*, s.v. 'Paris ¶ 3: 1725-89' by Rebecca Harris-Warrick.

CHAPTER FOUR

Some Social Issues: Power, Status Relationships, and Gender at the *bal public*

C'est donc le Public réuni qui devient le principal spectacle. Chaque classe de ce Public s'ennoblit, & toutes semble n'en faire plus qu'une; de même que les fleuves majesteux, les rivieres & les foibles ruisseaux réunis dans la mer, participent à sa grandeur sans y être distingués.

Anon. (1769)[1]

A chief characteristic of formal *bals particuliers* in the early eighteenth century was the important focus they placed on dances performed by one couple at a time. In 1725 the dancing master, Pierre Rameau, emphasized the role that status played in this focus, explaining how couples were to dance in order of descending social rank.[2] There were two basic kinds of couple dance: the 'generic' variety—the courante and menuet, for example—each featuring standard sequences of steps and floor patterns that could be accommodated to any courante, or any menuet accompaniment; and the 'figured' dance, in which the steps and floor patterns were fitted specifically to a particular piece of music. The latter were given special attention in annual collections of dances printed in Paris between 1700 and 1715 in the so-called Beauchamps-Feuillet system. During those years some sixty couple dances for the ballroom were issued,[3] a production that dropped sharply (perhaps not coincidentally) after the *bal public* was inaugurated in early 1716.[4] Beyond offering advice and instructions on the

---

[1]*Réponse d'une artitste a un homme de letters, qui lui avoit écrit sur les Waux-halls* (Amsterdam, 1769); from the *Bibliothèque de l'Arsenal*, Collection Rondel, R°12871: 'It is, then, the Public brought together that becomes the chief spectacle. Each class of this Public is ennobled, and all seem to form nothing but a single entity. [It is] just like majestic rivers, streams and gentle brooks brought together in the sea, participating in its grandeur, without being distinguished in it.'

[2]Pierre Rameau, *Le Maître à danser*, 'Du ceremonial que l'on observe au grand Bal du Roy,' 49-54; and 'De la manière de se conduire avec politesse dans les Bals reglez,' 55-59.

[3]The statistics have been compiled from the inventory of dances given in Meredith Ellis Little, and Carol G. Marsh, *La Danse Noble. An Inventory of Dances and Sources* (New York, 1992).

[4]Between 1715 and 1725 just 19 appeared. ibid.

performance of a repertoire of steps common to most of these couple dances, Rameau is otherwise silent about them. But he does give important information on the performance of the generic dances. Although he praised the courante as the *ne plus ultra* of couple dances, Rameau recognized that the menuet had become more popular, and he devoted considerably more space to describing its performance.[5]

There were also group dances at a formal ball, of course, but even these served to highlight rank, according to Rameau's prescriptions, for the dancers in the group were to be arranged according to social status. The only group dances for which he offers information are the *branle*—from his description, almost certainly the *branle à mener*—and its companion dance, the gavotte.[6] Both these were line dances in which the lead couple (of the highest social standing) retreated to the end of the line, and then worked its way up to the head of it again, at which point the dance concluded. It is strange, indeed, that Rameau should have described just these two dances in 1725, for they had become quite rare by that time,[7] whereas the newer contredanse had become all the rage. I believe he elected to describe the conduct of a branle (and its gavotte), rather than the contredanse, because of the ability of the former to project rank in a conspicuous way. In fact, it would seem that Rameau was a harsh critic of the contredanse precisely because of its inability to do so. In a discussion of the kinds of graceful dancing in groups that he endorsed, he wrote:

> It [graceful group dancing] can also be seen in the custom of [danc-ing] Branles, where each [couple] leads in its turn, which does not create confusion as in a number of those contredanses that I have seen danced that have no taste whatsoever, all of which diminishes the pleasure to be had from seeing good dancing.[8]

In the ideal conduct of orderly social dancing that Rameau championed—whether for couples dancing alone or in groups—a dutiful respect of rank was ever-present. In the case of masked balls, Rameau recommended that one treat those in disguise with the utmost respect, allowing them to dance first, because, he cautioned, costumes

---

[5]*Le Maître à danser*, 76-109.

[6]The evidence is reviewed in Richard Semmens, 'Branles, Gavottes and Contredanses in the Late Seventeenth and Early Eighteenth Centuries,' *Dance Journal*, 15/2 (1997), 35-62; see 39-40.

[7]ibid., passim.

[8]*Le Maître à danser*, 109: 'On a vû même l'usage des Branles où chacun menne à son tour, ce qui ne cause pas de confusion à nombre de ces contre-danses, que j'ai vû danser qui n'ont nul gout; ce qui diminue le plaisir que l'on a à voir bien danser.'

often obscured persons of the highest distinction.[9] Even this more egalitarian conduct was, for Rameau, still clearly based in a concern for social status.

No doubt recalling practices of the recent past, he even prescribed a 'correct' sequence of events in the proceedings of a formal ball. When those who were to dance had assembled, and the king and queen (or their surrogates) had taken up their positions, the group dances were to begin, and these were followed by the couple dances. But this plan may have only applied to 'royal' balls, because in his description of the sequence of events at *bals reglez* held anywhere, Rameau makes no mention of an opening group dance, and has the proceedings start with the 'first menuet.'[10] Such a practice is confirmed in an account of a ball that occurred in early 1708. The account, from the memoirs of the Marquis de Sourches, also makes it evident that both the courante and the branle were already falling out of fashion (if only at Versailles). In his entry for January 5, de Sourches wrote:

> The King had said that he wished reestablished the old custom of beginning balls with the *branle à mener* and courantes. But it [the custom] had been so thoroughly superseded that even the dancing masters who were then at Versailles could not demonstrate the *branle à mener* to the people who wished to learn it. And so one was forced to begin the ball with the menuet.[11]

Although this ball took place at Versailles, it is not clear from the description if it was a royal ball. But a royal ball most certainly did take place the following evening, the night of the 'Fête des Rois' (January 6) and it included as its featured dancers the King of England and his sister,[12] the duc d'Orléans (the future Regent), and other nobility of the highest standing. Even this ball, however, did not open with a group dance. The *Mercure galant* reports that 'Le Bal s'ouvrit par le

[9]ibid., 57: '...lorsqu'il arrive des Masques, de les faire danser des premiers, afin qu'ils prennent ceux de leur compagnie de suite. On doit faire l'honneur préferablement aux Masques, car très-souvent ce déguisement cache des Personnes du premier rang.'

[10]ibid., 56.

[11]Cited in Norbert Dufourcq, *La Musique à la cour de Louis XIV et de Louis XV d'après les Mémoires de Sourches et Luynes, 1681-1758*, 29-30: 'Le roi avoit dit qu'il vouloit qu'on rétablit l'ancienne coutume de commencer les bals par le branle à mener et par les courantes; mais elle avoit été si bien abolie que les maîtres de danse qui se trouvèrent alors à Versailles ne purent pas même montrer le branle à mener aux personnes qui voulurent l'apprendre: et ainsi on fut réduit à commencer le bal par le menuet.'

[12]England's monarch at the time, of course, was Queen Anne, but it was French policy not to recognize her legitimacy. Instead, they recognized the only surviving son of James II (a catholic), James Edward (later referred to as the 'Old Pretender'). James Edward, just 19 years old at the time, was enjoying safe haven at the French court in early 1708 with his sister, Louisa Mary (then 17 years old).

Roy d'Angleterre & par Madame la Princesse sa soeur.'[13] If the remarks of de Sourches from the previous day can be believed, it is hardly surprising that a branle was not performed. But why not a contredanse in its place? On the surface, this appears to have been a plausible alternative, for it is known that contredanses were performed at this ball elsewhere in the proceedings.[14] Once more, the *Mercure* reports: 'It is easy to imagine that all the dances that currently are most regularly performed were danced, and that contredanses were not overlooked.'[15]

Evidently a contredanse was not considered an appropriate way to open such a formal ball, and the reasons may have been close to the concerns Rameau implicitly voiced some seventeen years later. Such a dance did not project social status in the conspicuous and refined way that a branle did. Beginning directly with a couple dance, on the other hand, did. Although the contredanse superseded the branle as the most popular group dance at formal balls in the early eighteenth century, it is incorrect to conclude that it therefore assumed the role and function of the older dance. In 1725 Rameau had recourse to a description of the branle, it seems, because he felt obliged to offer at least some advice on the performance of group dances at formal balls— they were, after all, certainly a regular feature of them—and the branle was the only dance that suited his purposes, which included, among other things, an overriding concern for the issue of rank.

But Rameau also had recourse to a description of the opening branle at a royal ball, because even in the 1720s it was still encountered from time to time (notwithstanding the failing memories of dancing masters at Versailles earlier in the century). One of these occasions is described in good detail in the journal of Edmond Barbier, where an account of a royal ball celebrating the recent arrival of the Spanish Infanta[16] is offered. This ball took place on Sunday, 8 March 1722, and was mounted in the theatre (the *Salle des Machines*) of the Tuilleries Palace. Barbier's account presents a picture of ballroom routine that is so remarkably close to the prescriptions Rameau set down just three years

---

[13]*Mercure galant*, janvier (1708), 280. The ensuing commentary makes it clear that they were performing as a couple (probably dancing a menuet), and not leading a group dance.

[14]Rebecca Harris-Warrick, 'Ballroom Dancing,' 46, reports that this is the earliest occasion she has found evidence for contredanses being performed at a formal royal ball.

[15]*Mercure galant*, janvier (1708), 283: 'Il est aisé de s'imaginer, que toutes les danses qui sont aujourd'huy le plus en usage, furent dansées, & que les contre danses ne furent pas oubliées...'

[16]The Princess Mariana, young daughter of Philip V, had been betrothed to the 11 year old Louis XV in 1721. The betrothal was cancelled in 1723.

later, that it is tempting to imagine that the dancing master used it as his model, even if he was not himself a witness to it.[17]

Barbier reports that there were fifteen gentleman, including Louis XV, and fifteen ladies of the court who were named to dance. Apparently because there was a surfeit of princesses of blood in attendance, only a selection of them could be accommodated on the dance floor, but the remainder were nevertheless seated in a position of honour. On the other hand, 'not a single prince of blood was excluded from those [designated] to dance.'[18] The designated male dancers were seated behind the King's *fauteuil* at the head of the room. The female dancers were seated to the King's left, and the princesses of blood not named to dance were seated to his right. These latter two groups formed an oval along the length of the theatre, and framed the dancing space in which couples would perform, with Louis XV (when he was not dancing himself) as the centre and focus of their attention at the head of the room. The other seigneurs of the court were positioned in tiers behind those seated in the places of honour. Presumably the other on-lookers, including Barbier, were still further from the inner circle. Overall the disposition of those in attendance at this ball matches perfectly the description offered by Rameau (and depicted in an engraved plate of *Le Maître à danser*) of the ideal layout at a royal ball.[19] Even before any dancing began, such a layout displayed rank in the strongest possible terms, and set the stage for the dances that would proclaim this social order over and over again during the evening.

Barbier's account continues: 'First a branle was danced by all thirty dancers, in which each led the branle in his turn, starting with the King. Then he danced a menuet with Mlle de Charolais.'[20] This almost certainly initiated a series of couple dances, but Barbier offers no description. Instead, he immediately moves to an account of *menuets à quatre*, and these, too, were initiated by the King.[21] In fact, Barbier's

---

[17]In fact, the possibility of Rameau having witnessed this ball is not as remote as might be thought. On-lookers, even from untitled classes, were admitted to this event if they had a 'ticket,' which explains why Barbier, himself, gained admission. See *Journal de Barbier*, vol. 1, 133: 'On n'y entrait que par billets. J'y étais.'

[18]ibid.: 'Pas un prince du sang n'était de la danse.'

[19]A translation of the relevant passages and a reproduction of Rameau's plate can be found in Harris-Warrick, 'Ballroom Dancing,' 41.

[20]ibid., 134: 'On a dansé d'abord un branle des trente danseurs, où chacun a mené le branle à son tour: le roi a commencé, ensuite il a dansé un menuet avec mademoiselle de Charolais.'

[21]ibid.: 'Les menuets à quatre ont aussi été commencés par le roi avec mademoiselle de La Roche-sur-Yon, M. le duc d'Ossonne, amabassadeur d'Espagne, et madame la duchesse de Brissac.' Although not mentioned by Rameau, menuets performed two couples at a time had become a commonplace by the 1720s, either to accommodate more dancers, or to accelerate the proceedings. The evidence is reviewed in (cont.)

account offers precisions concerning the overall sequence of events at a royal ball overlooked (or perhaps rejected) by Rameau. The dances—at this ball, at any rate—were sequenced according to genre: first the branle, then the couple dance(s), then the menuets à 4, and then the contredanses, and in each case the new genre was announced by a performance from the King. 'The menuets à quatre were continued, and afterwards the contredanses were opened by the King, who danced a *cotillon* for four. It was already ten o'clock.'[22] For fully four hours (Barbier tells us the ball began at 8, and continued after the King's *cotillon* for another two hours), the court and other on-lookers were treated to a display of dancing of several kinds, grouped by genre, performed by the very highest stratum of society, all in an orderly way that Rameau, no doubt, would have applauded.

•   •   •   •   •

On almost every count, Rameau's paradigm for the orderly procedures of social dancing did not, indeed could not obtain at the *bal public*. There were no invited guests, let alone a list of individuals designated to dance, and therefore there could be no socially predetermined order in the proceedings. There was no surrogate king or queen as a *présence*, and therefore no focus for the performance of a couple dance, or even a group dance, for that matter. In fact, the only prescriptions among the many Rameau offered that might have applied were his observations concerning the masked ball. At the *bal public* that meant that everyone ought to be treated in more or less the same way. Rather than the 'preferential honour'[23] with which, Rameau advised, masquers normally were to be treated, those in attendance at an opera ball could expect no more than to be received 'with decency.'[24] Although one did not abandon rank upon entering a public ball, it would have been misguided to believe that one could go there expecting

---

Harris-Warrick, 'Ballroom Dancing,' 45-46. It has also been suggested that a vogue for menuets à quatre emerged as a consequence of the popularity of the contredanse. See Naïk Raviart, 'Le bal français du début du règne de Louis XIV à l'aube de la Révolution,' in *Histoires de bal* (Paris, 1998), 43.

[22]*Journal de Barbier*, 134: 'Ces menuets à quatre ont continue et, après, les contredanses ont été ouvertes par le roi, qui a dansé un cotillon à quatre. Il était alors dix heures.' It is possible that the 'Cotillon' mentioned here is the dance issued in 1705 as part of Feuillet's *Recüeil de Dances de Bal pour l'Année 1706*. It is titled 'Le Cotillon,' is for two couples, and in most respects behaves like a contredanse. See Semmens, 'Branles, Gavottes and Contredanses,' 40-44.

[23]See above, n9.

[24]The *Reglement* of 1716 prohibits violence, insult and indecency at the public ball. See Appendix 1, article IV.

to be treated in a special way. One of the apparent attractions of the *bal de l'Opéra* was the relaxation it offered to the rigorous rules of behaviour demanded by more formal occasions. As we saw in chapter one, Louis XV enjoyed his visit to the public ball on lundi gras, 4 March 1737, because he was able to move about (he was 'jostled') unrecognized.[25] Indeed the regulation that mandated attending in a costume[26] (a regulation that was not always strictly observed[27]) seems to have been designed to promote more fluid social interaction. But even if one elected to attend *sans domino*, there was no mechanism in place at the opera ball that could engage a special protocol in recognition of an individual's social position. It was this feature of the *bals publics*, perhaps, that explains why Rameau offered no advice on them.

It would be a mistake, however, to conclude that a typical opera ball was little more than a free-for-all, or an occasion at which polite conduct could be dispensed with altogether. It was, after all, a magnet for fashionable society (especially during carnival season) and, as a public event, it functioned as an arena for social discourse. It was a kind of social discourse, though, that was not normally encountered. A formal ball, such as the one described by Barbier in 1722, served to reaffirm the stability of the social order, to entrench its hierarchical structure, and to allow its component parts to interact in an idealized way. Attending a public ball, on the other hand, permitted one to engage society, or be engaged by it, on a much more individual level. The social discourse it nurtured favoured personal interaction over the behaviour of the group. While the focus of the formal ball was the dancing couple, its underlying motive was a collective affirmation of the whole. The *bal public*, on the other hand, celebrated the individual. Dancing had a part to play in this celebration, as we shall later see, but it was not allotted the critical focus that it enjoyed at a formal ball.

Shortly after the public balls were inaugurated in early 1716, the *Mercure galant* offered an unusually lengthy 'account' of them (it runs nearly 100 pages) in the February issue of that year. This account is difficult to characterize. It does not provide a real description, at least not of the kind I have cited frequently in the course of this investigation,

---

[25]See chapter one, n96.

[26]See Appendix 1, article II.

[27]There are several accounts of the Regent and members of his retinue, during the early years of the public ball, descending directly from his apartments to the ballroom, often in an inebriated state. That they were immediately recognized must mean they were undisguised. See, for example, *Mémoires de Saint-Simon*, vol. 29, 298: 'J'étois touché aussi d'éloigner M. le duc d'Orléans... de l'état auquel il se montroit souvent aux bals de l'Opéra.' As we saw in chapter one (n44), Saint-Simon had earlier observed that one could attend the public ball both 'masqué et non masqué'.

in which details of the venue for a ball, of those in attendance, of the attire worn by some, and occasionally of those who danced have formed the principal object. This account, rather, is satirically impressionistic and episodic, in short, a piece of tongue-in-cheek fiction. It should not be dismissed on that count, however, for in many ways it represents an important initial reaction to this new variety of social gathering. If the account is viewed as commentary on a perceived assault on the hegemony of courtly conduct (but this is only one of the possible readings), then I think it is fair to say that the initial reaction to the public ball was not altogether favourable.

The author of the account, who addresses us directly in the first person, and who uses the active voice, begins by recounting an 'adventure' in which a gentleman has received permission from his wife to attend an opera ball. His visit there is brief, however, for he has planned to use the occasion to see his mistress at her residence. That encounter proves inconsequential, in part because he finds her in bed and ready for sleep, and in part because his mistress has become quite jealous of his wife, and is annoyed with him. Eventually he decides to return home to his wife's bed. But his wife, who is evidently quite aware of her husband's infidelity, has planned a little trick to teach him a lesson. She has engaged the services of a gentleman neighbour to take her to the opera ball as well, and they have returned to her bed to complete the evening, and the ruse. When her husband returns and slips quietly into her bed, she leaps up, screaming, and feigns horror at being discovered. 'Save yourself, save me,' she cries, 'Monsieur, we are lost!' The household attendants rush into the room, and gaze in amazement at the threesome, while the husband can only believe that he is not alone in his unfaithfulness.[28] Our author then immediately admits that he has personally had a similar experience, but one in which there was no trickery at the conclusion, and one, moreover, whose outcome he finds preferable. He confesses frankly:

> The husband of a pretty wife with whom I spent the night while he was at the ball discovered me with her. He was neither frantic, nor shocked. He let me dress quietly, merely acknowledged the secret, and dismissed me with all the graciousness in the world. In his words, 'Get dressed, Monsieur, do not publicize this adventure. Go back to bed, Madame, and may heaven protect us from a greater misfortune.'[29]

---

[28]*Mercure galant*, février (1716), 179-184.

[29]ibid., 184-185: 'Le mary d'une jolie femme avec qui j'ay passé la nuit, pendant qu'il estoit au Bal, m'a surpris avec elle. Il n'a esté ni fou, ni étourdi, il m'a seulement recommandé le secret, & m'a congedié de la meilleure grace du monde. A son exemple habillez-vous, Monsieur, ne publiez point cette avanture; recouchez-vous, Madame, & le Ciel nous garde d'un plus grand malheur.'

These two stories, of course, tell us little about the opera balls. Rather, they seem to pass judgment on what can happen *because* of them, and the judgment, while somewhat sarcastic, is far from unequivocally disapproving, since it is mediated by the personal, somewhat matter-of-fact 'confession' of the narrator.

The two initial anecdotes, however, serve as prelude to a more thorough exploration of gallant adventures that occur at the opera balls themselves. Our narrator's tone becomes slightly more patronizing as he instructs us on what to expect. 'No matter where one turns at the Ball,' he explains,

> there are always people trailing about everywhere, and masquers who ask nothing more than to annoy others, or to be annoyed themselves. Timid souls or imbeciles die of boredom there. The former have insufficient courage to attempt an adventure, the latter lack the wits to pull it off.[30]

These general observations are followed by an even more patronizing set of 'instructions' on how to succeed at such an affair. As if to underscore the formality of our instructor's endeavours (and at the same time to impart, perhaps unintentionally, a certain foreign quality, an 'otherness,' to the conduct of the opera ball), each instruction is numbered in an ultramontane fashion: 'Primo,' 'Secundo,' and so on. 'First,' he insists, 'it is essential that every masquer possess audacity, and even impudence. Second, that he know at least a half dozen impertinent phrases to banter about.' There follows a lengthy excursion into the varieties of conversation used in a verbal assault on another masquer that explains how and what one is to 'yelp into the ears of the masquer being attacked' ['glapir dans les oreilles du Masque qu'on attaque']. 'Third, a different tone is taken to make a declaration of love to someone one doesn't even know.'[31] These three 'rules' of conduct form the basis for the (mis-)adventures that are exposed in the remainder of the *Mercure* account.

At the heart of all of them is a 'fear of being discovered' on the one hand, and a compulsive drive 'to uncover,' or to 'de-masque' on the

---

[30]ibid., 187: 'Qu'on se tourne d'un ou d'autre costé au Bal, il y a toûjours & partout des gens qui cherchent noise, & des Masques qui ne demandent pas mieux que d'agacer les autres, ou d'estre agacez eux mêmes. Les timides ou les imbeciles s'y ennuyent à la mort. Les uns n'ont pas le courage de tenter une avanture, les autres n'ont pas l'esprit de la soûtenir.'

[31]ibid., 188, 193: '*Primo*. Il faut qu'un Masque quelqu'il soit, ait de l'audace, & même de l'effronterie. *Secundo*. Qu'il sçache au moins une demie douzaine de phrases impertinentes pour les debiter à tort & à travers... *Tertio*. On le prend sur un autre ton pour faire une declaration d'amour à une personne qu'on connoît pas.'

other. Once these dynamics are understood, the account begins to make more sense. 'To annoy' a fellow masquer was to attempt to uncover her or his true identity. 'Being annoyed,' however, was not entirely undesirable because there was a certain thrill in the risk, so it was not uncommon for a masquer 'to ask' (to put herself/himself into a position) to be annoyed (discovered). It took 'audacity' to embark on an adventure at a public ball because it left one vulnerable to discovery, and that is why it was so important to be well disguised—in appearance, as well as in behaviour—and why it was advisable to use different modes of conversation. It was even possible in these adventures for a husband and wife both to be in attendance at a ball (but never knowingly together), and not to recognize each other. In the anecdotes recounted by our host at the opera ball, two players invariably try to 'trump' each other by uncovering the true identity of the other, or, if they have failed to do so, by trying to fool the other into believing that they really have 'discovered' them. All this is accomplished through witty conversation that aims to put the other on the defensive. A 'declaration of love' in these opera ball encounters is in reality an expression of sexual interest, and amounts to an offer to reveal one's identity, to take off one's mask.

What can be made of such a reaction to the new opera ball? The satirical tone certainly suggests disapproval, yet it is not nearly as dismissive a judgment as was passed, for example, by the Regent's mother, who in a letter of 12 November 1719 wrote:

> I learned yesterday that my son and Mme d'Orléans have permitted the duc de Chartres [their son] to go to this accursed *bal de l'Opéra*, so shameless. It will be the physical and moral ruin of this child who, up till now, has been so pious, for to go there or to a brothel is one and the same thing. The child has a delicate constitution, he's a little gnat, he can't endure the slightest fatigue, and in all his life has never stayed up past 11 o'clock. On top of this, the insane company that is attracted to the ball will certainly kill this poor boy.[32]

Madame's comments are blunt, hardly satirical, and utterly disapproving. The account of public balls in the *Mercure*, by comparison, is almost non-committal, beyond its satirical tone. It exposes a

---

[32]Olivier Amiel, ed., *Lettres de Madame, Duchesse d'Orléans, née Princesse Palatine, 1672-1722*, Le Temps retrouvé, vol. xxxii (Paris, 1981), 402: 'J'ai appris hier que mon fils et Mme d'Orléans ont permis au duc de Chartres d'aller à ce maudit bal de l'Opéra, si dévergondé. Ce sera la ruine physique et morale de cet enfant qui, jusqu'à ce jour, a été si pieux, car d'aller là ou au bordel c'est tout un. L'enfant a une santé delicate, c'est un vrai moucheron, il ne peut endurer la moindre fatigue, et de sa vie il n'a veillé plust tard qu'onze heures. Ceci joint à la vie insensée qu'on mène à ce bal, tuera bien certainement ce pauvre garcon.'

temporary re-ordering of class structure, or if not that, at least a significant re-definition of the status quo. The players in this new scheme are not distinguishable by rank, or even by gender, for that matter, (at any rate, not in any important way).[33] Power in the arena of the opera ball, rather, was measured by 'audacity,' and birthright yielded no advantages whatsoever to one's chances at 'success.' As in a royal ball, nevertheless, that of the opera house proclaimed class boundaries in no uncertain terms, and our narrator was quick to point these out at the very beginning of his discourse. Excluded from the inner circle of privileged participants at an opera ball were both 'timid souls' and 'imbeciles,' for they lacked either the fortitude or the cunning to succeed. The consequences of their failings were not banishment from 'court' (the opera house), nor loss of station—there was, after all, no station to lose. Their punishment, rather, was death by boredom!

Now all this is a very interesting subversion of courtly ballroom routine, one that might also have been understood by some as less than favourable commentary, not on the newly instituted public balls, but on the oppressive formality of the royal ball. Increasingly during the waning years of Louis XIV's reign unveiled discontent, sometimes described as boredom in the sources, was expressed about the predictable, unchanging, and humourless etiquette that attended the formal ball.[34] As early as the mid-1670s, in fact, Madame de Sévigné wrote frequently of a prevailing 'sadness' surrounding some of the formal balls she attended.[35] By the 1690s the future Regent's mother wrote that the formal ball was 'hors de mode,'[36] and in 1710 she remarked that 'it is boring for those who dance and for those

---

[33]In the account of the *Mercure* there is an interesting allusion to gender roles at the opera ball in the passage that explains the modes of conversation to be adopted there. *Mercure galant*, février (1716), 189: 'Sur ce principe, il luy dira, *bonjour Beau, ou Belle Masque*; la difference du sexe fait peut-estre celle du début. L'un est cependant plus en usage que l'autre. Il luy dira, *bonjour Beau Masque*...' ('In this regard he [or she—the reference is to the masculine noun 'masque'] will say to her/him, "Good day handsome, or pretty masquer". The difference in sex is, perhaps, that of an opening. Nevertheless, one is more common than the other. He [or she] will say to her/him, "Good day handsome masquer...") From this I infer that the more common opening presumed initially that the masquer 'under assault' was a gentleman.

[34]Evidence for this tendency is reviewed in Naïk Raviart, 'Le bal français,' 42.

[35]See, for example, Roger Duchêne, ed., *Correspondance / Madame de Sévigné*, 3 vols. (Paris, 1972), vol. 1, 667. In this letter from January, 1674, she writes: 'Le bal fut fort triste, et fini à onze heures et demie.' There are many other examples, some reviewed in Raviart, 'Le bal français,' 42.

[36]*Lettres de Madame*, 118. In a letter of May 1695: 'La danse est donc hors de mode partout?'

who watch.'[37] Seen in the light of these comments, the subversion of courtly conduct revealed in the *Mercure*'s 1716 account of the *bal de l'Opéra* was, perhaps, an exploration of much wider social practices. The primary target, nevertheless, was the newly created public ball. And there is an important difference between the boredom of a formal ball and that of a public one. In the former boredom was suffered by those in the 'inner circle' (those who had been invited to dance or to look on), and in the latter by those outside it (those who lacked the fortitude and cunning to participate).

Turned upside down in the 1716 account of the opera ball, as well, was the whole notion of personal display. At a formal ball it was *important* to be recognized, not so much for the purposes of flattering one's vanity (although that certainly was a factor), but rather so that one could be situated within the privileged hierarchy on display. While personal appearance and attire could draw particular attention to an individual, the likelihood of being recognized was essentially a matter of station. It had less to do with being better dressed, better coiffed, or more resplendently bejewelled than everyone else. In fact, it was frequently the case that all the ladies designated to dance at a royal ball wore the same (invariably sumptuous) costume,[38] *uniformed*, so to speak, to carry out their ritualized duties. This was not intended to obscure identities. It was intended, rather, to set a select few apart from everyone else, to situate them in a position of high distinction.

Even at a masked ball—according to Rameau's prescriptions—one was situated (albeit anonymously) by virtue of the fact that those in disguise were to be given the honour of dancing first. In these circumstances, of course, there was a chance that one could be situated incorrectly. In many accounts of masked balls, however, it is quite clear that true anonymity was no more than a fiction willingly agreed to by the participants, because the accounts regularly reveal the identities (or, if not that, at least the social positions) of the individuals in disguise. A striking example is found in a letter of the future Regent's mother, dated 8 February 1699. In it she describes a masked ball held at Marly, making observations such as 'A lady was seen entering as tall and wide as a tower. It was M le duc de Valentinois, son of M de Monaco.' Or,

M le Dauphin arrived with another troupe, all comically masked. They

---

[37]*Lettres de Madame*, 295. In a letter of November 1710: 'Combien le prince royal [the Duke of Hanover] a raison de ne pas aimer la danse française! C'est ennuyeux pour ceux qui dansent et pour ceux qui regarde.'

[38]There are numerous descriptions in the *Mercure galant*. See further Rebecca Harris-Warrick, 'Ballroom Dancing,' 44, and n9, where an invitation to a royal ball in January, 1739 even set down specific instructions for hairstyles.

changed costumes three or four times. His group was composed of the Princesse de Conti, Mlle Lislebonne, Mme de Chatillon and the duc de Villeroy. The duc d'Anjou and the duc de Berry with their companions made up a third band of masquers.[39]

Evidently Madame had no difficulties recognizing the masquers at this event, and by identifying them by name in her correspondence she was, in fact, doing them an honour.

At the opera ball described by the *Mercure*, on the other hand, being recognized was something to avoid, for it left one exposed, and in a vulnerable position. The dynamics of this exposed position are not difficult to fathom. It was one thing to carry on with others in a playfully impertinent way behind the protective barrier of a disguise (in the relative safety of a large crowd), and quite another to do so after having been recognized. With recognition came a loss of power, an inability to engage others with 'audacity.' There was also an undercurrent of sexuality in the dilemma, for a 'declaration of love' at the opera ball, as we have seen, was typically articulated through an offer to reveal one's identity. Allowing oneself to be recognized, then, was also in some ways 'being promiscuous.'[40] Once recognized, there was little one could do except, perhaps, to retreat to the loges, to take oneself *hors de combat*. But even that offered no protection against the social consequences of having been discovered once one was outside the opera house. And so it is that in one of the anecdotes recounted in the *Mercure* a gentleman's identity is revealed at the opera ball after he is deemed to have insulted another gentleman while chasing after a woman. He is challenged to a duel that takes place the next morning, and eventually is seriously wounded.[41] While the cause of the social disruption described in this anecdote was a perceived insult, the agency for its eventual unhappy outcome was the *mistake* of revealing one's identity. (In this case the mistake was especially egregious because the poor gentleman also gave out his address, and thus was easily found the next morning by his accuser). At the opera ball, then, *not* being recognized ultimately meant power, quite the opposite to the situation

---

[39]*Lettres de Madame*, 170: 'On vit entrer une dame haute et large comme un tour, c'était M. le duc de Valentinois, fils de M. de Monaco... M. le dauphin arriva avec une autre troupe tous bien drôlement masques: ils changèrent d'habits trois ou quatre fois. Sa compagnie était composee de de la princesse de Conti, Mlle de Lislebonne, Mme de Chatillon et le duc de Villeroy. Les ducs d'Anjou et de Berry avec leurs gens formaient la troisième bande de masques.'

[40]There is a hint of this in the remarks of the duc de Richelieu, quoted in chapter one: 'the majority of the ladies [at the opera ball], unmasking themselves with the pretext of being inconvenienced by the heat, cared only to have themselves admired.' See chapter one, n49.

[41]*Mercure galant*, février (1716), 234-243.

in a formal ball, where power (social distinction) *meant* being recognized.

As was the case at a private masked ball, of course, there must have been frequent occasions at the *bal public* when individuals were recognized without suffering any of the consequences reported in the account of the *Mercure*. If, for example, one was a frequent participant at the balls, but regularly wore the same costume, eventual discovery was a real likelihood. Indeed, Louis XV, who *was* recognized at the opera ball in 1737 (if only by a few in attendance) was in the habit of wearing a bat costume ('costume de chauve-souris') at masked balls during that period. He wore the same costume and, not surprisingly, was recognized once more at the opera ball held on the Thursday before mardi gras in 1739.[42] There is a kind of irony at work here: persons of truly distinguished rank were somewhat *disadvantaged* at the opera ball, for they were often *too recognizable* to remain anonymous for long. This kind of incidental recognition, however, was evidently of no consequence, especially if the individual who was discovered was not actively engaged in an 'adventure.' Under ordinary circumstances, though, safeguarding one's identity at the public ball was important, because it gave one licence to exercise power during the proceedings.

It may be concluded that two important forces were at work at the *bal de l'Opéra*, each propelling the other: an interest in engaging in a kind of behaviour that subverted (or at least was at odds with) the accepted norms of the upper end of the hierarchical social structure, and the danger of being discovered doing just that. The danger, more precisely, was in being found to be a *willing* participant in such behaviour, and one was a willing participant, of course, by virtue of the fact that one paid to gain admission. This, I believe, is what the 1716 account in the *Mercure* is trying to tell us in part. The message is disguised, however, like the participants in an opera ball. Its tongue-in-cheek tone is diverting, not moralistic, and there are features in the narrative that almost certainly were contrived to make it seem more like a piece of fiction than a serious exposé. For example, one of the players in the gallant adventures, a M de Verno, is made out to be a seasoned veteran of such affairs. He finds himself at the opera ball, we are told, 'according to his habit, in his costume of striped taffeta.' His adventure begins with an 'attack' on a lady he finds at his side, conducted in accordance with 'the great experience he has in these assemblies.'[43]

---

[42]Edmond Barbier, *Journal*, t. II, 215. He wore the same bat costume at a masked ball held at Versailles over the evening of 26-27 January the same year. See ibid., t. II, 217.

[43]*Mercure galant*, février (1716), 246-247, 247-248: '... M. de Verno, dis je, se trouvant selon sa coûtume, au bal de l'Opera, sous un domino de taffetas rayé... il attaqua une Dame qui se trouva sous sa main. La grande experience qu'il a dans ces assemblées, luy mit d'abord un joli compliment à la bouche.'

Now the original readers of this account in February, 1716 would certainly have recognized how fanciful this story was, for the opera balls were so new at the time—there had probably been fewer than a dozen of them—that no one could possibly have cultivated the experience M de Verno is supposed to possess.

It is precisely this kind of lie, however, that makes me think that the overall account in the *Mercure* was intended to convey something more, that there was a coded message lying behind the fanciful adventures. In its unadorned form the message goes something like the following. 'One goes to the opera ball to engage in subversive behaviour. It is subversive behaviour because one is engaged in it.' But the message is not unadorned. It is delivered in a humorously playful way that pokes fun at the participants of an opera ball. While many established courtly procedures are turned topsy-turvy, they are not, in their subverted form, presented as any immediate threat to the social order. They are held in check, restricted, for the most part, to the confines of the opera house ballroom. Because many of the players in the anecdotes are presented as experienced ball-goers, however, there is an implication that there may be some long-term consequences.

If my decoding of the message is correct, then the initial reaction to the opera ball (for the editor of the *Mercure*, at any rate) was that it represented an assault, but a fairly benign one, on the hegemony of courtly conduct in social gatherings. Such a reaction is hardly surprising, however, because the *Mercure galant* was certainly a conservative publication with a predisposition for praising courtly activities (especially royal ones) and conduct on every possible occasion. Although the opera ball was far from praiseworthy, it was nevertheless an interesting novelty, deserving of some commentary, and it generated the longest single piece (to my knowledge) that the *Mercure* had ever published on any topic up to that date.

Nearly fifty years later, in the issue of April 1764, the *Mercure* published another piece on the opera balls that is remarkably similar.[44] It recounts an amorous adventure—just a single one this time—of a gentleman at the ball, and it invokes precisely the same kinds of imagery that dominated the earlier account. The issues of trying to uncover another's identity, and the perils of being discovered are once more the central theme. But this adventure also explores the morality of marriage and faithfulness to one's spouse in some detail. In this

[44]*Mercure de France*, avril (1764), pt. 2, 23-32. Note the change in title of the journal here. During the seventeenth and eighteenth centuries, the *Mercure* had at least three different titles, and several editors. The journal, itself, gives a useful account of its own history and editorship in *Mercure de France*, mai (1760), 127-131.

adventure—titled 'Le Bal de l'Opera, Anecdote qu'on prendra pour un Conte'—a gentleman attempts to 'de-masque' (seduce) a young woman, seeks the aid of an acquaintance who is an expert in such things, and is then tricked into contemplating other potential conquests at the ball. While the gentleman considers these, his acquaintance successfully seduces the young woman (or so he thinks), and heads off to a loge with her. The gentleman follows them to congratulate his acquaintance on succeeding where he had failed, and discovers that the young woman is actually his wife. The message of this anecdote is essentially the same as those of 1716, but it is not nearly so covert. We are warned at the outset that the anecdote should be understood as a 'story' (a cue that compels us to hunt for a hidden meaning), and we are guided, further, through means of an early footnote that reads: 'All these remarks and those that follow are the remarks [proper to] a ball [at the opera], in which it is essential to take care to consider the morality of the author.'[45] Although the overall tone is still playful in this piece, its message is much more direct: the opera balls encourage a corruption of proper behaviour, and they compromise the stability of respectable social structures and institutions (marriage).

In the nearly fifty years that separated these two pieces, of course, the opera balls had established themselves as a very popular entertainment, patronized by the highest echelons of society, and even by the royal family. In the intervening years, as well, the *Mercure* had also begun to treat them (when it treated them at all) in a more accepting way. In fact, in the issue published just the month before the anecdote discussed above the *Mercure* praised the opera ball with unbridled enthusiasm. It reported on the newly opened facility at the *Palais des Tuilleries* as follows:

> The more [often] the new ballroom is visited the more its beauty is recognized. The greater number of masquers there only creates the liveliness required by [such] diversions and that kind of confusion that is the brilliance of balls, without which the inconveniences of a crowd [that is] too reserved is experienced there. It would be difficult to set out a more comfortable or better-appointed place for the most magnificent celebration.[46]

---

[45]*Mercure de France*, avril (1764), pt. 2, 25: 'Tous ces propos & ceux qui suivent sont des propos de bal, par lesquels il faut bien se garder de juger de la morale de l'Auteur.'

[46]*Mercure de France*, mars (1764), 170: 'Plus on fréquente la nouvelle Salle de Bal, & plus on en reconnoît la beauté. Le plus grand nombre de Masques n'y produit que la vivacité nécessaire à l'amusement, & cette sorte de confusion qui fait tout le brilliant des Bals, sans que l'on y éprouve les incommodities d'une foule trop reservée. Il seroit difficile de disposer un lieu plus commode & plus convenable pour la fête la plus magnifique.'

It is not easy to reconcile this clearly supportive notice with the anecdote published a month later. Here 'confusion' is reckoned to be laudable (certainly far removed from Rameau's view, which deplored confusion at a ball.[47]) This is exactly the same positive twist to the meaning of 'confusion' that was used by the young woman quoted in the opening of chapter two (drawn from the *Mercure*'s 1716 account of the opera balls). But here the *Mercure* uses this meaning of the word without recourse to a fictitious character as speaker. And if that were not enough, there is even a hint of criticism of *formal* balls in the passage, which are accused, it seems, of being 'too reserved.' What can be made of this abrupt change of position between March and April?

It may well be that the *Mercure* was merely reflecting a divided opinion on the opera balls. From their very inception, after all, the balls had been judged very differently: the Regent's mother abhorred them, while the Regent was a habitué. It is also possible, however, that the editor of the *Mercure* experienced a kind of *crise de conscience* at the conclusion of an unusually dazzling opera ball season (one that the journal itself had applauded), and felt obliged to offer up an opposing viewpoint. Although this possibility is perhaps less likely, it is worth exploring briefly.

The anecdote of April 1764 was published in the wake of the inaugural season of opera balls mounted in the new ballroom of the *Palais des Tuilleries*. The season's opening had been postponed several times while the new venue was prepared, so anticipation was especially pronounced.[48] As we have already seen, attendance overall that season was very strong, even though there was room for just twelve balls, owing to the season's late start. The new Tuilleries facility, which was praised for its spaciousness and sumptuous appointments,[49] no doubt played an important role in this success, and sparked a renewed interest in the public ball among Parisians. The opera balls, in short, had once more become a sort of novelty, and this may have prompted the *Mercure* to re-visit some of the satirically cautionary remarks that had been expressed when public balls had first appeared in 1716. I do not mean to suggest that the earlier account was literally consulted—although because the similarities between the two pieces are so striking, this is

[47]See above, n8.

[48]*Mercure de France*, janvier (1762), pt. 1, 151, reported to its readers that the opening of the season still, regrettably, could not be determined, although it noted that an opening in time for carnival season was 'indispensable.' In pt. 2, 176, it announced the first ball would take place on Sunday, 29 January. The first ball was actually delayed until Thursday, 2 February 1762.

[49]The new ballroom is described with glowing approval in *Mercure de France*, février (1764), 195-197.

far from out of the question—but rather that analogous events (the sudden faddishness of opera balls in a newly revamped venue) yielded a similar response.

As interesting as the variegated reception history of opera balls preserved in the pages of the *Mercure* in 1764 is the important fact that they were described in terms of adventures of disguise and unmasking, just as they had been in 1716. The persistence of this metaphor is conspicuous, and its use was not restricted to colourful narratives in the venerable Parisian journal. These kinds of adventures can also be found in descriptions of opera balls in the diaries and memoirs of the period. In these sources, of course, opera ball adventures are not so much a metaphor for an underlying social reality as they are the reality itself. The *Souvenirs* of the baron de Frénilly (1768-1848) provide a useful example, not only because they preserve an account of opera balls in the final decade of the *ancien régime*, but also because they reveal an interesting metamorphosis in the practice (and the social function) of disguise. It is true that the baron's *Souvenirs* should not be regarded as a completely reliable witness in all respects. They were written while he was in self-imposed exile during the final twenty years of his life, and they recall better days (as far as he was concerned) with some bitterness.[50] When he relates events in which he does not feel compelled to make himself out as a principal player, however—and this is the case in his account of the opera ball—his recollections seem perfectly trustworthy. His reminiscences of the opera ball are from the period dated 1780-1787 in his *Souvenirs*, but since he did not reside in Paris between 1785 and 1790,[51] he must be referring to the early 1780s. He recalls,

> A very different ball was that given at the Opéra. Its very name recalls the cream of the society of Paris at that brilliant period. Only the women were masked, and it was this which lent it piquancy and charm, for half of those present knew the others without being recognised themselves. Women had the pleasure of being bold and at the same time respected under cover of the mask, whilst the men had that of being given a puzzle to solve.
>
> Well-bred women were in black dominoes and masks, rarely white and never coloured. Even their feet, and especially their hair, were disguised. They arrived in Sedan chairs but returned in a sort of bath-chair. To conceal their identity was an important matter, and

[50]Arthur Chuquet, ed. *Souvenirs du baron de Frénilly, pair de France (1768-1828)* (Paris, 1908). English trans. by Frederic Lees, *Recollections of Baron de Frénilly, Peer of France (1768-1828)* (London, 1909). See Introduction, v-x.

[51]ibid., v-vi.

sometimes with good reason. Many a domestic plot and many a Court or State intrigue originated there. The crafty Rulhière was one of the lions of this ball. On one occasion he offered his arm to Mme. de Sénéchal, then in her first youth, and, seeing a vacant seat by the side of the Queen, whom he had recognized in spite of her mask, placed her there. He then began a conversation in which he passed in review all the ladies of the Court, and about whom he told such amusing anecdotes that Marie Antoinette, who gained much instruction at that *soirée*, was ready to die with laughter.[52]

There are some familiar ideas and themes in this account, but some important new developments, too, the most obvious of which is that disguise at the opera ball has now become gendered. The resultant shifts in power that might be expected from this development, however, are not at all straightforward. While de Frénilly allows that women, by virtue of their masks and costumes, were given licence to be 'bold' (the 'audacity' of the earlier accounts), men were evidently not weakened correspondingly in the absence of disguises. Indeed, they were empowered in a manner not available to women. De Frénilly does not comment directly on this empowerment, of course, but the social dynamics in his descriptions make its nature quite obvious. Men were now freed from 'fear of discovery' and the imperative of safeguarding their ballroom identities. Their energies were now focussed exclusively on pursuit. But there is more. Because the identities of the gentlemen were already known, women were effectively restricted to a defensive posture, for there was nothing for them 'to discover' (except, perhaps, the identities of other women). While they 'enjoyed the pleasure of being bold under cover of the mask,' there was, in fact, no longer any reason for them to *be* bold, to *exercise* that power. In short, the men had been made active players, and the women passive, as de Frénilly's anecdote certainly makes explicit. By pretending not to recognize Marie Antoinette, and using Mme de Sénéchal as his *prop*, Rulhière is able to seat himself next to the queen and say comical things about the women in her court. The end of the anecdote summarizes rather precisely the new configuration of power at the opera ball. If Marie Antoinette is laughing at the things she thinks she has learned by happy accident, then she has been duped. If she is laughing at the thought that Rulhière doesn't realize whom he is seated next to, then she has been duped as well! The very passive roles played by the two ladies here are given special emphasis. Mme de Sénéchal is a decoy, and the queen, the real object of the joke, is otherwise no more than a third party, an ear-witness to a one-sided conversation she believes she is not intended to hear.

[52]ibid., 23.

'De-masquing' the male population at an opera ball, then, resulted in a re-alignment of power that disadvantaged women. At any rate, the variety of power roles available to them in accounts of opera balls from earlier in the century (when they had been as actively engaged in adventures of discovery as the men) certainly had been reduced by the 1780s. At de Frénilly's opera balls women *receive* 'respect' as a consequence of their disguises (in a manner, interestingly, that is reminiscent of Rameau's advice about conduct at a masked ball); they no longer *command* it. And they are the *objects* of 'a puzzle to solve,' or of a trick to be played, as in the anecdote about Marie Antoinette. In terms of their social manoeuvrability at the opera ball, in other words, women had become essentially a single class. It does not seem incongruent to this new structure that it also became fashionable for the ladies to be attired in disguises of a single colour (although why *black* is difficult to fathom[53]): uniform colour in their costumes reflected the new social reality of the opera ball in a compelling way. Men, on the other hand, retained the ability to seize an opportunity for an adventure, and to differentiate themselves from others: Rulhière was one of the 'lions' of the opera ball. The admiration in de Frénilly's epitaph is unmistakable.

Although the dynamics of socializing at de Frénilly's opera ball now favoured men, the consequences of this activity (the stakes, so to speak) were reduced in proportion, because men were *not* disguised, and therefore not at liberty to engage in the somewhat outlandish behaviour that opera balls had formerly featured. De Frénilly enumerates three of the possible consequences—domestic plots, intrigues of court, and intrigues of state—but offers an example of only one (or perhaps two) of these, an intrigue of court (and, by extension, perhaps of state). The stories that Rulhière recounted about the ladies of Marie Antoinette's court were intended, no doubt, to engender intrigue. The immediate result of this intrigue, however, was a fit of laughter from the queen, a rather harmless outcome. There is no suggestion in de Frénilly's account that the

---

[53]It may be that black became fashionable as a deliberate subversion of the reigning preference for white gowns at private balls of the time. In the passage in de Frénilly's *Souvenirs* immediately preceding his account of the opera ball, he describes developments in private balls. 'Two years before the Revolution a sinister sign foreshadowed a change in these balls. Our gala costumes disappeared, and men no longer danced except in black dress-coats. The consequent mingling of crows and white-robed nymphs led to balls being nick-named "magpie" gatherings.' ibid., 22-23.

opera balls occasioned a temporary upset to the social order.[54] If there were an upset, it was to the institution of the masked ball, which had been transformed into one that was only partially masked, and gendered in the process. This was not viewed as a shortcoming, however, but rather as a feature that 'lent it piquancy and charm.'

In the nineteenth century a preference for partially masked balls at the opera house in Paris persisted. Surviving posters and tickets for these events sometimes indicate that wearing a costume was optional,[55] but much more frequently they give explicit instructions that a disguise was *required* for women. A ticket (for a gentleman's admission) for a ball held at the Académie Royale de Musique on mardi-gras, 4 February 1845 includes an instruction along one of its borders:[56] 'Les Dames ne seront admises qu'en Dominos ou costumées et masquées' (ladies will not be admitted except in dominos or costumed and masked). Along the facing border is written 'Le Controle refusera tout Costume qui ne sera jugé convenable' (the box-office will refuse any costume not deemed appropriate)! A poster announcing the 'Dernier Bal Masqué de l'Opéra' of the 1884 season transmits a similar message: 'Les Cavaliers, tenue de Soirée ou Costumés. Les Dames, en Dominos, Costumées et Masquées' (the gentlemen in evening dress or costume, the ladies in dominos, costumed and masked).[57] It may well be that tickets and posters for opera balls in the late eighteenth century gave the same kinds of instruction about attire, but, unhappily, such evidence has all but perished. I have been unable to locate any opera ball tickets from the period, and am aware of only a handful of surviving posters. One of these announces a ball on 12 February 1778.[58] None of these posters offers advice on attire, although they are chronologically proximate to the balls described by de Frénilly.

---

[54]Is his enumeration of consequences hierarchical by design: that is, home, court, state? If so, it is perhaps telling that he chose an illustration from the middle (or perhaps top) of the hierarchy to underscore the 'harmlessness' of the consequence.

[55]A poster announcing a 'Bal Masqué' to be held at the Academie Royale de Musique on 20 February 1830, for example, gives the following instruction: 'On pourra venir Masqué ou non Masqué.' See Agnès Terrier, *Le billet d'Opéra* (Paris, 2000), 58, for a colour facsimile of this poster.

[56]ibid., 59.

[57]ibid., 60.

[58]Preserved at the *Bibliothèque-Musée de l'Opéra* in a folder of operatic *affiches* under the shelf number Aff.Rés.22. I am extremely grateful to Elizabeth Bartlett for having drawn my attention to this collection of posters. It also includes an announcement for a ball on 31 January 1779, and one to be held in the 'Salle du Pantheon' on 2 February 1786. Other announcements for balls are typically appended to posters announcing operatic performances. A colour facsimile of the poster in question is given in Agnès Terrier, *Le billet d'Opéra*, 58. Its original dimensions are 37cm high by 49cm wide. I am most indebted to Mary Cyr for examining these posters, and for conveying her findings to me.

Yet even if such evidence were plentiful, it would not explain *why* the custom of segregated costuming emerged. It seems very unlikely that the practice arose only gradually, because if that were the case the early stages of such a development would certainly have been problematic. Just a handful of undisguised gentlemen among a majority who remained masked would surely have been untenable. The dynamics and typical behaviour of the opera ball either would have placed the minority in a terribly disadvantageous position, or cast them in the role of mere onlookers. It therefore seems more probable that the move to segregated costuming was rather sudden, precipitated perhaps by a new regulation (although I have found no supporting evidence for this), or triggered by some event that made wearing a disguise for gentlemen somehow undesirable. I can at least say with reasonable confidence that segregated costuming arose some time between 1764—the men in the *Mercure*'s account of that year are all disguised—and the early 1780s, the general time-frame of de Frénilly's recollection. Although it may not have been a motivation for the introduction of segregated costuming, one of the results of this development is clear: the conduct of opera balls was tamed. By the 1780s the gentlemen, now out of disguise, had to behave in a more genteel way, and the women, of necessity, had adopted a more passive stance. In short, the *bal de l'Opéra* had become *polite*.

•   •   •   •   •

Among the more striking features of the descriptions of opera balls considered so far (and in the vast majority of all the prose accounts of them that I have been able to consult) is that music and dancing are nowhere to be found. The absence of dancing in de Frénilly's reminiscences is particularly striking, because in the paragraph immediately preceding his account of the opera ball he describes fashionable private balls of the time, mentioning such dances as the menuet (which he claims had disappeared since his childhood) and the allemande.[59] I was initially surprised by the absence of dance in many accounts of opera balls, and tempted to conclude, as some scholars have, that dancing was only encountered sporadically at them.[60] Such a conclusion is understandable, given the paucity of references in many period sources, and the problem of the remarkably

---

[59]*Souvenirs*, 22.

[60]See, for example, Naïk Raviart, 'Le bal français,' 45. 'Sous le règne de Louis XV...la foule est telle qu'on n'y guère de place pour danser... Vers la fin du siècle on ne danse plus, ou quasi, au bal de l'Opéra.'

large crowds that attended the *bal public* from time to time, but it is a conclusion that is patently false. There most certainly was dancing at the opera ball, and a good deal of it, since it was, after all, a *ball*. That dancing is not mentioned in so many of the sources, therefore, deserves some examination, for this may tell us something about how eighteenth-century social constructions of the opera ball were originally conceived.

In the balls of the nobility in the eighteenth century—from the most informal to the most lavishly formalized—dance played a central role and, not surprisingly, it was often mentioned in accounts of them, however briefly or imprecisely. In the case of royal balls, commentators frequently provided additional details about dancing, as if the centrality of dance in these balls were somehow magnified. What *was* the role of dancing at these affairs? Earlier in this chapter I suggested that a formal ball served to legitimate the social order, to entrench its hierarchical structure, and to idealize the interaction of its component parts. That idea now needs further exploration. In making this claim, first of all, I am not suggesting that formal balls were organized in response to some nagging suspicion that, without them, the social order and its hierarchical structure were in imminent danger of collapsing. Such a notion is preposterous, of course, because social structures, while they are self-shaping, and to a large degree self-perpetuating, are by no means self-*standing* edifices requiring occasional support. Social structures and the practices they embrace, rather, are defined from within, and they are redefined constantly in many different ways. Among the primary ways society defined itself in early modern Europe was through class distinctions. In eighteenth century France these distinctions were particularly prominent, and, for the upper classes, the visible display of rank through dancing at a ball was certainly one of the more conspicuous ways in which that portion of society was able to demarcate its boundaries, to set itself apart from the others.[61] Dance was performed at a formal ball, in other words, *as though it were understood* by the individuals taking part to be an agent of class definition.

---

[61]Most sociologists who adhere to a social constuctionist model would argue that societies do not define their class boundaries consciously, as an act of collective will, but rather unconsciously: class boundaries are a product of deep-rooted habit. For a useful review, see David Swartz, *Culture & Power. The Sociology of Pierre Bourdieu*, especially chapter 5, 'Habitus: A Cultural Theory of Action,' 95-116. Norbert Elias takes this notion further, arguing that class structure and its reproduction in seventeenth and eighteenth century France was an unconscious response to a social imperative. See *The Court Society*, passim.

A useful illustration of how dance served as just such an agent, and how it was the locus for renegotiating class distinctions can be found in the *Mémoires* of the duc de Luynes. He describes a formal ball ('bal rangé') hosted by Louis XV at Versailles in late January 1739.[62] De Luynes lavished a good deal of attention on details of the dancing at this event, because it had a central role to play in the proceedings, to be sure, but also because the dancing at this ball gave visible expression to a renegotiation of class definition that became apparent to him as the evening unfolded. His account, interestingly, gives a rather different picture of ballroom procedure than that of the ball over which Louis XV had presided in 1722. In this ball Louis XV gave instructions on the ordering of dances, but did not himself take part in them. The ordering of the dances, other than opening menuets, seems no longer to have held any special significance, for contredanses were mixed liberally with menuets and other *danses figurés* for couples during the proceedings, evidently in no purposeful sequence.

> A contredanse was then danced. Next the King asked M de la Tremoille, who was behind him, to go dance *la mariée*[63] with Mme de Luxembourg. This dance was followed by a contredanse, after which M de Clermont d'Amboise and Mme la princesse de Rohan danced a new [figured] dance made up of a menuet and a tambourin. After this M le Dauphin [then just nine years old] and Madame [likely one of his three sisters, either one of the twins who were eleven at the time, or another sister who was ten] danced *la mariée*. There was a contredanse afterward, and when it was finished the King said that the collation [prepared] for M le Dauphin would be taken.[64]

[62]The ball, which was followed by a masked one, took place on Monday, 26 January, and is also described in *Mercure galant*, février (1739), 378-382. This is followed by a lengthy account of the masked ball.

[63]It seems very likely that the two references to a couple dance titled *la mariée* in this passage are to a dance choreographed by Pécourt and first notated and issued by Feuillet in 1700. The dance had been re-issued by Pierre Rameau in c1725, and again in c1728 and c1732, so it was enjoying a new vogue at the time. See Meredith Ellis Little, and Carol G. Marsh, *La danse noble*, No. 5360 in their inventory, and the commentary provided on p.124. It is also possible that this is a reference to one of two other known choreographies titled *La Nouvelle Mariée* (see Little/Marsh inventory Nos. 6360, 6380). See further, Rebecca Harris-Warrick, 'La Mariée: The History of a French Court Dance,' in John Hajdu Heyer, ed. *Jean-Baptiste Lully and the Music of the French Baroque: Essays in Honor of James R. Anthony* (Cambridge, 1989), 239-257.

[64]Reproduced in Norbert Dufourcq, *Mémoires de Sourches et Luynes*, 66: 'On dansa donc une contredanse; ensuite le Roi dit à M. de la Tremoille, qui étoit derrière lui, d'aller danser la mariée avec Mme de Luxembourg. Cette danse fut suivie d'une contredanse, après laquelle M. de Clermont d'Amboise et Mme la princesse de Rohan dansèrent une danse nouvelle, composée d'un menuet et d'un tambourin. Après cela, M. le Dauphin et Madame dansèrent la mariée; il y eut après une contredanse, et lorsqu'elle fut finie le Roi dit qu'on apportât la collation de M. le Dauphin.'

De Luyne's attention was drawn in particular, however, to features in the performance of menuets at this ball that were new to him, and he devoted considerable space to a discussion of them.

During all the menuets danced by M le Dauphin and Mesdames, everyone remained standing throughout. However, Madame la Duchesse [de Luynes, that is, de Luyne's wife], who has seen a great number of balls, since she started dancing at the age of five and continued until age thirty-six, told me she had never before observed that one remained standing during menuets and [other] dances. In the presence of the King, in truth, everyone rose when M le Dauphin or the princes and princesses got up to dance, but one sat down again during the dance. Mme la Duchesse told me, further, that the figure used today in the menuet had never been in use formerly. At present, after having made a reverence to the King, and then to the lady with whom he is dancing, the gentleman dances always keeping his hat in hand until he has arrived next to the King, [where], instead of turning, he dances facing the King, his hat still lowered, and he doesn't turn his back to the King until the second pass. Likewise, the lady, on the first pass, dances [with] her face inclined toward the King. The same is done for the Queen [or] M le Dauphin in the absence of their majesties, and for the princesses in the absence of M le Dauphin. Mme la Duchesse [once again, his wife] says that she has always observed that once the gentleman had made a reverence to the King and to the lady, he replaced his hat, then travelled in dance toward the King, after which he withdrew. And that was the only ceremonial observed, but one always turned his back to the King while passing before him. This new figure was invented by Lavalle, M le Dauphin's dancing master.[65]

---

[65]ibid.: 'Pendant tous les menuets que dansèrent M. le Dauphin et Mesdames, l'ont se tint toujours debout. Cependant Mme la Duchesse, qui a vu grand nombre de bals, puisqu'elle a commencé à danser à l'âge de cinq ans et qu'elle a continué jusqu'à trente-six, m'a dit qu'elle n'avoit jamais vu que l'on se tint debout pendant les menuets et danses; en présence du Roi, à la vérité, tout le monde se levoit quand M. le Dauphin ou les princes ou princesses partoient pour aller danser, mais que l'on se rasseyoit pendant la danse.

'Mme la Duchesse m'a dit encore que la figure que l'on observe aujourd'hui dans le menuet n'étoit point en usage autrefois. Présentement, après avoir fait la révérence au Roi, ensuite à la dame avec laquelle on danse, l'homme danse toujours le chapeau à la main jusqu'à ce qu'il soit arrivé devant le Roi, et lorsqu'il est arrivé auprès du Roi, au lieu de tourner, il danse en face du Roi, toujours le chapeau bas, et il ne tourne le dos au Roi qu'au second tour. De même la dame, au premier tour, danse le visage tourné du côté du Roi; on en use de même pour la Reine, pour M. le Dauphin en absence de LL. MM., et pour Mesdames en absence de M. le Dauphin. Mme la duchesse dit qu'elle a toujours vu que lorsqu'on avoit fait la révérence au Roi et à la dame, on remettoit son chapeau, qu'ensuite l'on venoit en dansant jusqu'auprès du Roi, après quoi l'on reculoit; et c'étoit là le seul cérémonial que l'on observoit, mais que l'on tournoit toujours le dos au Roi en passant en devant lui. Cette nouvelle figure a été inventée par Lavalle, maître à danser de M. le Dauphin.'

The new features in the menuet described here gave special acknowledgement to the King's presence. They were incorporated into the menuets performed by the Dauphin and his sisters, most certainly, and perhaps into all the other menuets danced as well, although the account is equivocal on this point. (The Dauphin and his sisters, in any case, were set apart from all others at this ball, since everyone remained standing throughout their dances.) Because the royal children (perhaps along with others) were seen by the assembled company to be honouring their father in this special manner, a heightened respect was accorded to him, and the Dauphin prepared the way, as well, for his own honorific treatment in the years to come. It was neither a calculated or spontaneous decision made by the Dauphin and princesses during their performances that produced the modification, however, nor even an unconscious response to possibilities inherent in the situation. It was, rather, an 'invention' of the Dauphin's dancing master. There can be little doubt that M Lavalle set this new figure into place with a view to honouring the King (and ultimately to honour himself for having devised it), but his design was never, surely, to effect some renegotiation of boundaries among the noble classes. Yet, for the duc de Luynes, and perhaps even more emphatically for his wife, that is precisely what occurred. The important dynamic at work here is not that changes were made to the menuet figure, or to the protocol of standing versus sitting during a royal performance, but the fact that these were *noticed*, and noticed quickly (however disapprovingly). Dance served as a potent social agent at this ball through its ability to communicate, in rather direct ways, a refinement in status relationships among those in attendance. The communication engaged more than the king, the dauphin, and the royal princesses; it engaged everyone present.

Dancing at formal balls is frequently mentioned in eighteenth century accounts, therefore, because it was understood to convey important meanings about social status. Although in a less dramatic way, this was true for masked balls as well, especially those of the nobility, where a semblance of order was maintained in various ways. It was common, for example, to station someone at the entrance of the venue for a noble masked ball to monitor admission. Each arriving guest (or occasionally a designated individual in each group of arriving guests) was to reveal her or his identity.[66] Another way in which a noble masked

---

[66]There are numerous examples of this procedure described in the journals and diaries of the time, for example, the account of a masked ball held at Versailles in February 1708 in *Mercure galant*, février (1708), 325: 'No one was allowed to enter the ball without making themselves known' ('Personne ne devoit entrer à ce Bal, sans s'estre fait connoître').

ball was subjected to a modicum of control was by issuing tickets for presentation at the door, but this procedure, unlike that of the public ball, was tantamount to issuing an *invitation*.[67] Even with such controls, however, mishaps occurred. Jacques Bonnet offers an account of one of these that demonstrates once more how central the issue of status was to dancing at a ball, even a masked one. He writes,

> A masquer also is at liberty to take the queen of the ball to dance, [even] if it were a princess of blood, undisguised, as I saw happen at a ball that the king [Louis XIV] gave at Versailles, where a mask disguised as a cripple, and draped in an old blanket, had the temerity to select Madame la duchesse de Bourgogne. She had the good grace to accept, so as not to disrupt order at the ball. It was learned subsequently that this mask was no more than a simple officer of the court. However, he was not blamed at all, because this is a licence the masked ball permits.[68]

What is important in this account is that the Duchesse de Bourgogne (and Bonnet) recognized that there was a degree of 'order' at this ball, and that it was susceptible to disruption if she refused to *dance* with the mask who had invited her. By agreeing to dance with him, however, she occasioned a mishap (the blame for which would have been *his* had it not been a masked ball) that revolved around the issue of rank. The nature of the mishap is easy enough to grasp: because the officer was of a social station far beneath that of a future queen (a future, of course, that was never to be realized), the critical role of dance as a status defining agent in *her* circles was rendered inoperative. Indeed, it had been compromised.

At the *bal de l'Opéra*, however, the situation was quite different, because conventional status relationships were *never* operative. In addition to the obscuring of rank produced by disguises (a feature common to all masked balls), there were other forces at work at the opera ball that not merely blurred class distinctions further, they negated them altogether. Everyone in attendance possessed exactly

---

[67]Dangeau describes this procedure at a masked ball given by the duc d'Ossone in 1713. See *Journal*, t.XIV, 349: 'masquers entered only with a ticket' ('les masques n'entraient que par billet').

[68]Jacques Bonnet, *Histoire générale de la danse sacrée et profane* (Paris, 1724), 148-149: 'Le masque a même la liberté de prendre la reine du bal pour danser, quand ce seroit une princesse du sang, non masquée, comme je l'ai vu arriver dans un bal que le roi donnoit à Versailles, par un masque déguisé en paralitique, et enveloppé d'une vieille couverture, qui eut la hardiesse d'aller prendre Madame la Duchesse de Bourgogne; elle eut aussi la complaisance de l'accepter, pour ne rompre l'ordre du bal: on sçut depuis que ce masque n'étoit qu'un simple officier de la cour; cependant il n'en fut point blâmé, parce que c'est une licence que le bal masqué autorise.'

the same qualification: they all had paid the six-pound admission price.
Everyone was in a single, large ballroom: there were no special rooms
in the facility to which those of great distinction (or anyone else for
that matter) could retreat if the crowd became too large or unruly.[69]
Everyone had the same access to the dance floor: there were no
designated dancers or designated spectators. And everyone was
engaged in the same game of cat and mouse, playfully trying to 'de-
masque' others in attendance, while safeguarding her or his own
identity. Most importantly, there was no re-stabilizing *conclusion* to an
opera ball. At daybreak the ballroom did not revert to some area in a
royal *palais* or fashionable *hôtel*, ready to receive company once more
from an ordered society that placed a high premium on status. It
reverted to an empty theatre. The opera ball was not an *event*, as was a
formal ball—masked or otherwise—that could be cherished in memory
if things had gone especially well, or compensated for if unfortunate
mishaps had occurred. It was not mounted to celebrate a particular
occasion or to honour an individual. The opera ball, rather, was more
like an on-going spectacle that was either playing or not playing at the
moment. The players in this spectacle were unranked.

Eighteenth century commentators on the opera ball were
preoccupied, more often than not, with exploring the workings of a
ball in which the issue of status was not evident. I believe their
explorations often fail to take notice of dancing simply because dance
had nothing to contribute to the social construction of the opera ball
they were trying to assemble. Dance was, in fact, rather an incongruity
at the opera ball, an orderly intrusion on an otherwise unordered
gathering. As I will argue more fully in the next chapter, the dances
performed at an opera ball were generally the same as those of a private
one (where they continued to have a central role to play, for the reasons
discussed above). Dancing at the opera ball, however, was neither a
focus of attention, nor even in the middle of the room normally, but
quite literally marginalized. In his article on the contredanse in the
Encyclopédie Louis de Cahusac relates that 'at the opera ball one dances
different contredanses at the two ends of the room.'[70] Although he

---

[69]In February 1700 the *Mercure* describes a masked ball put on by Madame la
Chancelière in honour of the duchesse de Bourgogne at which an unexpectedly large
group of unidentified masks arrived, forcing the hostess to move the duchess and her
party, who were becoming 'un peu dérangé,' to a separate room that had been
prepared for just such a contigency. This is but one of several examples of segregated
areas prepared for noble balls. See *Mercure galant*, février (1700), 192.

[70]*Encyclopédie ou dictionnaire raisonné des sciences, des arts, et des métiers*, (Paris, 1751-1780),
s.v. 'Contredanse'. The article is signed (B) and is therefore by Louis de Cahusac, and
is included in one of the volumes issued in 1754: 'Au bal de l'Opera on danse dans les
deux bouts de la salle des *contredanses* différentes.'

offers no explanation, the likely reasons are as follows: dancing was relegated to the two ends of the room because that is where the two orchestras were located and, moreover, because the center of the room was often packed with 'people trailing about everywhere,' as the *Mercure* put it.[71] Indeed, in his *La Danse ancienne et moderne* of 1754 Cahusac rather ironically confirms this observation in his brief chapter on 'Des Bals publics.' He writes, 'the two ends of the room are attended by a few obscure masquers, who follow the airs the orchestra plays. All the others jostle, jumble, and push themselves about.'[72] It was, therefore, on the center of the room that the gazes of eighteenth century commentators seem typically to have been fixed.

One of the eighteenth-century sources that *does* mention dancing at the opera ball does so in a way that lends support to my proposal that, while it was there in good quantity, dance did not have a central role to play at the opera house ballroom. The source is a play, printed in 1777 but evidently never staged, entitled *Le bal de l'Opéra, Comédie en un acte, en prose, ornée de chants & de danses* by Le Chevalier DuCoudray.[73] The play, as might be expected, is set entirely at an opera ball, and its plot is little more than a series of amorous adventures involving a Chevalier, a Marquis, and their wives. The adventures are of exactly the same nature as those we have already seen at the opera ball, with disguise and mistaken identity serving as principal ingredients. The songs and dances that 'adorn' the play are, in fact, entr'actes (perhaps *entre-scènes* might be more accurate) that have nothing to do with the action of the piece. On this count alone one might argue that dancing, for the purposes of this play, has been set apart from the central activity of an opera ball. But it is not just *any* dancing that DuCoudray calls for, it is the dancing of a public ball, and throughout the play it is contrived to *interrupt* the action. Near the conclusion of scene nine, for example, the attentions of both the Chevalier and the Marquis have been directed toward a 'courtesan' who, though in disguise, seems vaguely familiar to them. The Marquis heads off to investigate, leaving the Chevalier with the Marquise. The final lines of the scene are spoken by him: 'Et nous, Madame, rangeons-nous de ce côté, pour faire place à ce quadrille qui se prépare.' ('And we, Madame, let us stand aside for this quadrille being prepared.') Scene ten opens with the following

[71]See above, n30. Some of the implications of Cahusac's interesting observations will be treated in chapter five.

[72]Louis de Cahusac, *La Danse ancienne et moderne, ou traité historique de la danse*, 3 vols. [in one], (LaHaye, 1754). Part 2, 'Livre Second,' 177: 'Les deux côtés de la salle sont occupés par quelques Masques obscurs, qui suivent les airs que l'Orchestre joue. Tout le reste, se heurte, se mêle, se pousse.'

[73]Le Chevalier DuCoudray, *Le Bal de l'Opéra, Comédie en un acte, en prose, ornée de Chants et de Danses*, [bound with] idem., *Essai sur la comédie, la farce et la parodie* (Paris, 1777).

stage instructions: 'Contredanse caractérisée. La Marquise & le Chevalier se rangent d'un côté du théâtre; la contredanse finie, ils se levent.' ('Characterized contredanse. The Marquise and the Chevalier place themselves to one side of the stage; the contredanse finished, they rise.')[74] Pursuit of the mysterious courtesan then resumes. At this fictional opera ball dancing was, at best, a diversion from the principal activity in the proceedings or, at worst, an intrusion on it.

When eighteenth century commentators offered descriptions of balls, therefore, they generally seem to have felt obliged to mention dancing when it contributed to an understanding of status relationships. The more distinguished the company, the greater was the inclination to offer additional details, because on these occasions dance served to articulate status relationships in an especially compelling way. When status relationships were not an issue—and this was certainly the case at opera balls—the attention of the commentators was directed elsewhere. But how did the participants at an opera ball view dancing? How did they negotiate the incongruity of a status-shaping activity at a social gathering that was in all other respects devoid of class structure? I have already hinted at an answer: they set it off to the side, and indulged in it just the same.

---

[74]ibid., 33.

Music and Dancing at the *bal public*

*Toute est tranquille, comme à l'ordinaire; tous les spectacles sont pleins;
mais, à la vérité, il n'y a aucune assemblée de danses dans les maisons
particulières de Paris: il y a seulement le bal de l'Opéra.*

E.-J.-F. Barbier (1757)[1]

Although the *bals reglés* (regulated balls) of the nobility such as the
kinds that Rameau described in 1725 generally had a standard
sequence of events, and observed a typical protocol, scholars remain
less informed about many of the details in the proceedings than might
be hoped. It is not always clear, for example, just who decided what
couple dances were to be performed by the designated dancers: if it
were not to be a 'standard' menuet, further uncertainties arise. De
Luyne's account of the ball held at Versailles in late January, 1739,
described in the previous chapter, exposes many of the difficulties.

> A contredanse was then danced. Next the King asked M de la
> Tremoille, who was behind him, to go dance *la mariée* with Mme de
> Luxembourg. This dance was followed by a contredanse, after which
> M de Clermont d'Amboise and Mme la princesse de Rohan danced a
> new [figured] dance made up of a menuet and a tambourin. After
> this M le Dauphin and Madame danced *la mariée*. There was a
> contredanse afterward, and when it was finished the King said that
> the collation for M le Dauphin would be taken.[2]

Did M de la Tremoille and Mme de Luxembourg *know* that the King
was going to request that they dance 'La Mariée'? Or did Louis XV
happen to know that was a dance they both knew, and merely made a
decision about *when* it would be performed? It is difficult to know all
the preparations that allowed M de Clermont d'Amboise and the
Princesse de Rohan to perform a new couple dance (consisting of a
menuet and a tambourin). Was it made to newly composed music? If

---

[1]Edmond-Jean-François Barbier, *Journal*, vol. iv, 199: 'All is quiet, as usual. All the
shows are full, but, in truth, there is not a single gathering for dancing in the private
households of Paris; there is only the opera ball.' The rather gloomy mood that Barbier
reports attended this carnival season was precipitated by an assassination attempt on
Louis XV earlier in the winter.

[2]See chapter four, n64 for the original French of the passage.

so, how did some individual gain access to the music in advance of the occasion, in order to make performing parts for the musicians? Who decided what couples would participate in the contredanses at this ball, and how did those who did participate organize themselves into contredanse 'sets' (groups of four, eight, or twelve dancers)? How were any of the dances mentioned in the passage begun? Was there some kind of cue?

Questions such as these will likely never be answered with any kind of certainty, because a formal ball was a rather special occasion, and each yielded a fresh set of circumstances that, while fitted to a general procedural mould (emphasizing rank), were not necessarily applicable to any other ball. The opera ball, on the other hand, only rarely was required to accommodate special circumstances, so the musical and dancing routines that it developed remained comparatively stable. As we shall see, for example, the size, make-up, and deployment of the opera ball orchestra became standardized by 1727 in a way that persisted until the early 1770s. Yet although the *bal public* featured a number of long-lived routines, there remain many questions about the conduct of its music and dance. It is not easy to imagine how a dance at the opera ball was taken up, or how the participants managed to manoeuvre themselves into an appropriate space (at precisely the correct time) to begin it. Were the dances to be performed at any given ball known by those in attendance in advance? Or did the orchestra simply offer up dance music in some pre-determined sequence, in the hope of attracting couples to the dance floor? Did it sometimes happen that a dance was played that attracted no dancers at all? In the following paragraphs I will explore some possible answers to these questions, beginning with what is known with at least some degree of certainty: the make-up and disposition of the opera ball orchestra.

During the first decade of the *bals publics* the orchestra—of a size and make-up that I have not been able to discover—was deployed as a single group that played in an alcove at the stage end of the theatre.[3] This disposition evidently was found to be deficient in some ways, for when the remodeling of the facility was completed by the beginning of the 1727-1728 season the orchestra is known to have been divided into two groups, each consisting of fifteen instrumentalists, that were placed at either end of the room: one at the oval-shaped loges end of the auditorium (at the far end of the amphitheatre), and the other at

[3]According to the *Mercure galant*, novembre (1727), 2514: 'Elle [the room] formoit un quarré étroit du côté du Théatre, avec un alcove dans le fond, où la Symphonie étoit placée.'

the foot of the (slightly raised) *salon demi-octagone* located on the stage.[4] It may be that, as the popularity of the opera ball grew during these early years, larger crowds made it difficult for the single orchestra to be heard by those who were not close to the stage. Ball goers, at any rate, would not have been unfamiliar with an orchestra divided into smaller, integral groups, since this often was the case in private balls, but normally only when there were several rooms in a household set up to accommodate dancing.[5] A double orchestra in a single ballroom, on the other hand, was rather more rare. In the royal ball held in the theatre of the Tuilleries palace in 1722 (described on pp.88ff), a sizable orchestra of 150 instrumentalists was divided into two groups. Barbier's account of this ball relates that the two groups played in alternation on this occasion, except in those dances in which Louis XV performed, when they played together.[6]

At the opera ball, too, the double orchestra sometimes played as a single unit on stage (in the 'salon demi-octagone'), not for any honorific reasons, and never to accompany dancing, but, rather, to formally announce the commencement of the proceedings with some opening orchestral music. The *Mercure* reports that these performances lasted about a half an hour, that they included trumpets and timpani, and that the repertoire consisted of 'grand symphonic works by the best masters.'[7] This general practice may have been a regular feature of the opera ball, but the inclusion of trumpets and timpani was almost certainly an occasional occurrence, for the few surviving rosters of the opera ball's orchestral personnel never include trumpets (although a roster from 1781 does list two drum players—'tambours'—in the regular ensemble).[8] It is not impossible that one or two of the string players had sufficient skills to play trumpet as well when required, but because the numbers in the ball orchestra were somewhat smaller than the full orchestra of the *Académie Royale de Musique*—thirty in total *versus*

[4]ibid., 2519: 'Trente Instrumens placez, quinze à chaque extrémité de la Sale [sic], composent la Symphonie pour le Bal.' My arguments for the placement of the stage-end group in the *salon quarré* (as opposed to the *salon demi-octagone*) are explored on pp.47-48.

[5]Such was the case, for example, in the ball of February, 1700 described briefly in chapter two (see n45), where seven rooms were utilized: three for dancing (each with a group of violins and oboes), two for relaxation, and two for buffets and collations.

[6]*Journal*, I, 134-135: 'Il y avait deux orchestres dans les côtés de la salle, composés de cent cinquante instruments, qui se relayaient: quand le roi dansait, tout jouait.'

[7]*Mercure galant*, novembre (1727), 2519: 'Mais pendant une demie-heure, avant qu'il commence, ces Instrumens s'assemblent dans le Salon octagone, avec des Timbales & des Trompettes, & donnent un Concert composé de grands Morceaux de Symphonie des meilleurs Maîtres.'

[8]*Archives Nationales*, AJ[13]-28, dossier 8.

forty-four to forty-six[9]—it seems more likely that supernumeraries were hired if trumpets and timpani were needed.

Opening a ball with some ceremonial orchestral music is a practice that is not normally mentioned in the literature, but there is some evidence that, for royal balls at least, such opening music may have been expected. In the second installment of the *Suite de dances* [sic] *pour les violons et hautbois qui se joüent ordinairement à tous les bals chez le Roy*, prepared c1712, and sometimes attributed to André Danican Philidor, l'aîné,[10] the first two pages of the collection (only a *partie de dessus* is given in this volume) present seven different 'Ouvertures' from ballets or incidental music to plays of the 1660s.[11] These are followed by the main body of the work, headed 'Danse pour les Bals,' beginning on page three, making it clear that the opening material was *not* intended to accompany dancing. Whoever compiled the collection nevertheless associated this music with the other repertoire that was played 'ordinairement à tous les Bals chez le Roy.'[12] The opening music of the opera ball, therefore, was likely modeled on a procedure of the royal ball that has been typically overlooked in the sources.

After 1727 the orchestra of the *bal public* was deployed in two, equal sized groups for most of the evening, a feature that became so entrenched that it remained characteristic of the public ball in Paris, even in the nineteenth century.[13] Rosters of the orchestral personnel employed by the opera ball from the 1750s and 1760s not only confirm the size (and deployment) of the two groups reported by the *Mercure* in 1727, but they offer additional precisions about the instrumentation, as well. An 'Etat des Simphonistes des Bals de l'Opera pour l'année 1757 à 1758'[14] offers the information set out in table 5.1.

[9]See, for example, Graham Sadler, 'Rameau's Singers and Players at the Paris Opéra. A little-known inventory of 1738,' 464.

[10]Rebecca Harris-Warrick, 'Ballroom Dancing,' 46. This volume, however, is not included in the Philidor works list prepared by her in *The New Grove Dictionary of Music and Musicians*, 2nd ed.

[11]Paris, BN (Musique) Ms. fr. Vm⁷3555. All seven overtures are by Lully.

[12]The first of the seven overtures is headed 'Pour le Roy et la Reine d'Angleterre par ordre de Sa Majesté.' Was this overture played at the opening of the ball on the Fête des rois in 1708 which, it will be recalled, 's'ouvrit par le Roy d'Angleterre & par Madame la Princesse sa soeur'? (See chapter four, n13.)

[13]It was not uncommon in posters announcing an upcoming ball to draw special attention to a double orchestra. Such is the case in the poster reproduced in Victor Rozier, *Les bals publics à Paris* (Paris, 1855), 46, which announces '2 Orchestres.' This imprint is exceedingly rare. A copy is preserved in *Bibliothèque-Musée de l'Opéra* with the shelf number [C.2941. Another surviving poster—this time from 1884—is reproduced in Agnès Terrier, *Le billet d'Opéra*, 60. It announces the final ball of the year with 'Deux Orchestres' conducted by 'MM. O. Metra [and] Darasz-Miska.'

[14]*Archives Nationales*, AJ¹³-1, dossier 4, pièce A21.

Table 5.1 Personnel Roster for Opera Ball Orchestra, 1757-1758

Côté du théâtre			Côté de l'amphithéâtre		
Violons			Violons		
	M^rs	Jalodin,		M^rs	Parin, Pere,
		Perin,			Houbaut, Pere,
		Berot,			Parin, fils,
		Loullier,			Houbaut, fils,
		Boucher,			Leliare,
		Letellier,			Giguet,
		Feuillade			LeRoy,
		Taupin [or Topin],			Gobert,
		Laurent,			Mongaultier,
		Montigny,			Mercier,
hautbois		Jérôme,	hautbois		Laumonier,
		Joblin,			Simouin,
Basses		Marcelles,	Basses		Dan [?Dun]
		Linterlin [?Tinterlin],			Moulinquin, pere,
		Moulinquin, fils,			Barroin [?Barrois]

This roster indicates that the two groups of fifteen musicians had precisely the same instrumentation, and were positioned in the auditorium in the way I have suggested they had been thirty years earlier, one on the stage end ('côté du théâtre') and the other on the amphitheatre end ('côté de l'amphithéâtre'). Each group had ten violinist/violists, two oboists, and three cello/double bass players. Although I have been unable to find evidence to support the suggestion, it seems likely that the strings were organized in a way patterned after that of the larger opera orchestra. That ensemble, of course, was evolving in significant ways during the first decade or so of the *bal public*. Among other things, the strings of the *grand choeur* underwent a realignment that, by the mid-1720s, saw the middle voices (played by violas and often referred to as the *parties*) of the traditional five-part string texture reduced from three to two parts.[15] A five-part texture was not thereby abandoned, however, because the violins had been divided into firsts and seconds since 1700 at least (although they most often had played in unison). A complete set of performance parts— the earliest such set to have survived—for Louis La Coste's *Télégone* (1725) is preserved in the *Bibliothèque-Musée de l'Opéra*.[16] The string

[15]The *quinte de violon* was suppressed, leaving the *haute-contre de violon* and *taille de violon*. See Jérôme de LaGorce, 'L'orchestre de l'Opéra et son évolution de Campra à Rameau,' *Revue de Musicologie* 76/1 (1990), 23-43.

[16]Louis La Coste, *Télégone* (1725) MAT. 18 [249 (67-92). La Gorce, 'L'Orchestre de l'Opéra,' 35-38, (Annexe I.A) offers an exceptionally useful inventory of all surviving performing parts in this collection that were used in premieres at the Paris opera from 1700 to 1764.

group in this set of parts is represented by four copies of a *1ᵉʳ dessus de violon*, four copies of a *2ᵉ dessus de violon*, two copies of an *haute-contre de violon*, two copies of a *taille de violon*, and four copies of a *basse du grand choeur*. Since it is known that the string ensemble of the *grand choeur* of the time was comprised of 16 violinists, 6 viola players, and 8 bass players[17] (cellos, double basses, *basses de violon*), it can be assumed that these musicians performed two to a part, except the viola players, who performed three to a part.

The size and make-up of this string ensemble, like that of the opera ball, remained remarkably stable for much of the eighteenth century (until the 1770s). An 'Etat present des personnes qui composent l'Académie Royale de Musique' from 1752 gives the following information on the strings of the *grand choeur*.[18] (See table 5.2.)

Table 5.2 Composition of the String Group of the Opera Orchestra, 1752

16 [sic, i.e. 15] Violons.

Messieurs

Aubert,	Caraffe, 3. [?Charles-Placide]
Langlade,	Exaudet,
Caraffe, L.	Perrier,
Aubert, F.	Despreaux, F.
Vallée,	Le Miere,
Dupont,	Tarade,
Travenol,	Piffet, *neveu.*
Labbé, F.	

8 Basses du grand Choeur
Messieurs

Capperan,	Dun, L.
Antheaume,	Dun, C.
Forcade,	Sallantin, L.
Saublay,	Davesne,

6 Parties
Messieurs

Plessis, C.	Dun, F.
Paris,	Chauvet,
Champion,	Simon,

Using the above information as a model for the opera ball ensembles (and referring to the roster of 1757 given in table 5.1), it seems a

---

[17]ibid., 26.

[18]*Almanach historique et chronologique de tous les Spectacles* (Paris, 1752), 88-89.

reasonable assumption that the two mini-orchestras of the *bal public* had the make-up set out in table 5.3. I believe it is a reasonable suggestion because approximately the same proportions among the five essential voices in the ensemble of the larger opera orchestra are preserved in this smaller group.

Table 5.3 Likely Make-up of each 15-member Orchestral Group at the Opera Ball

First violins:	4	(plus one oboe doubling)
Second violins:	4	(plus one oboe doubling)
violas:		
haute-contre	1	
taille	1	
cello(s)/double bass(es):	3	

The bass instruments in these ensembles likely included at least one *contrebasse de violon* (double bass), and perhaps (for a time) the *basse de violon*, besides cellos.[19] Of particular interest in these ensembles is the absence of bassoons. In terms of the common orchestral practice for operas and ballets, this is a most unusual feature: where there were oboes there were invariably bassoons. The absence of bassoons in the opera ball orchestra was an anomaly, rather than the reflection of a common practice in ballroom music making (if, indeed, a common practice can be said to have existed). A large engraved plate (one of three in different perspectives) depicting a public ball held at the *Hôtel de ville* in late August 1739, in honour of Louise Elizabeth de France (Louis XV's first-born daughter) and Don Philip (of Parma), shows good detail of the orchestra that played at these festivities.[20] The orchestra in the main ballroom—it played as a single unit—was located in a raised gallery overlooking the dance floor. The engraving

[19]See Mary Cyr, '*Basses* and *basse continue* in the Orchestra of the Paris Opera 1700-1764,' *Early Music* 10/2 (1982), 155-170. Cyr, 161, suggests that after 1733 the cello and double bass were the favoured bass instruments in the opera orchestra (in place of the more varied earlier practice that often included the *basse de viole* and the *basse de violon*). The earliest reference that I have seen that specifies the precise mixture of cellos to double basses is a roster of the *Grand Choeur* from 1773. It lists five 'Basses du Grand Choeur' (Labbé, Renaudet, Sallantin l'aîné, Lobry, and Desplanques) and four 'Contre-basses' (Malbrancq, Holfedlt [sic], Gaspard, and Louis). See *Les Spectacles de Paris, ou calendrier historique & chronologique des théâtres*, pt.22 (Paris, 1773), 17.

[20]A copy of this plate is preserved in the *Musée Carnavalet* in Paris: Cabinet des arts graphiques, TOPO G.V.15/GC.

depicts an orchestra of thirty-three performers: thirteen violins/violas, eight oboes, three cellos, four double basses, three bassoons, a drum, and one other wind instrument that I cannot identify. The three bassoons were played at the rear of one side of the gallery in a grouping behind the eight oboists.

The surviving rosters of the opera ball orchestra, on the other hand, strongly suggest that bassoons were probably *never* a regular part of the ensemble. The make-up of the orchestra for the 1766-1767 season (given below in table 5.4) is precisely the same as it had been a decade earlier, with four oboists, but no bassoon players.

Table 5.4 Personnel Roster for Opera Ball Orchestra, 1766-1767[21]

	Côté du théâtre		Côté de l'amphithéâtre
M[rs]		Violons	
	Perin		Parin, P[ère]
	Bojeau		Parin, f[ils]
	Loulier		Houbaut
	Joublay, f[ils]		Viëhard
	Feuillade		Laurent
	Blanchard		LeRoy
	Girard		Théry
	Boival ou Dechain [in substitution]		Florist
	Guison		Despreaux, f[?ils, ?rère]
	Duport		Guillermont
		hautbois	
	Gallion		Despreau, p[ère]
	Lefort		Gibes
		Basses	
	Mercier		Marcelles
	L'Empereur		Moulinquin, P[ère]
	Montigny		Barrois

Even as late as the 1780-1781 season, when the opera ball orchestra had grown to forty musicians, including two percussionists, bassoons did not figure in the regular ensemble (see table 5.5).[22] It does not appear likely that this was merely an oversight (and a consistent one, at that) in the documentation, for the same sources also provide

[21]'Etat des Simphonistes des Bals de l'Opera 1766 a 1767,' *Archives Nationales*, AJ[13]-1, dossier 4, pièce A21.

[22]'Etat du Payment a faire aux Symphonistes de l'Academie Royale de Musique employés aux 17 Bals donnés dans la Salle de l'Opéra du Dimanche 12 Novembre 1780 au Mardy 27 fevrier 1781,' *Archives Nationales*, AJ[13]-23, dossier 8.

information about the opera orchestra, and *always* include information about the bassoon players—usually four, or occasionally five—in a listing that is distinct from either the other bass instrumentalists, or the oboists. [23] And it surely cannot be that there were no bassoonists available for employment in the ball orchestra, since bassoons were always plentiful in the orchestra of the parent institution (although, as we shall see shortly, there was normally only sporadic overlap in personnel between the orchestra of the opera and that of the opera ball). I can only conclude, therefore, that bassoons were not considered to be a needed resource in the opera ball's ensembles. Whatever the circumstances may have been that led to this outcome, they certainly were long-lived.

Table 5.5 Opera Ball Orchestra Personnel and Salaries, 1780-1781

Name	Number of Balls Played	Rate of pay per ball	Net Pay
Violons (ensemble 1)			
Regnier, père	17	12 livres	204
Sauton	17	10	170
Regnier, fils	17	8	136
Perrier	17	8	136
Dossion	17	8	136
Thierry	16	10	160
Goy	17	8	136
Guilles	17	8	136
Pinçon, l'[aîn]é	17	8	136
Adnet	17	8	136
Gogo	17	8	136
Pinçon, c[ade]t	17	8	136
Barriere	3	8	24
Caron	[?14]	8	112
Violons (ensemble 2)			
Duport	17	12	204
le Dez	17	10	170
LaHante	17	10	170
Deham	17	10	170

(cont.)

[23]See LaGorce, 'L'Orchestre de l'Opéra,' 26.

Table 5.5 (cont.)

Name	Number of Balls Played	Rate of pay per ball	Net Pay
Granger	17	8	136
Maze	17	12	204
le Roux	17	8	136
Denis	17	10	170
Loulier	17	10	170
Landrin [?l'aîné ?cadet]	17	8	136
le Fevre	17	8	136
Rognon	17	10	170
Boete	17	8	136
Maupin	17	8	136
hautbois			
Martin	17	10	170
Cabur	17	10	170
Blin	16	8	128
Rostêne	16	8	128
tambours			
Guichon	17	10	170
LaValliere	17	10	170
Basses			
Cailteau	17	12	204
La Cuisse	17	10	170
Carelle [signs himself 'Carel']	17	8	136
Landrin, Père	17	10	170
Tinterlin	17	8	136
Landrin, fils	17	8	136

Of interest, as well, in the rosters of the opera ball orchestra presented above is the absence of a harpsichord player, or any other chord playing instrument to add harmonic support to the ensembles. By contrast, a salaried *claveciniste* remained a regular component of the larger opera orchestra until 1776.[24] In his provocative study—now over twenty years old—of continuo practices at the Paris Opéra through 1776 and the

[24]Graham Sadler, 'The Role of the Keyboard Continuo in French Opera, 1673-1776,' *Early Music* 8/2 (1980), 148-157; here, 153. LaGorce, 'L'Orchestre de l'Opéra,' 25, does not dispute the claim.

role of the harpsichord, Graham Sadler argued that the harpsichord (and the theorbo, too, earlier in the century) did not customarily play during dances ('airs de ballet').[25] While the evidence he cited in support of his claims was solid, it was also rather slim: the number of surviving *basse-continue* performing parts from operatic productions of the eighteenth century (these served as his principal point of reference) is simply too small to be a reliable predictor.[26] And yet I believe Sadler was probably correct, at least in the case of the accompaniment to dances. Indeed, the practice of French dance—both theatrical and social—from the mid-seventeenth century on favoured a full ensemble of strings or oboes (or both) that required no additional harmonic support. In the case of social dance (which very likely informed at least some practices of the theatre) the absence of chordal instruments, and especially harpsichords, was often a matter of practicality. Even if a harpsichord were available in a household, the space for musicians at a formal ball was typically very cramped, but nevertheless, of necessity, located proximate to the area(s) set aside for dancing. This often prompted the construction of risers, positioned in as unobtrusive an area as possible, maximizing the space for dancing, and also effectively minimizing the space for musicians.[27] A harpsichord, more often than not, could not be accommodated in such circumstances. While such practical concerns may have had a role to play in the exclusion of harpsichords from the opera ball orchestra—two of them, after all, would have been required in the two-group layout—it was just as likely to have been a matter of custom. On less formal occasions, of course, especially if a full ensemble of musicians was unavailable, a smaller grouping of instruments, including a harpsichord, was often encountered. Such a situation is depicted in several illustrations of the seventeenth and eighteenth centuries, even in outdoor venues.[28] But for large gatherings it seems to have been the rule for the ballroom orchestra to play without the support of chordal instruments. The

[25] ibid., *passim.*

[26] See n16 above for a source that reviews some of the surviving performing parts.

[27] Harris-Warrick, 'Ballroom Dancing,' 45, reproduces a floor 'plan' prepared for a royal ball in Versailles in 1697, held in the *Gallerie des Glaces*. The musicians were situated in a bank of risers that literally spilled into the area of the next room, 'behind' the famous wall of mirrors (into Louis XIV's chambers). The plan codes this area as for 'Haubois & Violons.'

[28] For example, the oil on canvas painting, 'Gesellschaft im Freien' by David Vinckeboons, reproduced in Walter Salmen, ed. *Tanz im 17. und 18. Jahrhundert*, (Leipzig, 1988); Bd. IV, Lieferung 4 of *Musikgeschichte in Bildern*, Werner Bachmann, general ed. See illustration 134 (page 161). In this pastoral scene a couple dances in a grove while others look on. The accompanying instruments include flutes, a lute, and a spinet-like instrument, played by a woman who is seated with her back to the dancers.

depiction of the orchestra that played for the public ball held at the *Hôtel de ville* in 1739, discussed earlier (see above, n20), includes no harpsichord.[29]

The opera ball orchestra, in summary, consisted of two modestly sized string bands that were mixed with a pair of oboes and that played without a *basse-continue*. It is, perhaps, not a coincidence that this is an instrumentation that matches exactly that of the two largest collections of ballroom dance music from the first decade or so of the eighteenth century: the two installments of Philidor's *Suite de danses pour les violons et haubois qui se jouent aux bals chez le roy*, of 1699[30] and c1712.[31] Unlike that of c1712 which, as I mentioned earlier, preserves just a *partie de dessus*, the 1699 collection has a bass part as well. It is unfigured.

A comparison of the personnel rosters for 1757-1758 (table 5.1) and 1766-1767 (table 5.4) suggests that at least some members of the opera ball orchestra held their positions for quite some time. Eight of the violinists/violists—Perin, Parin père, Parin fils, Houbart, Loulier, Feuillade, LeRoy and Laurent—and three of the cellists/bassists—Barrois, Marcelles, and Moulinquin—appear on both lists, so they served for at least ten years (assuming they were members of the orchestra on a continuing basis during the intervening years, for which records, unfortunately, have not survived). The violinist/violist Duport of the 1766-1767 roster also appears in the 1780-1781 list. Loulier, in fact, appears in all three of the rosters, although it is not clear that this is just one individual. Who were these musicians, and how did they come to serve in this orchestra?

My observations are based, admittedly, in a very small sampling of documents that offer information about individuals who played for the opera balls, but I believe nevertheless that they are defensible. The rosters suggest that a majority of those who were engaged for service in the opera ball did not also hold appointments in the *Académie Royale de Musique* (or if they did, as we shall see, they did so only briefly.) Only three, or perhaps

---

[29]In our time this convention is almost never respected in so-called historically informed concerts of French baroque dance music. A striking example is the recording of 1994-1995 (issued by Erato in 1995) with the title *Musiques à danser* (Erato Musical Compact Discs, 0630-10702-2). This recording, under the supervision of Francine Lancelot, presents dance music for both the theatre and the ballroom, for most of which there are surviving eighteenth century choreographies. The theatrical dance music is performed by 'Les Talens Lyriques,' directed by Christophe Rousset. The ensemble includes both theorbo and harpsichord. The ballroom dance music is performed by 'La Simphonie du Marais,' directed by Hugo Reyne. It also includes a theorbo and harpsichord.

[30]Paris, BN (Musique), Vm⁷6765.

[31]See above, n11.

four,[32] of the thirty individuals who played in the 1757-1758 season may have also played for the opera at some point in their professional careers. The violinist/violist LeRoy may very well be the LeRoy who played *taille de violon* in the opera orchestra for a single season (1754-1755). The Mongaultier from the same roster may be the violinist who played a *partie de dessus* at the opera in 1742, or perhaps the violist with that orchestra after 1764. And Mercier (again from the 1757-1758 list) may be the *haute-contre de violon* who played in the opera orchestra between 1725 and 1738.[33] In these three cases, of course, it is conceivable that the LeRoys or the Mongaultiers or the Merciers were not the same individual, but merely members of the same family: as in the opera orchestra, that of the opera balls featured several family dynasties (some members of which performed during the same years) whose service literally spanned decades. In all three of these cases (if they are all, in fact, just one individual) the service to the opera ball did not overlap with employment in the larger opera orchestra. This is a significant point because the season of opera balls *did* overlap with that of the opera, and an individual playing for both entertainments would have found himself on call some days for over twelve hours of service, with no more than a three- or four-hour break between the opera's conclusion and the start of the ball. Indeed, in the 1757-1758 season thirteen of the fourteen balls offered occurred on the evening following an operatic performance.[34] This would have been particularly grueling on Thursday evening balls (of which there were four that season) because Fridays had become the most popular day to attend the opera among Parisians, and performances that day (which still commenced at about five in the afternoon) had to be especially well delivered.[35]

One can only admire the stamina of the two or three individuals that the rosters suggest did, in fact, take on simultaneous employment in the opera ball and the opera orchestras. If the 'Dan' listed in the 1757-1758 roster really is the 'Dun cadet' who played as a *basse du Grand Choeur* in the opera orchestra from 1741 to 1759 (he is listed as

---

[32]The 'Dan' among the 'Basses' of the 1757-1758 roster might be the bassist 'Dun l'aîné' who played in the opera orchestra from 1741-1752, or the 'Dun cadet' who served from 1741-1759. My information on players in the orchestra of the *Académie Royale de Musique* is drawn principally from LaGorce, 'L'Orchestre de l'Opéra,' 39-43. This useful appendix is an alphabetic listing of 'Musiciens ayant fait partie de l'orchestre de l'Opéra entre 1704 et 1764.'

[33]Although over thirty years of service to the *Académie Royale de Musique* may seem far-fetched, it is certainly a possibility. Nicolas Baudy, for example, the famous first violinist in the orchestra, enjoyed a distinguished and lengthy career, from 1696 to 1738. See further, Sadler, 'Rameau's Singers and Players,' 464.

[34]As documented in *Archives Nationales*, AJ[13]-9, dossier 141.

[35]From 1752 through the 1780s something like the following is regularly included in the theatrical calendars, this one taken from *Spectacles de Paris* (cited in n19) of 1773, p.[iv]: 'mais c'est le Vendredi surt-out, qu'on voit jouer les bons Acteurs.'

'Dun C.' in table 5.2), then he managed the double duty for at least one season. It is a certainty, however, that the two 'Despreaux', father and son, of the 1766-1767 opera ball season (see table 5.4) accomplished the feat. Jean-François Despréaux (1693-1768) had played oboe (and flute) in the orchestra of the Opéra since 1727. He retired from this position (not surprisingly!) in 1767[36] at the conclusion of a season of double service. His son, Claude-Jean-François (d1794), began playing in the opera orchestra in 1750 as a violinist, and after 1771 became *premier dessus de violon* and principal violin soloist in the group.[37] It is also possible, however, that Despreaux f[ils] in the 1766-1767 roster is Louis-Félix Despréaux (1746-1813), another son of Jean-François, who played viola in the opera orchestra starting in 1765.[38] In either case one of the sons, too, managed to play in both orchestras for at least that season. This accomplishment is quite remarkable when one considers that there were seventeen balls in the 1766-1767 season, nine of them between February 2 and March 3.

But the surviving rosters by themselves do not tell the whole story. The employment history of Despréaux fils (Claude-Jean-François, that is, the violinist) is an interesting case in point. There is every indication that when he first joined the opera orchestra for the 1750-1751 season, he also began playing for the opera ball. By the beginning of the 1752-1753 season he requested and was granted leave to resign his duties at the *bal public*. A document from early November 1752 reads:

> Mr Despreaux fils, one of the violinists of the *Académie Royale de Musique*, requests to resign from the 'Orchestre des Bals.' It is proposed to replace him with Mr Topin, a dancing master and very good violinist for balls. Mr Rebel, who has auditioned him, having been informed [of the request], reports [favourably] on his ability and accuracy to fulfill these duties.

The official ruling of 13 November:

> Decreed at the City Office that Mr Topin will be admitted into the orchestras for balls in place of Mr Despreaux fils who has requested to be relieved.[39]

---

[36]According to Fétis, *Biographie universelle des musiciens*, 2nd ed. (Paris, 1874).

[37]He retired in 1782, once more according to Fétis, ibid.

[38]*The New Grove Dictionary of Music and Musicians*, 2nd ed., s.v. 'Despréaux, Louis-Félix' by Michael Barnard.

[39]*Archives Nationales*, AJ[13]-1, dossier 22: 'Le Sr Depreaux [sic] fils l'un des Violons de l'Orchestre de l'Academie Royale de Musique demande a se retirer de l'Orchestre des Bals. On propose pour le remplacer Le Sr Topin—Maitre a Danser et tres bon Violon pour les Bals. Le Sr Rebel qui l'a entendu répond de sa capacité et de son exactitude a remplir ses devoirs s'en etant informé. (cont.)

The roster of 1757-1758 (table 5.1)—the earliest complete one I have discovered for the opera ball orchestra—still includes 'Taupin' among the violinists.

It is understandable why Despréaux fils may have wished to be excused from his duties at the opera ball in 1752, even if it did mean a loss of income: double service must have been very fatiguing. But because it is difficult to fathom why he would have chosen to take up service in both orchestras again by 1766, it seems more likely that the 'Despreaux f' of table 5.4 is not the violinist, but rather Despréaux f[rère] (Louis-Félix), the viola player. As for the father, I can only imagine that he decided to join the opera ball orchestra in 1766 (and perhaps in the previous few years as well) in anticipation of his retirement in 1767, to earn additional income. Did he enjoy some preferential access to a position with the opera ball orchestra because he was a member of *Académie Royale de Musique*? I believe the answer is 'yes.'

By the mid-century, certainly, initial employment with the opera orchestra seems to have carried with it at least the possibility of appointment to that of the opera ball. (The converse was evidently *not* the case.) As we saw above, Despréaux fils decided to resign from the opera ball group just two years after entering the service of the *Académie Royale de Musique*. The case of another violinist who also began his employment with the opera in 1750, a Mr Le Miere, is more complex:

> Mr Le Miere, one of the violinists of the *Académie Royale de Musique* [also] playing at the opera balls, requests no longer to perform this latter service. Mr Rebel proposes for his replacement that Mr Tinterlin, a violinist at these balls who plays in place of Mr Bourque, and as a consequence pays half of his fee for each ball to this Mr Bourque, will [now] enjoy full payment for a full position. Instead of Mr Tinterlin, Mr Laurent, a very good ball violinist, [will now] play in place of Mr Bourque for half pay.
>
> Mr Laurent has played previously at the opera ball, and performed his duties there very well every time he was hired. He was prevented [from full employment] only to keep the position open for one of the members of the *Académie [Royale de Musique]* who claimed priority for a position at the ball over an *externe*.

The official ruling:

> On 23 November 1752. Decreed at the City Office, in conformity with the proposal of Mr Rebel, that Mr Tonterlin [sic] will be em-

---

Du 13 9bre 1752

Arresté au Bureau de la Ville, que le Sr Topin sera admis dans les orchestres pour les Bals en la place du Sr Despreaux fils qui a demandé sa retraitte.'

ployed in the ball orchestra in place of Mr Le Miere, and that Mr Laurent will be be admitted in place of said Mr Tonterlin.[40]

This document conveys much information about a complicated practice of player substitution in the opera ball orchestra. An *externe* was an individual who sat in for another and received a portion (half, if this particular document is representative of the wider practice) of the per service fee that the notional *holder* of the position would normally earn. The practice evidently could involve an arrangement that spanned an entire season (or perhaps longer): Mr Tinterlin substituted for Mr Bourque on a long-term basis, it seems. Mr Laurent, on the other hand, apparently enjoyed just occasional employment in the opera ball orchestra before 1752.

The document also reveals a kind of pecking order in access to employment with the opera ball orchestra. An instrumentalist of the *Académie* could 'hold' or 'reserve a position,' if one became available, for his own use ('demandaient alors la preference d'une place au Bal'), or at least enjoy first refusal before an *externe* was hired. A member of the ball orchestra— Mr Bourque, for example[41]—could hold a position, but hire it out to someone else who, if they performed well, might eventually graduate to a fulltime appointment when a vacancy occurred: in this case, Mr Tinterlin. And an occasional 'hire' might aspire to a position of fulltime 'subsitution,' as happened with Mr Laurent. Mr Laurent is still listed on the roster of the opera ball orchestra in 1757 (table 5.1), and indeed in 1766 (table 5.4), as well—whether or not continuing as a substitute for Mr Bourque I cannot say. Mr Tinterlin, on the other hand, who *must* have been a violinist (since Laurent took over his 'substitution' and is listed in both

---

[40]*Archives Nationales*, AJ[13]-1, dossier 22: 'Du 23 9bre 1752. Le Sr Le Miere l'un des Violons de l'orchestre de l'Academie Royale de Musique jouant au[x] Bals de l'Opera demande a ne plus exercer cette fonction. Le Sr Rebel propose pour son remplacement que le Sr Tinterlin l'un des Violons desdits Bals qui joüe a la place du Sr Bourque et qui par consequent rend la moitié de sa paye par chaque nuit audit Sr Bourque jouisse du payment total d'une place entiere et que le Sr Laurent tres bon Violon de Bal joüe pour le Sr Bourque a demiepaye au lieu du Sr Tinterlin.

Le Sr Laurent a cy devant joué au Bal de l'Opera et y a tres bien rempli ses devoirs tous le tems qu'il y a été employé. Il n'en a été exclus que pour accorder sa place a un a [sic] des sujets de l'Academie qui demandaient alors la preference d'une place au Bal sur un Externe.

Du 23 9bre 1752. Arresté au Bureau de la Ville Corformement a la proposition du Sr Rebel que le Sr Tonterlin sera employé dans l'orquestre pour le[s] Bals en la place du Sr Le Miere, et que le Sr Laurent sera admis a la place du Sr Tonterlin.'

[41]Beyond the fact that he evidently played violin, and held an official position in the ball orchestra starting some time before 1752, I have no additional information on Mr Bourque. He seems never to have held a position in the opera orchestra (according to the listing of opera orchestra personnel given in LaGorce, 'L'Orchestre de l'Opéra,').

1757 and 1766 among the 'violons'), either became a cellist/bassist (the 'Linterlin' of table 5.1), or left the opera ball orchestra some time between 1752 and 1757. The name 'Tinterlin' does not appear in the 1766 roster, but *does* in that of 1780-1781, again as one of the *basses*.

Rosters—as important as they have proved to be in studies of orchestral practices at the Paris opera[42]—can often paint a picture of the performing personnel that is considerably more stable than was actually the case. In the opera ball orchestra of the 1750s, at any rate, membership was somewhat volatile, in part because some members of the orchestra of the *Académie Royale de Musique* chose regularly to resign a concurrent appointment to the ball, and in part because there was an active trade in substitutions. But this volatility was also the result of another important factor: playing at the opera balls does not seem to have been an entirely desirable employment for some.

A few documents from the early 1750s reveal discontent among the ball orchestra ranks. A Mr Béry, for example, who played violin at the opera ball 'among those who are *externes*,' decided at the beginning of the ball of 12 November 1752 that he no longer wished to attire himself in the livery of the orchestra, nor to play at the ball, so he left. He was subsequently dismissed, of course.[43] Another violinist, Piffet neveu (most likely Louis-François-Barthélemy Piffet, 1734-1779),[44] evidently caused even more disruption at the same ball. He had been appointed to the *Académie* orchestra in October 1751 as a substitute for his uncle, Joseph-Antoine Piffet, who wished to resign his duties (but apparently not his position) after twelve years of service. The uncle lobbied hard for this outcome, drawing attention not only to his nephew's skills as a violinist, but also to his talents as a composer, some of whose works had been directed by him in public and even in the *Chapelle du roi*.[45]

---

[42]Along with surviving performing parts, rosters have been of central importance to the work of Graham Sadler, 'Rameau's Singers and Players,' and LaGorce, 'L'Orchestre de l'Opéra.'

[43]*Archives Nationales*, AJ[13]-1, dossier 19: 'Le Sr Béry... qui joue du violon au Bal dans le nombre des Externes apres avoir refusé au Sr Rebel de se placer hier dimanche 12 Novembre... a quitté son vetement du bal et s'en est allé ayant dit au Sr Rebel qu'il ne vouloit plus jouer au Bal... le Sr Bery sera privé par forme d'amande du payement pour le Bal du 12 9bre et en outre [sera] exclus pour l'avenir de ce service.'

[44]He was known alternately as 'le neveu' or 'le fils'. See *The New Grove Dictionary of Music and Musicians*, 2nd ed., s.v. 'Piffet' by Jeffrey Cooper.

[45]*Archives Nationales*, AJ[13]-1, dossier 22: 'Piffet qui sert a l'orchestre de l'Opera depuis 12 années ne pouvant plus pour les raisons de famille exercer son employ, suplie très humblement Vôtre Grandeur vouloit bien luy accorder sa retraitte et pour le recompenser accorder au jeune Piffet son neveu sa place à titre de surnumeraire; les talens du jeune homme sont connus, joüant superieurement du Violon, ainsi fait chanter un Motet a la Chapelle du Roy, et plusieurs de ses ouvrages dans le public...'

The request was granted and, indeed, 'Piffet neveu' is listed among the 'Violons' of the opera orchestra of 1752 (see table 5.2). This appointment, once again, seems to have been concurrent with one to the opera ball, for we find him at the first ball of the 1752-1753 season, Sunday, 12 November. On that evening

> As soon as Mr Rebel had withdrawn from the ball… Mr Piffet Lefils [or 'neveu', see n44] abandoned the violin position that he was required to fill all night long to walk about in the ball. And he responded to Mr Marchand—charged with overseeing the conduct of the orchestra on the amphitheatre side—that he no longer wished to go to the trouble of playing at the ball.[46]

A report on this incident, dated 18 November 1752, offers some additional details that suggest even more strongly that Piffet neveu was not at all happy about playing for the balls.

> Mr Piffet fils, a symphonist in the orchestra of the *Académie Royale de Musique* playing violin at the opera ball, having abandoned his duties there for three-quarters of the night of the last ball, and having confirmed to Mr Rebel what he had told Mr Marchand—that he did not wish any longer to play at the ball—added to this offence the one of saying that the fine imposed on him in this matter[47] was of little consequence, because he had [already] determined to quit his position at the ball, [finding it] quite beneath him.[48]

This incident, interestingly, does not seem to have had any impact on his position in the larger opera orchestra, where he continued to serve from 1752-1754, 1757-1759, and from 1761 until sometime after 1764.[49]

---

[46]*Archives Nationales*, AJ[13]-1, dossier 21: 'Des que le Sr Rebel s'est retiré du Bal Dimanche 12 novembre le Sr Piffet Lefils a quitté sa place de violon qu'il devoit remplir toute la nuit pour se promener dans le Bal et a repondu au Sr Marchand—chargé de veiller au service de l'orchestre du Costé de l'amphithéatre qu'il ne vouloit plus se donner la peine de jouer au Bal.'

[47]He was not paid for the ball, and was instructed in no uncertain terms to be 'plus exact a son devoir dans les Bals' in the future. ibid.

[48]*Archives Nationales*, AJ[13]-1, dossier 20: 'Le Sr Piffet fils l'un des Simphonistes de l'Orchestre de l'Académie Royale de Musique et jouant de violon au Bal de l'Opera apres avoir manqué a son service les trois quarts de la nuit dernier Bal et apres avoir Confirmé au Sr Rebel comme il l'avoit dit au Sr Marchand qu'il ne vouloit plus jouer au Bal a ajoute a ce tort celuy de dire que l'amende qui luy a été imposée a ce sujet devenoit tres indifferente puis qu'il étoit determiné a quitter sa place au bal fort dessous de luy.'

[49]According to LaGorce, 'L'Orchestre de l'Opéra,' 42. He also played for the *concert spirituel*. See n44.

Whether minor insurrections such as these were a commonplace at the opera ball I cannot say. It is clear, though, that the opera management believed the conduct of the ball orchestra should be monitored rather closely. In the two incidents described above Rebel himself was present for at least the opening of the ball (perhaps only because it was the first of the season). François Rebel (1701-1775) and François Francoeur (c1698-1787) served as 'Inspecteurs' of the *Académie Royale de Musique* from 1743 until 1753, and were named its co-directors from 1757 through 1764.[50] Rebel, especially, seems to have been concerned with the operations of the opera ball, as many of the preceding documents have demonstrated. He was actively involved with the personnel, auditioning instrumentalists, and making recommendations on matters of hiring and dismissal (in the late 1740s and 1750s his recommendations were to the city of Paris—administrators of the Opéra—through the *Prévost des Marchands*).

Rebel, however, was not the only individual to keep a close eye on the day-to-day functioning of the opera ball. On the ballroom floor itself there were four individuals at each ball whose specific duties were to monitor the conduct of the two orchestras. We have already encountered one of these—Mr Marchand, who challenged Piffet when he abandoned his post on 12 November 1752 (see n46, above). During that season Marchand was teamed with Mr Joublay (or 'Jaublay') on the amphitheatre side of the ballroom, while Mssrs Paris and Champion evidently monitored the group who played at the stage end. Two of the four—Mssrs Paris and Champion—were members of the opera orchestra at the time, serving as violists (both individuals are included in the *Académie* roster from that year, a portion of which is reproduced in table 5.2). Mr Joublay was to become a violinist with the opera ball orchestra by 1766 (see table 5.4), but in 1752 did not yet hold such a position. The identity of Mr Marchand is less clear. It does not seem likely that he was the Marchand who played flute and oboe in the *Académie Royale de Musique* for a single season in 1732. It is possible that he is the 'Le Marchand' who played bassoon in the group in 1756, or who served as *tambouriniste* from 1762-64.[51] But in the early 1750s none of the four individuals was engaged at the opera ball as an instrumentalist. A letter dated 12 March 1751 and addressed to Mr Neuville, chief cashier of the Opéra, gives an interesting account of what was expected of them:

---

[50]*The New Grove Dictionary of Music and Musicians*, 2nd ed., s.v. 'Francoeur, François' by Michelle Fillion, and Catherine Cessac, and 'Rebel, François' by Catherine Cessac.

[51]See LaGorce, 'L'orchestre de l'Opéra,' 42.

It has come to my attention, sir, that Mrs Marchand and Jaublay, engaged to control the symphonists under the accounts of 'gratiffications des bals' at the rate of 2 *sols* apiece for each ball, and Mssrs Paris and Champion, employed under the same accounts at the rate of 50 *sols* apiece for the conduct of the symphonists, were not diligent in fulfilling their duties and in supervising the performance of the orchestra to the public's satisfaction. Given this lapse in diligence I entreat you, as a consequence, to suspend payment of their salaries until further notice.[52]

It might reasonably be concluded from this letter that discipline in the orchestras sometimes broke down, and as a result that performances suffered to such a degree that they no longer met with 'the public's satisfaction.'

To be fair to the musicians, on the other hand, playing for the opera balls cannot have been a particularly gratifying experience, even if it did *not* entail lengthy overnight performances. There certainly was little challenge to a player, beyond the test of stamina and endurance. The principal repertoire, however tuneful it may have been, was by its very nature rather predictable (at least in its phrase structures), and it favoured *contredanses* that required multiple repetitions, in most cases, to accommodate the choreographies. Eighteenth century commentary on the nature of contredanse music often reflects—more often than not in a positive way—on its inherent simplicity and attractiveness. These characteristics, in fact, were often regarded as a *requirement* of the genre. In his *Dictionnaire de Musique* (1768), for example, Jean-Jacques Rousseau wrote:

> The airs of contredanses are most often in duple time. They must be rhythmically well marked, brilliant and gay, and nevertheless have much simplicity, for, because they are repeated very often, they would become intolerable if they were full of substance.[53]

[52]*Archives Nationales*, AJ[13]-1, dossier 5: 'Il m'est revenu, Monsieur, que les Srs Marchand & Jaublay employés sur l'etat des gratiffications des Bals a raison de 2" chacun pour chaque Bal pour le Controlle des Simphonistes, et les Srs Paris et Champion employés sur ce même etat a raison de 50" chacun pour la conduite des Simphonistes n'ont pas été exacts a remplir leurs devoir[s], et a veiller a l'execution de la Simphonie a la satisfaction du Public, je vous prie de vouloir bien en consequence, attendu leur peu d'exactitude, suspendre le payement de leurs gratiffications jusqu'a nouvel ordre.' The two (quite dramatically different) rates of pay recorded in this letter might be explained by the fact that Mssrs Paris and Champion held fulltime appointments in the opera orchestra at the time, while Marchand and Joublay did not.

[53]Jean-Jacques Rousseau, *Dictionnaire de Musique*, (Paris, 1768); reprint ed. (Hildesheim, 1969), s.v. 'Contredanse.' Rousseau's remarks are repeated *verbatim* in his contribution to the article on 'Contredanse' in the Supplement to the *Encyclopédie*, vol. II, 575: 'Les airs des *contredanses* sont le plus souvent à deux temps: ils doivent être bien cadencés, brillans & gais, & avoir cependant beaucoup de simplicité; car, comme on les reprend très souvent, ils deviendroient insupportable s'ils étoient chargés.'

Contredanses, to be sure, were neither restricted to duple meter, nor were they the only dances encountered at the *bal public*. A consideration of the type and range of repertoire of the opera ball will be the focus of the following pages.

•   •   •   •   •

One can imagine musicians in the opera ball orchestras playing from parts copied for their use, and compiled by a librarian or copyist into 'books' of ballroom dances. The books must have required frequent updating, with new repertoire added on a regular basis, and older material discarded when it no longer was needed. In most other respects, though, the preparation of performing part books for the opera balls was probably rather straight-forward: there were none of the texted items, cues, or special doublings found in the performance parts for dramatic stage works. I believe the musical materials of the opera ball were prepared and updated by the copyists of the Opéra, who must have been obliged to include such work among their normal duties.[54] This seems a real likelihood because in the few surviving payment records for employees of the opera ball that I have examined there is never any indication of a salary for a copyist.[55] In contrast, fees for copying music for the *concerts spirituels*, or the annual concert on St Louis's day (August 25)—in both of which artists from the *Académie Royale* were featured—are often found among surviving payment records.[56]

Given the longevity of the opera ball, and the sizable repertoire it must have accumulated during the course of the eighteenth century, it is disappointing that no traces of original performing parts have survived. An idea of what those parts probably looked like, however, is offered by a surviving first violin part, titled 'Livre du Bal. Dessus de violon.'[57] According to a pencilled note (seemingly in a twentieth-century hand) this part book is principally the copying work of [André

[54]For a useful review of the copying activity and practices of the Opéra for much of the eighteenth century (through the mid-1770s), see Lois Rosow, 'Lallemand and Durand: Two Eighteenth-Century Music Copyists at the Paris Opéra,' *Journal of the American Musicological Society* 23/1 (1980), 142-163. Rosow's study offers no evidence of copying for balls, but the *bal public* was not a critical consideration for her.

[55]For example, the 'Etat du Payment a faire aux Employés et Préposés de l'Academie Royale de Musique pour les 17 Bals donnés depuis le Dimanche 12 Novembre 1780 jusqu'au Mardi 27 fevrier 1781,' *Archives nationales*, AJ[13]-23, dossier 8.

[56]Rosow reproduces a receipt signed by Lallemand in 'Two Eighteenth-Century Music Copyists,' 149. The document is dated 29 August 1749, and almost certainly was for music Lallemand prepared for the St Louis day concert that year.

[57]*Bibliothèque-Musée de l'Opéra*, Ms. fr. Rés. 1187.

Danican] Philidor [l'aîné]. I am inclined to agree with this assessment, not only because of the appearance of the musical and textual script, but because this anthology has a good sampling of dances by Philidor himself, and includes a number of concordances with Philidor's two collections of *Suite de danses*. It seems a good possibility that this violin part book was copied sometime after 1712 (the supposed date of Philidor's second *Suite*), because a number of dances that had been included in the 1712 collection are marked 'déchirée' (literally 'torn out') in the part book.[58] I do not wish to suggest that the partbook was prepared from Philidor's 1712 collection, or even that the two sources have some common lineage (beyond Philidor's evident involvement), despite the significant amount of shared music. I am merely proposing that a partbook that transmits much of the same repertoire as the 1712 collection, but that deliberately excludes *some* of it, is more likely to have been prepared at a slightly later time. Such pruning, of course, does not necessarily represent an effort to *modernize* the ballroom repertoire the partbook transmits. But it certainly indicates an intentional editing of materials from some previous iteration of the partbook. This is made especially clear in one entry in the table of contents which reads: 'le menuet sans N° de page, déchirée.'

Whatever the provenance of this partbook, there is no more than a remote possibility that it is a copy (or even a copy of just a portion) of a performing part used by the first violinists in the opera ball orchestra. I think the possibility is remote, first, because Philidor is not known to have had any direct connections with the *Académie Royale de Musique* in the eighteenth century (he was otherwise heavily committed to duties in the royal musical household)[59] and, second, because some of the repertoire contained in the 'Livre du Bal' is not well suited to the opera ball, as we shall see shortly. There are, for example, two suites of multi-sectioned branles (of the late seventeenth century variety[60]), and no fewer than sixteen courantes (not counting the six included with the

---

[58]Such is the case, for example, for some of the chaconnes found in a grouping from pages 44 to 49 in the 1712 collection: these include the 'Chaconne de Phaeton,' and the 'Chaconne de M[adam]e la P[rince]sse de Conty.' In the partbook, however, the table of contents lists these two chaconnes (along with five others) as 'déchirée;' indeed, all the chaconnes have been removed.

[59]The most complete biographical information on André Danican Philidor is found in Rebecca Harris-Warrick, and Carol G. Marsh, *Musical Theatre at the Court of Louis XIV. Le Marriage de la Grosse Cathos* (Cambridge, 1994), 14-21. Philidor's son, Anne Danican (1681-1728) had close connections to the Opéra, founding the *Concerts spirituels* in 1725, and likely the 'Philidor le cadet' who played flute and oboe in the opera orchestra from 1717-1726.

[60]For developments in the suites of branles in these years see Richard Semmens, 'Branles, Gavottes, and Contredanses,' 35-62.

suites of branles). Dances such as these were only rarely performed in the eighteenth century. This source, nevertheless, gives a good idea of what a performer's book of ball music looked like, and how it was organized.

The 'Livre du Bal' is arranged in such a way as to make accessing individual dances easy. In a table of contents at the front of the volume each dance is assigned both a number and a page reference. Presumably the assigned number was to make identification of a dance to be played quick and accurate. This table is organized by dance types arranged alphabetically: 'airs de danses détachés,' 'bourées' [or 'basques'], 'branles,' 'canaries,' 'chaconnes,' 'contredanses,' 'courantes,' 'menuets,' 'passepieds,' 'rigodons' [sic], and 'vieilles danses.' Additionally, at the conclusion of the volume the title of each dance (with a page reference) is listed in alphabetic order. The arrangement of the volume overall, however, is by genre, but without any other discernible purpose in ordering: branles, courantes, rigaudons, contredanses, chaconnes [empty], sarabandes, bourées, gigues, canaries, 'vieilles danses,'[61] menuets, passepieds, and finally 'pièces détachées.' In each group music has been entered onto paper lined with music staves, and there are several empty pages (also lined) at the conclusion of sections, into which, presumably, more dances of that genre could be added at a future time.

While I have been unable to locate original music with definitive connections to the *bal public*, there is no shortage of music with strong indirect links to it. Beginning as early as the mid-1720s Parisian publishers printed a great many anthologies of dance music that included a phrase like 'as performed at the opera ball' in their titles.[62] Most of these imprints were issued in series, more often than not without indication of a date of publication. Because the repertoire they transmit is shared by other anthologies, however, or is datable (if only approximately) through other means, it becomes possible to compile an inventory of literally hundreds of eighteenth-century dance tunes with close associations with the public ball.

The earliest datable collection that I have discovered comes from 1725 (and through its companion volume perhaps slightly earlier).

---

[61] There are thirty-two dances in this section, some of them, such as the courante 'La Duchesse,' or the 'branle de mets [Metz]' and 'branle de champagne,' very venerable, indeed.

[62] For example, *Premier recueil de contredanses telles qu'elles ont été dansées au bal de l'Opéra. Pour les violons, flûtes et hautbois* (Paris, nd). *RISM*, see *Recueils imprimés. XVIIIe siècle* (Munich, 1964), 324, suggests a date of c1754, but since the Boivin firm ceased publications in 1753, this seems in error. Guilcher, *La contredanse*, 229, claims the series was compiled by Maupetit, and was begun as early as c1745.

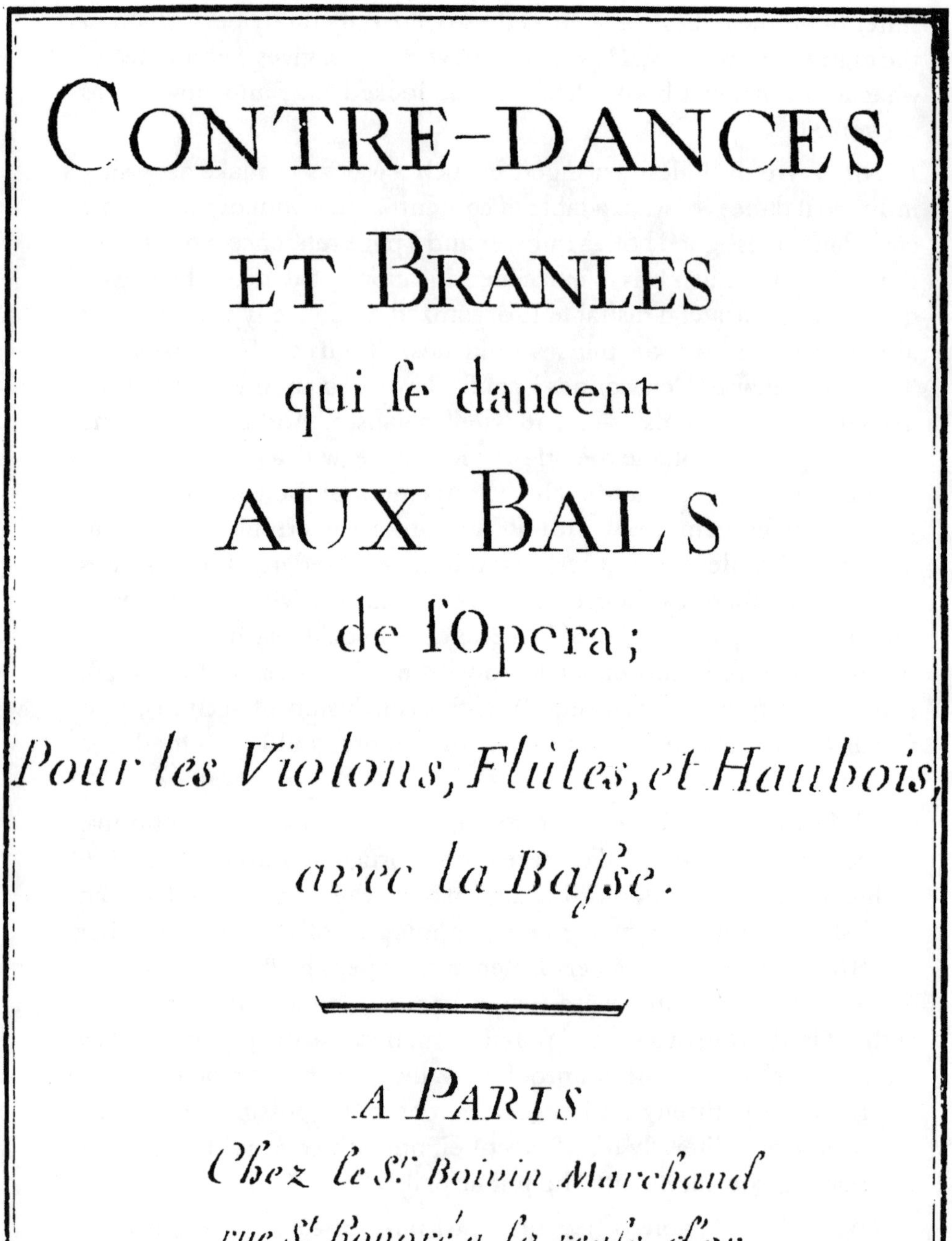

CONTRE-DANCES
ET BRANLES

qui se dancent

AUX BALS

de l'Opera;

Pour les Violons, Flûtes, et Haubois,

avec la Basse.

A PARIS

Chez le S.ͬ Boivin Marchand

rue S.ͭ Honoré a la regle d'or.

Prix, 5 ʃol. en blanc.

Illustration 4. Title page from Montéclair's *Contre-dances et Branles qui se dancent aux bals de l'Opera. Pour les violons, flûtes, et haubois, avec la basse* (Paris, nd.)

Ascribed to Michel Pinolet de Montéclair (c1667-1737) as either composer or compiler, it is the second volume of a collection of menuets: *Menuets, tant anciens que nouveaux, qui se dansent aux bals de l'Opéra. Deuxième recueil, contenant cent & un menuets…mis en ordre avec la basse chiffrée par Mr Montéclair* (Paris, 1725), issued by François Boivin (c1693-1733), Montéclair's nephew. The first volume, with a slightly different title,[63] must have been issued slightly earlier, but it is undated. According to James Anthony this series went into six volumes, the last four of which are now lost.[64] Anthony's assessment, however, is in need of revision, at least on some counts. Even though the second volume of menuets bears the date 1725 on its title page, Anthony proposes that the entire series may have been issued before 1709. This is an impossibility, of course, not only because Boivin did not purchase his music printing interests until July 1721,[65] but more especially because the titles in this series of menuet anthologies link the music specifically to the opera balls, and these were not inaugurated until 1716.[66]

Anthony also proposes a date of publication before 1709 for another collection of opera ball music by Montéclair—this time contredanses and branles: *Contre-dances et Branles qui se dancent aux bals de l'Opera. Pour les violons, flûtes, et haubois, avec la basse* (Paris, nd). Because this imprint was issued by 'Sr. Boivin' according to the title page (see illustration 4) and not by his widow, who after his death in 1733 continued to issue music under the name 'la veuve Boivin,' the collection must date from between 1721 and 1733. It, too, had a companion volume that is now lost.[67] The one that has survived, however, transmits a repertoire that includes many dances from earlier in the century. There is music for fifty-two contredanses,[68] and just

---

[63]*Menuets, tant anciens que nouveaux, qui se dansent aux bals de l'Opéra. 1er recueil contenant cent et un menuets disposés en dix suittes par Mr Montéclair* (Paris, nd).

[64]In the works list he compiled for the composer: *The New Grove Dictionary of Music and musicians*, 2nd ed. s.v. 'Montéclair, Michel Pinolet de' by James Anthony. Anthony apparently surmised the existence of the missing four volumes through the published catalogue of the Boivin music firm, *Catalogue général des ouvrages publiés par Boivin* (Paris, 1742).

[65]See *The New Grove Dictionary of Music and Musicians*, 2nd ed., s.v. 'Boivin, François' by Sylvette Milliot.

[66]His proposal is all the more curious because in his ground-breaking book on French baroque music, he claims the first *recueil* was issued in 1725. See James R. Anthony, *French Baroque Music from Beaujoyeulx to Rameau*, rev. ed. (New York, 1978), 321-322.

[67]See the Boivin firm's *Catalogue général* cited above, n64.

[68]Although there are fifty-three numbered contredanses, numbers 29 and 30 form a single, bi-partite dance, 'La Blonde et la Brune.' A choreography for two gentlemen and two ladies to this music (of unknown provenance) is catalogued in Meredith Ellis Little and Carol G. Marsh, *La Danse Noble. An Inventory of Dances and Sources*, 11 (item 1400).

four 'branles.' Of the contredanses, twelve had either been included in one (or more) of the musical collections discussed above—Philidor's two suites of ballroom dances of 1699 and c1712, and the undated 'Livre du bal'—or they had been included in one of the two large printed collections of contredanse choreographies that were issued in Paris before the inauguration of the public ball in 1716. The latter are Raoul-Auger Feuillet's *Recüeil de contredances mises en Choregrahie* (Paris, 1706), containing thirty-two dances, and Jacques Dezais's *Recüeil de nouvelles contredanses mises en Choregraphie* (Paris, 1712), containing twenty-seven dances.[69] Three of the four 'branles' also appeared in earlier collections. Table 5.6 sets out the concordances among the dances included in Montéclair's anthology of the 1720s or early 1730s and these five earlier sources.

Table 5.6 Montéclair's *Contre-dances et branles* and earlier collections

Montéclair	Philidor (1699)	Feuillet (1706)	Philidor (c1712)	Dezais (1712)	Livre du bal
Contredanses					
2. la Jeunesse			(72)		
3. la Cristine				(64)	
5. Jeanne qui saute	(18)		(65-69)	(51)	(61)
15. la Badine			(56)	(21-23)	
18. la Jalousie		(5-8)	(59)		
21. la Coquette			(59)		
22. la Boulangere			(57)		
23. la Chasse		(166-176)	(62)		
39. la Valentine	(15)	(100-106)	(50)		
40. le Prince Torge [=George]		(33-38)	(62)		
43. les Manches vertes	(19)	(17-24)	(51)		(65)
50. les Sept sauts			(29)		
Branles					
1. la Sissone			(22)		(96)
2. les Tricotets					(100)
4. la Cassandre			(26)		

In this table the numbers for the dances in the Montéclair collection are those given in the imprint; page references to the earlier anthologies are given in parentheses.

[69]Six additional contredanse choreographies had been included with Feuillet's *VIme Recüeil de danses et de contredanses pour l'année 1708* (Paris, 1707). See Meredith Ellis Little and Carol G. Marsh, *La Danse Noble. An Inventory of Dances and Sources*, 99-100, for bibliographic information on this collection.

Over one quarter of the Montéclair compilation (fifteen of fifty-six dances) shares repertoire with sources dating from before the establishment of the *bal public*.[70] In conjunction with the dozens of menuets preserved in the two surviving volumes from the mid-1720s (neither of which actually contains the 'cent & un menuets' promised in the title), Montéclair's *Contre-dances et branles* gives an important glimpse into the musical repertoire of the opera ball in its formative years. For the most part, that repertoire seems to have been the same as that of any other ball, not only in its general make-up—a preponderance of menuets and contredanses—but in a significant amount of specific material that is shared as well. Do the Montéclair publications really give a representative sampling of the opera ball repertoire in its early years? An account of carnival activities of 1727 reported in the *Mercure galant* suggests that this is, indeed, the case.

> Many people have remarked that carnival has been more widely celebrated this year in Paris than it has been for some time... The public balls given in the theatre of the Opera have been rendered more pleasing by diverse masquerades introduced there at the conclusion of carnival, and these have given much pleasure. Besides menuets for two and for four, many other special dances were performed, [as well as] a good many contredanses, in which eight, twelve, and up to sixteen persons dance together with much vivacity and a great variety of steps and *attitudes*. Some of the names of these dances that have been retained [by the reporter] will perhaps seem rather entertaining, like 'les Rats,' 'Jeanne qui saute,' 'l'Amitié,' 'le Poivre,' 'la Silvie,' 'la Blonde & la Brune,' 'le Cotillon qui va toujours,' 'l'Insulaire,' 'la Favorite,' 'Liron-Lirette,' 'la Capricieuse,' 'la Calotine' etc.[71]

The dances specified at the conclusion of this interesting account are all contredanses, and five of them—the 'Cotillon qui va toujours,' 'Jeanne qui saute,' 'les Rats,' 'le Poivre,' and 'la Blonde et la Brune'— were included in Montéclair's anthology.[72] At least two others—

[70]That fourteen of the fifteen dances have a concordance in the Philidor collection of c1712 is particularly striking.

[71]*Mercure galant*, février (1727), 392-393: 'Bien des gens ont remarqué que le Carnaval a été plus célébré cette année à Paris, qu'il ne l'avoit été depuis quelque temps... Les Bals publics qu'on donne sur le Théatre de l'Opera, ont éte rendus beaucoup plus agréables par diverses Mascarades qu'on y a introduites sur la fin du Carnaval, & qui ont fait beaucoup de plaisir. On y a dansé, outre les Menuets à deux & à quatre, plusieurs autres danses particulières, quantité de contre-danses, dans lesquelles, huit, douze & jusqu'à seize personnes dansent ensemble avec beaucoup de vivacité, & une extrême varieté de pas & d'attitudes. Quelques noms de ces danses qu'on a retenus, paroîtront peut-être assez plaisans, comme les Rats, Jeanne qui saute, l'Amitié, le Poivre, la Silvie, la Blonde & la Brune, le Cotillon qui va toûjours, l'Insulaire, la Favorite, Liron-Lirette, la Capricieuse, la Calotine, &c.'

[72]Respectively, numbers 1, 5, 17, 26, and 29 of the collection. Only number 5, 'Jeanne qui saute,' is listed in table 5.6, because of its conconcordances with earlier sources.

'l'Amitié,' and 'la Silvie'—also have concordances with earlier musical or choreographic sources with strong connections to the ballroom.[73] The music transmitted in these Montéclair imprints, in other words, is not merely a repertoire *anthologized* by virtue of its popularity (although there is certainly an element of that here). It is music that was actually *performed* at balls, including those of the Opera.

The establishment of the *bal public*, therefore, did not precipitate the creation of an entirely new repertoire of dances somehow fashioned to suit a new set of circumstances. It drew, rather, on some (but certainly not all) of the musical and choreographic materials that had found a popular place in private balls by the second decade of the eighteenth century. Even the masquerade, a standard feature at the time of masked balls among the nobility, found a place at the opera ball, as the preceding passage makes clear.[74] Yet though it drew, in its early years, on practices and even some of the repertoire found in balls of noble households, the opera ball was apparently not able to accommodate the dancing couple (typically performing menuets) as successfully as it was the dancing *group* (typically performing contredanses). By the 1740s printed collections of music 'performed at the *bals de l'Opéra*' only rarely were dedicated to the menuet.[75] Even single menuets contained in larger anthologies of dances are rather scarce.[76] This is in sharp contrast to imprints that have no definitive links to the opera ball, in which menuets continue to be be featured well past mid-century. The Parisian music printing firm of the Frères LeClerc, for example, issued literally dozens of volumes of menuets between c1742 and 1760.[77] Collections

---

[73]'L'Amitié' likely refers to 'la Bonne Amitié' from Feuillet's 1706 *Recüeil de contredances*, 1-4, while 'la Silvie' is included in Philidor's *Suite* of c1712, 71.

[74]Although the 'introduction' of masquerades to the opera ball at the conclusion of the 1727 carnival season may have seemed novel to the correspondent reporting for the *Mercure*, and although such masquerades would remain comparatively rare (see below, pp.162-64), they had made occasional appearances even earlier: in a special ball, for example, mounted in August 1724. See chapter one, n75.

[75]The last large collection with clear links to the opera ball that I have discovered is the series entitled *Minuetti diversi*, only volumes five through nine of which have survived. *Minuetti diversi. Ve [-IXe] recueil de menuets nouveaux français et italiens tels qu'ils se dansent aux bals de l'Opéra* (Paris, c1745). The latest (rather small) collection overall comes from a slightly later period, and seems rather isolated: *Suite de menuets pour les violons, flûtes, hautbois avec l'accompagnement de basse ou de basson tels qu'ils s'exécutent au Bal de l'Opéra. Mis en ordre par M. d'Avesne* (Paris, c1763).

[76]The *Deuxieme Recueil de Contredanses Telles quelles ont étées Dansées au Bal de l'Opera. Pour les Violons Flûtes, et Hautbois* (Paris, nd.) opens with a Menuet in g minor, and a Rigaudon in g major. These are followed by thirty titled contredanses; the volume concludes with three Cotillons.

[77]An inventory of the LeClerc publications is given in Anik Devriès, *Édition et commerce de la musique gravée à Paris dans la première moitié du XVIIIe siècle* (Geneva, 1976), 209-211. The firm also issued collections of contredanses in similar abundance during the same years.

of contredanse music associated with the opera ball, on the other hand, were issued with great regularity from the 1720s on. Table 5.7 sets out all the printed collections mentioning opera balls in their titles that I have been able to examine. The list does not claim to be a comprehensive inventory, but it does give a good idea of the importance of eighteenth-century opera ball repertoire to the Parisian marketplace, and indicates, further, just how dominant the contredanse was in that repertoire. In all, these printed collections contain well over a thousand dance tunes, although many of them, to be sure, are transmitted in more than one source, so the actual number of dances is somewhat less.

Table 5.7 Printed collections of eighteenth-century opera ball music

1a. Montéclair, Michel Pinolet de. *Menuets tant anciens que nouveaux qui se dansent aux bals de l'Opéra, 1er recueil contenant cent et un menuets disposés en dix suittes par Mr Montéclair.* Paris: Boivin, nd. [c1725].

1b. _____. *Menuets, tant anciens que nouveaux, qui se dansent aux bals de l'Opéra, deuxième recueil, contenant cent & un menuets... mis en ordre avec la basse chiffrée par Mr Montéclair.* Paris: Boivin, 1725.

2. _____. *Contre-dances et branles qui se dancent aux bals de l'Opéra; pour les violons, flûtes, et haubois, avec la basse...* Paris: Boivin, nd. [before 1733].

3. *Minuetti diversi. V [-IXᵉ] recueil de menuets nouveaux françois et italiens tels qu'ils se dansent aux bals de l'Opéra.* Paris: Madame Boivin, s.d. [c1745].

4a. [Maupetit, Jean-Baptiste Edmonde]. *Contredanses Nouvelles Tel quils ont etés Dansés au Bal du Roy et au Bal de l'Opera. Pour les Violons flutes et Hautbois et autres instruments. 1e Recueil.* Paris, nd. [series begins c1745]

4b. _____. *Septieme Recueil de Contredanses telles qu'elles ont étés Dansés aux Bals de versailles et de l'Opera.* Paris, nd. [?volumes 2 – 6 lost]

4c. _____. *Huitieme Recueil de Contredanses telles qu'elles ont étés Dansés aux Bals de versailles et de l'Opera.* Paris, nd.

4d. _____. *Neuvieme Recueil de Contredanses telles qu'elles ont étés Dansés aux Bals de versailles et de l'Opera.* Paris, nd.

4e. _____. *Dixieme Recueil de Contredanses Telles qu'elles ont étés Dansés aux Bals de St Cloud et de l'Opera. Pour les Violons, Flûtes et Hautbois.* Paris, nd.

4f. _____. *Onzieme Recueil de Contredanses Telles qu'elles ont étés Dansées aux Bals de St Cloud et de l'Opera. Pour les Violons, Flûtes et Hautbois.* Gravée par Mlle Bertin. Paris, Lyon, nd.

4g. _____. *Douzieme Recueil de Contredanses Telles qu'elles ont étés Dansées aux Bals de l'Opera Pour les Violons, Flûtes et Hautbois.* Gravée par Mlle Bertin, Paris, Lyon, nd.

5a. *[1er] Suitte de Contredances pour les Violons Flutes Haubois et avec l'Accompagnement de Basse telles qu'elles s'executent au Bal de l'Opera. Recueillies avec soin.* Paris, nd. [series begins after 1752]

5b. *[5e] Suitte de Contredances Pour les Violons Flutes Hautbois et avec l'Accompagnement de Basse telles qu'elles Sexecutent au Bal de l'Opera. Recueillies avec soin.* Paris, nd. [?volumes 2 - 4 lost]

5c. *[6e] Suitte de Contredances Pour les Violons Flutes Hautbois et avec l'Accompagnement de Basse telles qu'elles Sexecutent au Bal de l'Opera. Recueillies avec soin.* Paris, nd.

6a. *Premier recueil de contredanses telles quelles ont été dansées au bal de l'Opéra. Pour les violons, flûtes et hautbois.* Paris, nd. [series begins c1754].

6b. *Deuxieme Recueil de Contredanses Telles quelles ont etées Dansées au Bal de l'Opera. Pour les Violons Flûtes, et Hautbois.* Paris, nd.

6c. *Nouvelles Contredanses Telles quelles ont etées Dansées au Bal de l'Opera et au Bal de son Excellence l'Ambassadeur d'Espagne. Pour les Violons Flutes Hautbois et autres Instruments. IIIe Recueil.* Paris, nd.

6d. *Quatrieme Recueil de Contredanses Telles quelles ont etées Dansées au Bal de l'Opera. Pour les Violons Flutes et Hault-bois.* Paris, nd.

6e. *Cinquieme Recüeil de Contredanses Telles quelles ont etées Dansées au Bal de l'Opera. Pour les Violons Flutes et Haut-bois.* Paris, nd

6f. *Sixieme Recueil de Contredanses Telles quelles ont eteés Dansées au Bal de Versailles et au Bal de l'Opera. Pour les Violons, Flutes, et Hautbois.* Paris, nd.

6g. *Septieme Recueil de Contredanses Telles quelles ont eteés Dansées au Bal de Versailles et au Bal de l'Opera. Pour les Violons, Flutes, et Hautbois.* Paris, nd.

6h. *Huitieme Recueil de Contredanses Telles quelles ont eteés Dansées au Bal de Versailles et au Bal de l'Opera. Pour les Violons, Flutes, et Hautbois.* Paris, nd.

6i. *Neuvieme Recueil de Contredanses Telles quelles ont etées Dansées aux Bals de St Cloud et de l'Opera. Pour les Violons, Flutes et Hautbois.* Paris, nd.

6j. *Dixieme Recueil de Contredanses Telles quelles ont etées Dansées aux Bals de St Cloud et de l'Opera. Pour les Violons, Flutes et Hautbois.* Paris, nd.

6k. *Onzieme Recueil de Contredanses Telles quelles ont étées Dansées aux Bals de St Cloud et de l'Opera. Pour les Violons, Flutes et Hautbois.* Paris, nd.

6l. *Douzieme Recueil de Contredanses Telles quelles ont étées Dansées aux Bals de St Cloud et de l'Opera. Pour les Violons, Flutes et Hautbois.* Paris, nd.

6m. *Treizieme Recueil de Contredanses Telles quelles ont étées Dansées aux Bals de St Cloud et de l'Opera. Pour les Violons, Flutes et Hautbois.* Paris, nd.

7a. *IXme Recueil de Contredanses avec la Basse Chiffrée; et la Table par Lettres Alphabetiques. Qui se dansent au bal de l'Opera, et de St Cloud.* Paris, nd. [?first 8 volumes lost]

7b. *Xe Recueil de Contredanses avec la Basse Chiffrée; et la Table par Lettres Alphabetiques. Qui se dansent au bal de l'Opera, et de St Cloud.* Paris, nd.

8a. *Recueil des Contredanses à la Mode dansées au bal de l'Opera & de St Cloud.* Paris, nd.

8b. *IIe Recueil des Contredanses à la Mode Dansées aux bals de l'Opera, de St Cloud, et de Vincennes.* Paris, nd.

8c. *IIIe Recueil des Contredanses à la Mode Dansées aux bals de l'Opera, de St Cloud, et de Vincennes.* Paris, nd.

9. *Les Nouvelles Contre-danses qui se dansent aux Bals de l'Opera Pour le Violon, Flûte, Hautbois avec la Basse chiffrée.* Paris, nd.

I have grouped these collections (where appropriate) by series—for example, 4a, 4b, 4c, etc.—when it is clear that this is how they were originally issued. Usually the strongest evidence is not that of a passepartout title page, or even a uniform title (notice the variety in titles in series '4' as a case in point), but rather that of sequenced pagination in the imprints. I have suggested that the three volumes of my series '8' belong together for a variety of different reasons. They are bound together (along with a grouping of dances issued singly, it seems);[78] and all three have the phrase 'à la mode' in their titles, although the titles are not otherwise uniform. Perhaps more compelling evidence, however, is that all three volumes were issued without a bass line (they are the only three among these collections issued in such a way). In those few cases in table 5.7 where I have named a compiler (not counting the Montéclair collections), I have relied on suggestions by Jean-Michel Guilcher.[79]

I have also attempted to present the collections of table 5.7 in what I believe is a possible chronological sequence, but because there are so many lacunae in this respect, the chronology is very tentative. The dates for items '3' and the first volume of '4' once more have already been suggested by Guilcher.[80] The date for the first volume of '6' has been suggested in *RISM*.[81] Series '5' is dated 'after 1752' because two

---

[78]The entire compilation is preserved in the *Bibliothèque Nationale* (Musique) with the shelf number V^m Crlt 844(1-4).

[79]In his *La contredanse*, 229 (a listing of the musical sources he consulted). Guilcher likely based his assessments on information provided by unknown librarians, who have suggested the names of compilers (as well as likely dates of printing) in the catalogues of the collection they have prepared. In the absence of any other confirming evidence, they should be regarded as no more than suggestions.

[80]See n79, above.

[81]*Recüeils imprimés. XVIIIe siècle*, 324. The date, c1754, is probably out a year or two, because the Boivin firm ceased its operations in 1753. See above, n62.

of the dances it trasmits are from Rousseau's *Le Devin du village*.[82] The first volume of this series, therefore, must date from after the initial production of the work in October 1752 (and probably after 1753, following the first production in Paris at the Opéra). It is tempting to surmise that those collections in table 5.7 with titles that mention both the 'Bal de l'Opéra' and 'de St Cloud' ('4e', '4f', '6i' through '6m', series '7' and series '8') date from after 1785. Like the titles that mention 'Bals de Versailles,' 'de Vincennes,' or 'du Roy,' those with 'St Cloud' might have been designed to link the opera ball repertoire with that of *royal* balls. The chateau at Saint Cloud, however, became a royal residence (the preferred one for Queen Marie Antoinette) only in 1785, when it was purchased from the d'Orléans household and refurbished lavishly.[83] The renovations, though, were not completed until early 1788. Do the titles with 'St Cloud' in table 5.7 *all* date from the final two or three years of the *ancien régime*? I am inclined to think not. There are twelve such volumes in total, after all, over one third of the repertoire I have examined. Earlier in the century, moreover, the 'original' chateau and its grounds had been fashionable venues for both indoor and outdoor *fêtes*.[84]

The thirteen volumes comprising series '6' very likely spanned many years. The anomalous title (relative to all the others) of '6c'—making reference, as it does, to the ball of the Ambassador of Spain—may help in dating this volume. It is almost certain that the ambassador's ball mentioned here was not just a single event, but a veritable 'season of balls.' (The 'Opera ball' in the title is also given in the singular.) I believe this volume may have been issued in, or shortly after, 1762, because in February of that year the *Mercure* drew attention to a series of balls offered by 'Ambassadeurs':

> We note with satisfaction that the weekly balls given by the *Académie Royale de Musique* are more crowded and better attended this year than in previous ones, despite the superb balls of the Ambassadors, that might be considered [rather] like public *fêtes*, as a result of the

---

[82]Numbers 22 and 23 of the first volume: 'La villageoise du Devin de village,' and 'l'Allemande du Devin de village.' The former is Colette's air with chorus, 'Allons danser' that concluded the original production. The latter is based on the 'Allemande tres gai' that precedes the final number.

[83]My information has been gathered from a very useful account of the history of St Cloud on the internet: Les Amis du Parc de Saint Cloud, 'Saint Cloud: résidence princière, royale et impériale,' in *L'Histoire de Saint Cloud* © 2000. Available from: http://saintcloud.histoire.free.fr.

Internet. Accessed 22 July 2001.

[84]ibid.

magnificence that reigns there, and the great number of invited guests.[85]

Although a Spanish ambassador is not specifically mentioned in the passage, the balls in question are equated to very popular and well attended public *fêtes*, making a title like that given in '6c' both timely and appropriate.

Individual dances within these collections are occasionally transmitted in more than one source. This is undoubtedly an indication of their popularity. It is quite possible, however, that new choreographies were involved when a dance tune was reissued, and that the popularity was more a factor of the *tune* (with its title), than it was the *dance*. Three series of table 5.7 are particularly rich in concordances among the dance tunes they contain. So numerous are they, in fact, that it is difficult not to conclude that the volumes are somehow related. They are the *Contredanses nouvelles* of c1745 ('4a' in table 5.7), the *Premier recueil de contredanses* of c1754 ('6a') and *Les Nouvelles Contre-Danses* ('9'). Table 5.8 sets out the concordances in these sources. The three volumes are identified by the inventory number assigned in table 5.7, and next to this I have indicated the suggested date of the collection (if discernible) and the number of dances it contains. The first column offers a complete inventory of '4a' by title, numbering the dance tunes in the order in which they appear. The second and third columns show where the concordances occur (by item in the volume) in '6a' and '9'.

---

[85]*Mercure galant*, février (1762), 161-162: 'On remarque avec satisfaction que les bals que donne chaque semaine l'Académie Royale de Musique, sont plus nombreux & plus fréquentés cette année que les précédentes, malgré les superbes bals des Ambassadeurs qui peuvent être considérés comme des fêtes publiques, par la magnificence qui y regne, & par le grand nombre des personnes invitées.'

Table 5.8 Concordances among three opera ball contredanse anthologies

4a [c1745] (29 dances)	6a [c1754] (28 dances)	9 [nd] (14 dances)
1. Les Fruits	2	
2. La Volage		
3. La Villageoise	3	12
3a. Tembourin de suitte	4	13
4. Le Martingal (here in g minor)	5 (here in g minor)	6 (here in a minor)
5. Le Mouton noir	6	
6. La Darincourt	7	
7. La Chapelliere	8	8
8. La Belle de nuit	9	11 (minor variants)
9. La Neuvaine	10	
10. La Galante Contre-dance	11	
11. Le Cors-de-Chasse	12	
12. Loyseau Roialle	13	
13. Le Mitron (here G major)	14 (here G major)	3 ('La Mitronne', here E major)
14. La Marseilloise		
15. La Ba Bas		
16. La Mariniere	17	14
17. La decoupure (here d minor)	18 (here d minor)	4 (here a minor)
18. La Nouvelle Provançalle	19	
19. la Jardiniere (here G major)	20 (here G major)	7 (here A major)
20. La Boucquiere		
21. La Seraille		
22. Le Microscope		
23. Le Mediateur	22	
24. La Gacente ou la Latrimouille	23	
25. Cottillion Couleur de Rose	24	
26. Nouveau Cotilon en pot poury	25	
27. Cottillion de la Samaritaine	26	
28. La Magnotte (here D major)	27 (here D major)	1 (here in D but without signature)
29. Cottillion d'Auphin	28	

The relatedness of '4a' and '6a' is made quite explicit in this table. Not only does '6a' share much of the repertoire of '4a'—twenty of its twenty-eight dances—but it duplicates the ordering of the shared repertoire as well. If the dating of these two sources is indeed accurate (or even approximate), it is easy to imagine the compiler of '6a' discarding just a handful of the dances in the '4a' anthology, replacing them with new ones, but otherwise assembling the new collection with the older one as a direct model. The relatedness of '9', on the other hand, is less pronounced. Still, a high proportion of its repertoire—ten of fourteen dances—duplicates material found in both '4a' and '6a'. A significant number of the dances '9' shares with '4a', interestingly, have been modified. Six of the ten dances common to all three sources have either been transposed in '9', or they display other minor variants,[86] suggesting that the compiler of '9' had sources other than '4a' or '6a' as exemplars. The density of the concordances among these collections indicates that many of the contredanse tunes linked to the opera ball became, and remained popular for some time.

Two other series from table 5.7 also share a significant amount of material. Of the sixty-two dance tunes transmitted in the two volumes of series '7' only six do not have a concordance in one of the three volumes of series '8'. But since the latter are sizable anthologies—forty-eight, fifty-two, and fifty-four dances, respectively—the proportion of concordances to the total repertoire in any single volume is not as striking as is the case in the collections of table 5.8. Because just over ninety per cent of the dances of series '7' has a concordance in series '8', on the other hand, it might be argued that the former was compiled from the latter. I believe this is unlikely, because series '8' transmits only a melody part, while the dances in series '7' are provided with a 'basse chiffrée' as well.

Series '8' shares some repertoire with another important source for opera ball dances, this time a choreographic one: Le Répetoire des bals issued by Sieur de La Cuisse, beginning in 1762.[87] (This significant

---

[86]The transposition of 'Le Mitron' (4a.13, and 9.3) to E major is striking. Of the more than a thousand dances I have examined in the anthologies listed in table 5.7, the key of E major occurred only ten other times.

[87]Le répertoire des bals, ou Théorie-pratique des contredanses, décrites d'une manière aisée avec des figures demonstratives pour les pouvoir danser facilement, auxquelles on a ajouté les airs notés. Par sr. de La Cuisse (Paris, 1762 and following). The first three volumes of the de La Cuisse anthology are available on line at the 'An American Ballroom Companion' website of the Library of Congress. The following url gives access to the main bibliographic page for all three volumes: http://memory.loc.gov/musdi/213, in which 'musdi/213' represents the digital identification of the de la Cuisse volumes. Each page of the entire volume must be opened separately (as a 'tif file'), and has a unique url, beginning with the address given above, and followed by an extension '/000X.tif', where X is the number of each page in sequence. Because there are nearly 500 separate pages in the three de la Cuisse volumes (none of them numbered), working through the volume page by page can become tedious.

series of publications will be discussed in greater detail below.) Four of the dance tunes transmitted in '8c' and one in '8b' can be found with a choreography among the first and third *recueils* of *Le Répertoire des bals* (1762 and 1765, respectively).[88] Although de La Cuisse never specifically claimed to his readership that his publications offered contredanses performed at the opera ball, the compiler of series '8' *did* make just such a promise, so it may be concluded that these five dances (and almost certainly many, many more in the de La Cuisse anthologies) were actually performed at the *bal public*.

Before turning my attention to the dancing of the opera ball, however, I want to make one final observation concerning its music. A good proportion of the dance music performed at the opera ball was drawn from theatrical productions, either currently playing or of the recent past. Cahusac made this observation in 1754 with reference to productions at the Opéra:

> Contredanses are made to all the newest tunes that have gaiety. That of *Les fêtes de Polimnie*, the ballet by M. [Jean-Philippe] Rameau performed in 1745 [for which Cahusac had provided the libretto], was so popular that one has hardly put on a ballet ever since without a contredanse. It is with this that the final *divertissement* is usually concluded, in order to send the spectator off with a piece of gaiety.[89]

In fact, there are no contredanses labeled as such in *Les fêtes de Polimnie*, but there are a number of dances throughout, any of which may have been treated to a contredanse choreography. As for placing a contredanse at the conclusion of the ballet, as Cahusac suggests became customary, the evidence is scant, at least in Rameau's oeuvre. The final two items of the concluding *divertissement* in *Les fêtes de Polimnie*, for instance, are menuets. In *Platée*, another Rameau ballet from 1745, however, there *is* a piece labeled 'contredanse' in scene iii of the Prologue, and it found its way into one of the opera ball anthologies listed in table 5.7: 'La Platée' from the *Xe Recueil de contredanses... qui se dansent au bal de l'Opera et de St Cloud* (#5 of '7b'). Again, this ballet concludes not with a contredanse, but with the repetition of a chorus and dance. If Cahusac is to be believed, then, I

---

[88]They are: 'La Victorieuse' (#45 of '8c' and #5 of de La Cuisse/1), 'La Nouvelle Angloise' (#49 of '8c' and #10 of de La Cuisse/1), 'La Dubois' (#52 of '8c' and #16 of de La Cuisse/1), 'La le Franc' (#41 of '8c' and #27 of de La Cuisse/1), and 'La Marseilloise' (#28 of '8b' and #16 of de La Cuisse/3).

[89]*Encyclopédie*, s.v. 'Contredanse': 'On fait des *contredanses* sur tous les airs nouveaux qui ont de la gaïeté. Celle des fêtes de Polimnie, ballet de M. *Rameau*, représenté en 1745, fut si goûtée, qu'on n'a guere fait depuis de ballet sans *contredanse*; c'est par-là qu'on termine pour l'ordinaire le dernier divertissement, afin de renvoyer le spectateur sur un morceau de gaïté.'

must conclude that the custom to which he refers was a convention of *performance* rather than one of compositional design. It may well be, in other words, that following the final chorus and dance of *Platée* the contredanse from the Prologue was reprised as a kind of after-piece.

Sometimes the title of a contredanse was evidently only *suggestive* of an association with a ballet. The one titled 'La Hébé,' for example, from the *Douzieme Recueil...* (#28 of '4g'), has a melody that I have been unable to find in Rameau's *Les Fêtes de l'Hébé* of 1739. Other times the title is positively *misleading*. 'La Ramoneuse Tembourin de Dardanus' (#10 of the *Deuxieme Recueil...*in '6b') is not from Rameau's *tragédie* of 1739, but is actually the '1er Tambourin' from Act I of *Les Fêtes de l'Hébé* (scene v)!

It was not just ballets by Rameau, however, that furnished musical (and likely choreographic) materials for contredanses eventually performed at the opera balls. We have already seen that two contredanses were created from Rousseau's *Le Devin du village*,[90] and eventually included in the collection given as '5a' in table 5.7. Indeed, a choreography for one of these, the 'Allemande,' is preserved in the third *recueil* of the *Répertoire des bals*. The four engraved plates that transmit this choreography are reproduced below, pp. 152-55. Productions in other Parisian theatres also furnished materials for the ever-growing repertoire of contredanses performed in public balls, at the Opéra and elsewhere. The de La Cuisse publications make frequent references to theatrical sources for many of the contredanses transmitted in them. For example, 'La Bionni' from the first volume of the *Répertoire des bals* was first performed, de La Cuisse informs us, in a pantomime ballet entitled *Wauxhall Hollandois* produced at the Théâtre Italien on 28 November 1761. Its choreography was modified slightly for performance as a ballroom contredanse.[91] Another contredanse from the second *recueil* (1763) has the following on its title page (See p. 156):

[90]See n82, above.

[91]This contredanse was prepared for publication before the first volume of the *Répertoire des bals* went into production, and along with one other dance in the collection was treated to a special presentation. All the figures of the dance are depicted in a beautifully engraved illustration, with verbal instructions given above them, and the corresponding music underneath. Guilcher, *La Contredanse*, 99, claims the engravings were by Saint-Aubin. Information on the origins of the dance, and its slight modification is given in a 'Remarque sur cette Contredanse.' The entire dance as presented by de La Cuisse is reproduced in ibid., plate bound between pages 88 and 89.

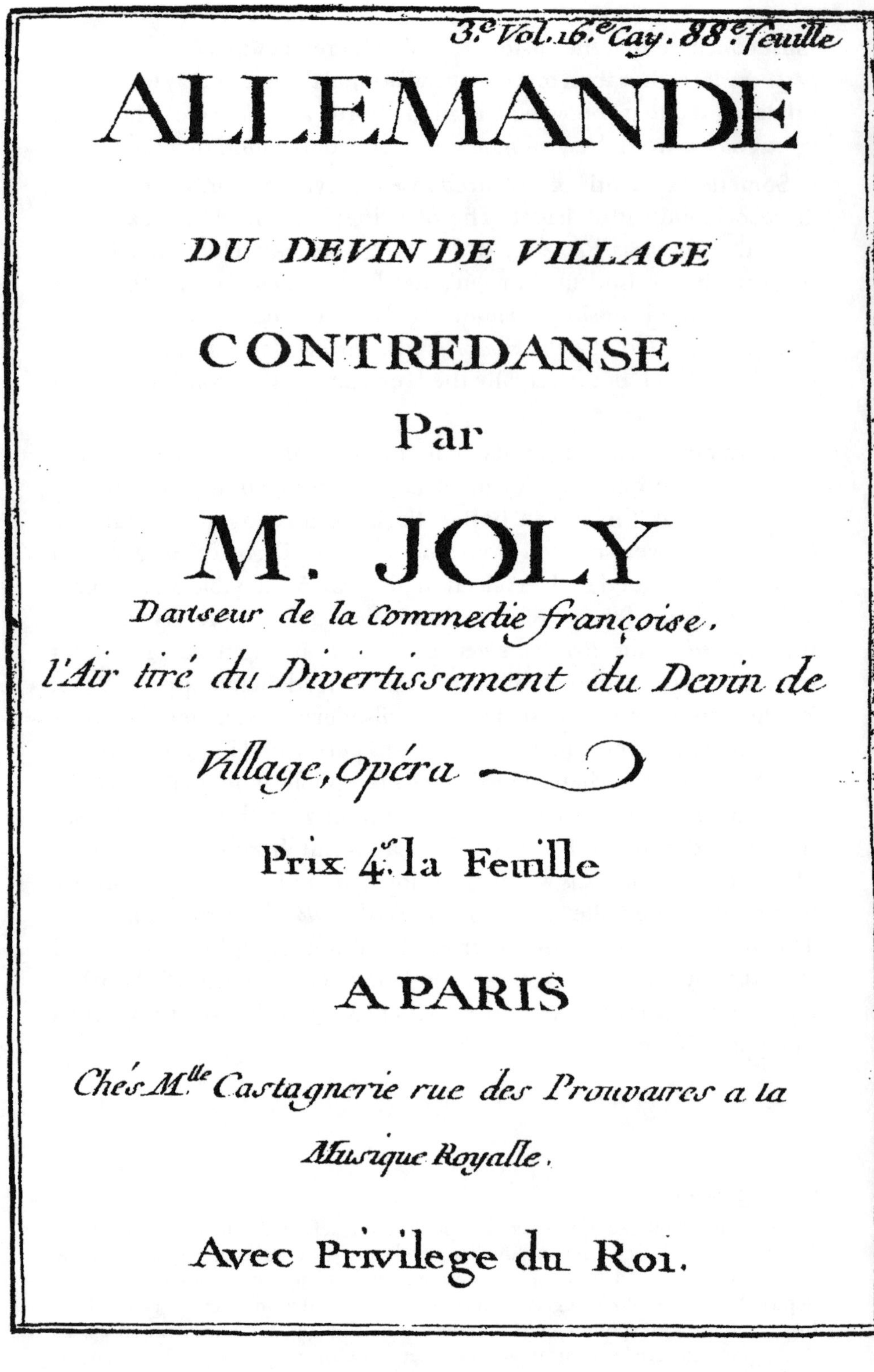

3.e Vol. 16.e Cay. 88.e feuille

ALLEMANDE

DU DEVIN DE VILLAGE

CONTREDANSE

Par

M. JOLY

Danseur de la Commedie françoise.

l'Air tiré du Divertissement du Devin de Village, Opéra

Prix 4.s la Feuille

A PARIS

Chés M.lle Castagnerie rue des Prouvaires a la Musique Royalle.

Avec Privilege du Roi.

Illustration 5, 4 plates. 'L'Allemande' from De la Cuisse, *Le Répertoire des bals*, vol. 3, (Paris, 1765).

ALLEMANDE

DESCRIPTION
Des Figures de la Contredanse

Cette Contredanse doit etre dansee toute en pas d'Allemande. Elle est tres jolie et nulement difficille.

1º Le Rond ordinaire.

2º Les 4 Dames vont en pirouettant au milieu se présenter
les mains en rond.

3º Dont elles font un demi tour, et presentent le bras
droit au Cavalier des places vis a vis avec qui ....

4º Elles tournent un tour d'allemande à la fin de la quel-
le les Cavaliers les fonts pirouetter.

5º
6º } Les Cavaliers, la même chose que les Dammes c'est
a dire pirouettent et demi tour de rond, mais en place de l'Allemande ils donnent ....

7º
8º
9º } La main droite a leur figurante, tournent un demi tour,
presente le bras gauche à la Dame du coin a droite,
tournent un tour d'Allemande, et redonnent la main
droite, à leur figurante pour rentrer a leur place; ce qui
forme une espece de petite chaine a trois

10º Alors deux figurans font a leur volonté, un pas de deux
au milieu avec quelques passes et pirouettes allemandes,
pendant toutes les vingt mesures du mineur les autres
restent imobilles a leur places

11º Puis tous font un demi tour de course jusques a leur places

12º La Main et au tour suivant ce sera deux autres figurans qui feront le pas de deux et ainsi de tour en tour les
uns après les autres.

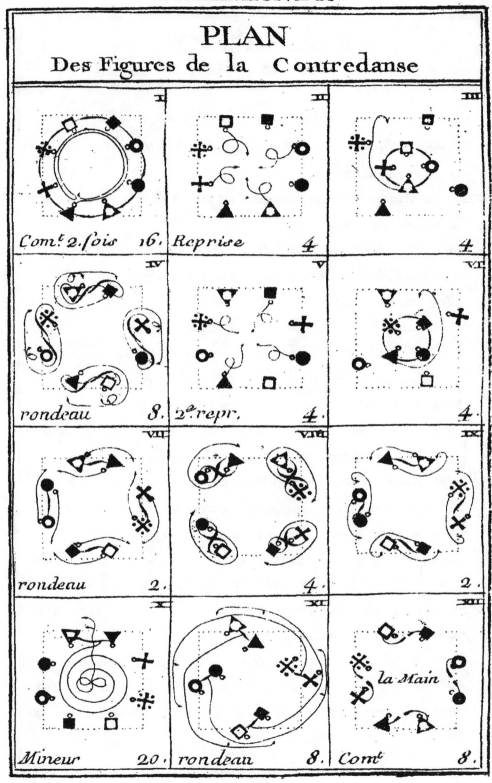

PLAN
Des Figures de la Contredanse

I — Com.^t 2. fois   16.
II — Reprise   4
III — 4
IV — rondeau   8.
V — 2e repr.   4.
VI — 4.
VII — rondeau   2.
VIII — 4.
IX — 2.
X — Mineur   20.
XI — rondeau   8.
XII — Com.^t   8.

la Main

ALLEMANDE
Contredanse

en rondeau

LES QUADRILLES
ou
Contredanses extraites
du Divertissement du Bal dans le 5ᵉ. Acte du
Bourgeois-Gentil-homme, Comédie

PAR Mᴿ. DESHAYES

Mᵗʳᵉ. des Balets du Théâtre françois,
la Musique, tirée du même divertissement
par Mʳ. Gervaise Musicien

Whether either of these dances was ever performed at the opera ball I cannot say, but it is clear that a good deal of the contredanse repertoire had origins in theatrical productions, and that these furnished not only music, but choreograhies as well.

• • • • •

Dances performed at the *bal de l'Opera*, unlike the music, were never anthologized in dedicated publications of the eighteenth century. In fact the publication of choreographies of any kind in Paris, let alone those that might be associated directly or indirectly with the public ball, are remarkably scarce between the early 1720s and the early 1760s. From the musical sources surveyed above, however, it seems fairly certain that in the first three decades or so of the *bal public*'s history (1716 –c1745) a judicious mixture of menuets and contredanses formed the principal repertoire danced at balls, and that thereafter contredanses became predominant. In the absence of any other hard evidence, the eyewitness account of dances performed at the opera ball during one carnival season (preserved in the *Mercure galant* of February 27, cited earlier) deserves closer inspection.

The *Mercure* reported, it will be recalled, that

Besides menuets for two and for four, many other special dances were performed, [as well as] a good many contredanses, in which eight, twelve, and up to sixteen persons dance together with much vivacity and a great variety of steps and *attitudes*.[92]

[92]*Mercure galant*, février (1727), 392-393: 'On y a dansé, outre les Menuets à deux & à quatre, plusieurs autres danses particulières, quantité de contre-danses, dans lesquelles, huit, douze & jusqu'à seize personnes dansent ensemble avec beaucoup de vivacité, & une extrême varieté de pas & d'attitudes.'

This is the only evidence I have discovered stating explicitly that couple dances (here 'menuets à deux') were performed at the opera ball, but it remains unclear if they were danced one couple at a time (as was the case in the formal ball). That 'menuets à deux' and 'à quatre' were danced is hardly surprising. Not only were they a staple of the ballroom in general, as we have already seen, but they also possessed a standard choreography (subject to some variation and ornamentation, to be sure) that fit any menuet music.

In the menuet à deux described by Pierre Rameau in 1725, after an opening reverence performed to music, the couple begin the dance facing each other, and then make a series of 'Z' figures, maintaining eye contact throughout. Since each sideways and each crossing path in the 'Z' figure normally took two menuet steps, and each menuet step occupied two measures of music, the music needed to be organized in phrases of an even number of measures, typically six, eight, twelve, or sixteen. Dancing the 'Z' figure served as a frame for the presentation of right and then left hands during the crossing path. In these the dancers circled each other while holding hands. The 'Z' figure is resumed before the dancers offer each other both hands on a final crossing path that serves as a climax to the dance.[93]

On the surface the menuet à deux was ideally suited to the public ball. Eighteenth century instructions on its performance make it quite clear that the number of 'Z' figures to be performed before and after the presentation of right and left hands was quite flexible. They admit, moreover, of variants in the 'Z' figures that accommodated more than just two menuet steps in any of the sideways or crossing paths. The number of steps used in the circling figures for the presentation of hands was also a discretionary matter. In other words, beginning the dance (or any of the subsequent 'Z' and hand presentation figures) precisely at the opening of a musical phrase was not required. Indeed, the dancing masters praised those whose skill permitted them *not* to make the menuet's patterns coincide with the phrase structure of the accompanying music. Kellom Tomlinson, for example, noted in 1735 that it was preferable to commence the opening 'Z' figure without waiting for the beginning of a musical phrase.

> Instead of standing to wait the Close or Ending of a Strain of the Tune, begin upon the first Time that offers [itself], in that it is much more genteel and shows the Dancer's Capacity and Ear in distinguishing of the Time, and from thence begets himself a good Opinion from the Beholders, who are apt to judge favourably of the fol-

[93]A detailed and informative analysis of Rameau's menuet is given in Wendy Hilton, *Dance and Music of Court and Theatre*, 291-308.

lowing Part of his Performance; whereas the attending the concluding or finishing of a Strain has the contrary Effect.[94]

The danced menuet, in summary, was of variable length, it could begin with something other than the opening phrase of music, and it could even conclude at any point. Tomlinson contended that the menuet:

> is no more than a voluntary or extemporary Piece of Performance... there is no limited Rule as to its Length or Shortness, or in Relation to the Time of the Tune, since it may begin upon any [part of a phrase that is the first of a two-measure unit] that offers [itself], as well within [that is, in the middle of] a Strain as upon the first Note or commencing thereof. It is the very same with Respect to its ending, for it matters not whether it breaks off upon the End of the first Strain of the Tune, the second, or in the Middle of either of them...[95]

Because the menuet was so flexible, therefore, I can imagine a couple deciding to begin a menuet at the opera ball well after the accompanying music had started. The dancers were at liberty, as well, to complete their menuets when it suited them. It does not seem probable that couples felt obliged to perform the danced reverences normally encountered before and after the menuet at the formal ball. These reverences were directed to the 'presence'—indeed, they were the only moments in the menuet when the attention of the dancers was not focused intently on each other—but since there was no 'presence' at an opera ball, performing this stylized bow surely would have been rather pointless.

I hinted above that it was a possibility that more than one couple danced menuets at the same time at the opera ball. While this possibility cannot be ruled out of the question, I believe it is a very remote one. The principal difficulty, it seems to me, unless all the participating couples somehow organized themselves to finish at the same time, would have confronted the musicians, who would certainly have had difficulty knowing when and how to bring the menuet to a conclusion. New couples joining in while others were bringing their dance to a close would have created the real potential for an exceedingly long menuet! The great flexibility in the menuet that Tomlinson, among others, described did *not* include the possibility that the music might stop *before* a couple had completed the presentation of both hands. So

[94]Kellom Tomlinson, *The Art of Dancing Explained by Reading and Figures* (London, 1735); reprint ed. (London, 1970), 124.

[95]ibid., 137.

how could the dance ever have been concluded if new couples kept deciding to join in?

Menuets à deux danced by several couples at once seem a remote possibility, finally, because the dance had already developed derivative types that *did* accommodate more than a single couple. In Pemberton's *An Essay for the further Improvement of Dancing* (London, 1711), for example, menuets for four, five, six, eight, and twelve performers (unusually, all women in this publication) are notated. Pemberton remarked that they were suitable for 'Entertainment[s] of Publick Dancings [sic].'[96] The 'menuet à quatre' was dominant among these menuet derivatives in Paris, however, and the account in the *Mercure* of 1727 makes specific reference to its performance at the public ball (see above, n92).

There is every reason to believe that the menuet à quatre offered dancers almost as much flexibility in performance as did the menuet à deux. By 1706, when Feuillet issued his *Vme Recüeil de danses de bal pour l'année 1707* the menuet à quatre was already 'so much in vogue that no assembly is formed where it is not danced.'[97] The menuet for two couples that he notates in this collection was evidently one that had already established itself as a ballroom standard. It unfolds in a sequence of figures that seemingly could be varied—lengthened, shortened, or ornamented—at the discretion of the dancers. Guilcher has observed that the dance was in every respect like a contredanse insofar as its figures were concerned.[98] Although Feuillet's notation has it begin and end with the music, the menuet à quatre is not really a figured dance, because its choreography could work effectively with *any* menuet music. And, as was the case with the menuet à deux, Feuillet's menuet à quatre, it seems, could be started and concluded successfully *anywhere* in the accompanying music.[99]

Why, then, did the menuet all but disappear from anthologies of opera ball music after about 1745 (see above, n75 and n76)? Of all dances it was certainly the one best suited to a spontaneous decision to dance at

[96]See Carol Marsh, 'French Court Dance in England, 1706-1740. A Study of the Sources,' PhD dissertation (The City University of New York, 1985), 196-200.

[97]Raoul Auger Feuillet, *Vme Recüeil de danses de bal pour l'année 1707*, preliminary material: 'Le Menuet a quatre est si en vogue qu'il ne se fait aucune assemblée où il ne soit dansé.'

[98]*La Contredanse*, 84. Marsh makes much the same observation about country dance figures in Pemberton's *For the further Improvement of Dancing* in her 'French Court Dance in England,' 200.

[99]This is in contrast to the 'Menuet a quatre' by Louis Pécourt included in the *Nouveau Recüeil de dance de bal et celle de ballet* (Paris, c1713) issued by Gaudrau. See Little, and Marsh, *La Danse Noble*, inventory number 5560. Pécourt's choreography is much more clearly aligned with its accompanying music.

the opera ball, requiring neither special preparation nor careful coordination with the accompanying music. I can only guess that the menuet fell from grace at the *bal public* first, because it was the spectator dance *par excellence*, and second, because it could not accommodate many dancers. These two points are related, but I will first address the second. It is not an anachronistic imposition of a more recent set of values to suggest that at gatherings such as the opera ball in the mid-eighteenth century accommodating more dancers was a concern. Cahusac made exactly this point in his article on the contredanse in the *Encyclopédie* in 1754. After observing that 'different contredanses are danced at the *bal de l'Opéra* at the two ends of the room' (a point to which I will return), he goes on to claim:

> At balls or at assemblies one hardly [ever] executes [couple dances such as] 'La Bretagne,' 'l'Allemande,' [or] 'La Mariée' etc., which were formerly fashionable. The contredanse is more gay, it accommodates greater numbers, and its execution is easy. It is hardly surprising that it has prevailed over all the others.[100]

The three couple dances he specifies in this passage were all choreographed for the ballroom by Pécourt in the early eighteenth century. All enjoyed a long-lived popularity, and all were re-issued in manuscript and print sources many times in the course of the century.[101] Cahusac could easily have added the menuet à deux to these three couple dances to make his point about the contredanse accommodating more dancers, but he could *not* claim that the menuet was a dance that was '*formerly* fashionable' (as he could for the Pécourt choreographies), because the menuet was still an important fixture of the formal ballroom in the 1750s.[102] At the opera ball of that time, on the other hand, couple dances of any kind—I would argue including the menuet—had become less desirable than contredanses. Cahusac, at any rate, does not claim that '*along with the menuet* the contredanse prevailed over all the others,' only that 'it' [the contredanse] had done so.

---

[100]*Encyclopédie*, s.v. 'Contredanse': 'Au bal de l'Opera on danse dans les deux bouts de la salle des *contredanses* différentes. On n'exécute guere dans les bals ni dans les assemblées, la Bretagne, l'Allemande, la Mariée, &c.qui étoient autrefois à la mode. La *contredanse* est plus gaie; elle occupe plus de monde, & l'exécution en est aisée: il n'est pas étonnant qu'elle ait prévalu sur toutes les autres.'

[101]See inventory items 1200 (l'Allemande), 1620 (La Bretagne), and 5360 (La Mariée) in Little, and Marsh, *La Danse Noble*.

[102]Indeed, new menuet choreographies were issued or re-issued in the 1760s, and even as late as the 1780s and 90s. See, for example, the following inventory items in ibid.: 5520, 5640, 5660, 5680, 5740.

As the principal couple dance at formal balls throughout much of the eighteenth century, the menuet accumulated status as the single most important dance to be mastered by those who aspired to acceptance in genteel circles. It had the ability to impart distinction upon those who danced it well, or to compromise the social standing of those who did not. The well-known advice of Lord Chesterfield (1694-1773), conveyed in a letter to his son, gives compelling testimony to the importance of dancing menuets well.

> As you will be often under the necessity of dancing a minuet, I would have you dance it very well. Remember that the graceful motion of the arms, the giving of your hand, and the putting on and pulling off your hat genteelly are the material parts of a gentleman's dancing. But the greatest advantage of dancing well is that it necessarily teaches you to present yourself, to sit, stand and walk genteelly; all of which are of real importance to a man of fashion.[103]

In order for the menuet to impart distinction upon those who danced it, of course, it had to be *observed* approvingly by those looking on. Moreover, when it *was* observed at gatherings in polite society, it was scrutinized rather critically (in the broadest sense) by individuals who themselves knew all the details of a menuet's elegant performance, and all the pitfalls of a performance that fell short of the mark.

The performativity of the eighteenth century ballroom menuet, in other words, engaged onlookers every bit as much as dancers. I argued in the last chapter, however, that dancing at the opera ball was not the central focus of attention that it was in more formal social gatherings. I believe this feature was a critical force in the decline of the menuet at the *bal public*. Deprived of attentive observers, the menuet would have lost a critical component in its execution, and therefore some of its very essence. Even if danced well, it would have been no more meaningful than a polished and eloquent oration delivered to an audience that was not listening. Such a compromise to the menuet's performativity, in conjunction with a growing desirability to accommodate more individuals on the dance floor at the same time, sealed the fate of the ballroom menuet at the public ball. Its decline must have been quite speedy. In 1727 they were danced there, as we have seen, and anthologies of menuet music with opera ball connections

---

[103]Cited in Selma Jeanne Cohen, *et al, International Encyclopedia of Dance* (New York, Oxford, 1998), s.v. 'Minuet' by Wendy Hilton. Hilton goes on to quote a passage from the journal of the duchess of Marlborough that demonstrates the negative consequences of flawed menuet performances: 'I think Sir S. Garth is the most honest and compassionate, but after the minuets which I have seen him dance... I can't help thinking that hee may sometimes bee in the wrong.'

were still being issued. After c1745, however, such anthologies (with the one exception given in n75) were no longer prepared, even though collections of menuets with no apparent opera ball connection remained popular. If menuets were still danced at the *bal public* after c1745, then Parisian publishers—quite unaccountably—must have become disinterested in capturing such a market. In contrast, contredanse anthologies with title pages that linked their contents to the public ball were issued on an ongoing basis by Parisian publishers for the remainder of the century (as table 5.7 suggests). This contrast is striking enough to make me confident that my conclusions about the decline of the menuet at the *bal public* are probably correct.[104] Because menuet music for the opera ball had disappeared from the marketplace by mid-century, moreover, it seems very likely that the menuet à quatre suffered the same fate as its couple dance parent at approximately the same time.

Menuets, therefore, formed an important portion of the opera ball's repertoire of dances, but only for the first three decades or so of its history. As for other dances performed there, the observer for the *Mercure*, in his report on opera balls in the 1727 carnival season, also witnessed what he termed 'plusieurs autres danses particulières' (again, see n92). What 'other special dances' might he have been referring to? Although other interpretations are possible, it seems probable that this is a reference to dances performed either as a part of, or detached from, the masquerades that were reported to have adorned opera balls near the end of that season: 'the public balls given in the theatre of the Opéra have been rendered more pleasing by diverse masquerades introduced there at the conclusion of carnival, and these have given much pleasure.'[105] One nineteenth-century journalist's brief history of the opera ball reported (without citing a source) that such masquerades were first introduced in 1724 by dancers from the Opéra 'to execute *danses de caractère* and to lend to these balls the attractions of a spectacle.'[106] I believe that this may be a reference to an extraordinary ball that occurred over the evening of 24-25 August 1724, reported in

---

[104]My conclusion, however, cannot be made without qualification. In *bals payants* other than those of the opera, menuets may well have remained quite popular. My guess is that they remained popular principally because the attendance at such affairs was never as large as that of the opera balls, so menuets could indeed be observed. At any rate, as we saw in chapter one, Charles Burney observed 'a very elegant room, in which the company dance *minuets, allemandes, cotillions,* and *contre danses*' in 1770, when he visited the Waux-hall d'hiver in Paris. See chapter one, n107.

[105]See n71, above.

[106]E. M. deLyden, Untitled newspaper article, from the 'Collection Rondel,' *Bibliothèque de l'Arsenal*, R°13033: 'pour former des mascarades plaisantes, pour executer des danses de caractère et donner à ces bals les attraits du spectacle.'

the *Mercure* as having been introduced by 'a little *divertissement*, entitled *Le Bal des dieux*,' that was 'followed by an ordinary ball at which there was a very large and attractive crowd.'[107] (This ball was mentioned briefly in chapter one: see n75.) It is not clear, however, if the masquerades put on in 1727 were performed by dancers from the Opera, or by non-professionals who had prepared them in advance. If they *were* put on by non-professionals, then they would have had to prepare music for the orchestra, and have it copied and distributed to the players before the event, at best an unlikely circumstance, but certainly not impossible.

I do not believe that references to *divertissements* and masquerades in the 1720s reflect a *normal* occurrence at the opera ball, however. I think, rather, that balls with prepared masquerades were somewhat exceptional events that made an appearance only occasionally (and more often than not *outside* the normal opera ball season). In at least three seasons from the late 1750s and early 1760s, nevertheless, opera balls with prepared entertainments were indeed mounted as a substitution for the standard 'benefit evenings' of the *Académie Royale de Musique*. These benefits (usually performances of highlights of the most popular productions of the season just passed) were put on prior to the Easter closure, and the proceeds of these gala performances went to the personnel of the *Académie*. But in April 1760 the *Mercure* reported that 'for the *capitation* [benefit] of the actors [this year] three balls will be given, each preceded by a concert, as was done last year. The first of these balls will be given on Tuesday, 15 April, the day of the reopening [of the theatre].'[108] In 1761 the more usual format for the benefit was resumed.[109] In 1763, however, balls were once more offered up.

> The [benefit prior to the] closure of the theatre which will take place this year on Saturday, 19 March [will be] for the profit of the *Académie*, and not for the actors, as has been the custom. The latter have decided that it would be more profitable to the benefit evening, commonly called [the] *capitation*, to put on some balls after the re-open-

---

[107]*Mercure galant*, août (1724), 1811: 'La nuit du 24. au 25. Aoust il y eut sur le Theatre de l'Opera un petit divertissement, intitulé *le Bal des Dieux*, qui fut suivi d'un Bal ordinaire, où il y eut une très-belle & très-nombreuse assemblée.'

[108]*Mercure galant*, avril (1760), 197: 'On donnera pour la Capitation des Acteurs, trois Bals, précédés chacun d'un Concert, comme on a fait l'année derniere. Le premier de ces Bals sera donné le Mardi 15 Avril, jour de la rentrée.'

[109]See *Mercure galant*, février (1761), 213-215.

ing [of the theatre]. They have planned the first of these for the twelfth of the present month of April.[110]

It is a testimonial to the consistent attractiveness and popularity of the opera ball (and perhaps less than favourable commentary on the lacklustre offerings of the Opera in 1759, 1760, and 1763) that the singers and dancers of the *Académie Royale de Musique* felt more confident about generating decent benefit earnings through balls rather than gala evenings of operatic highlights in those years. These balls almost certainly featured prepared pieces, likely with what had been termed 'plusieurs danses particulières' in 1727. There is no evidence that exceptional opera balls were ever mounted as benefits before or after the three years discussed above; neither have I found any other mention of masquerade-like entertainments adorning opera balls beyond the those of August 1724, and February 1727 (discussed in the foregoing paragraphs), and the ball of June 1721 at which the 'Prologue' to Lully's *Bellérophon* was performed (discussed in chapter one, pp.16-17). When 'special dances' were performed from time to time at the opera ball, I believe they were most probably theatrical choreographies performed by professionals.

The last dances described in the *Mercure*'s account of 1727 were contredanses, and it is to this dance type that I will finally turn my attention. Our eye-witness observed 'a good many contredanses, in which eight, twelve, and up to sixteen persons dance together with much vivacity and a great variety of steps and *attitudes*.' He went on to name several of the contredanses that were performed at the opera ball that carnival season (see n71, above). Since this description allows for a variable number of couples—from eight to sixteen dancers—it is certain that at least some of the dances described here (and perhaps even *all* of them) were *longways* contredanses. Two of the dances specified, moreover—'Jeanne qui saute' and 'l[a Bonne] Amitié'—have surviving choreographies (of the longways variety) in the first printed collection of contredanses to be issued in France (in 1706).[111] The longways contredanses were the first type of the family to have been imported into France from England in the mid-1680s, and they quickly became so popular that by 1706 Feuillet declared that 'they constitute the largest part of the diversions at assemblies where one dances.'[112]

[110]*Mercure galant*, avril (1763), 178: '...la clôture de son Théâtre, laquelle s'est fait cette année, le samedi 19 mars, pour le compte de l'Académie, & non pour les Acteurs, comme il étoit d'usage. Ceux-ci ont pensé qu'il seroit plus utile au produit du *Bene-fit* vulgairement nommé *Capitation*, de donner quelques Bals à la rentrée; ils ont indiqué le premier pour le 12 du présent mois d'Avril.'

[111]Raoul-Auger Feuillet, *Recüeil de contredances mises en Choregraphie*.

[112]ibid., unpaginated preliminary material [p.i]:'En effet elles font presentement la plus grande partie des divertissemens des assemblée[s] ou l'on danse.'

In the longways contredanse couples arranged themselves in a column, with the gentlemen on the left and the ladies on the right. The very basic description that follows makes use of some of the strategies employed by Feuillet in his 1706 account of the conduct of the dance. Like Feuillet, I will assume a contredanse 'set' (all of the dancers taking part organized in their columns) of just four couples, labelled A, B, C, D.

	Top of the Set	
	(Gentlemen)	(Ladies)
position 1	A	A
position 2	B	B
position 3	C	C
position 4	D	D
	Bottom of the Set	

Each contredanse was composed, usually, of from four to eight choreographed figures that were repeated in sequence over and over. With each repetition of a complete sequence of figures, a couple moved *down* one position in the set, and advanced the couple that had been below *up* one position. A couple that is moving *down* the set is an active one; those moving *up* the set are not active. Couple A initiated the first figure—a crossing pattern, for example—and continued through all the remaining figures of the contredanse. While it often happened that one or more of these figures engaged couple B, only couple A was considered 'active.' Indeed, couples C and D usually did nothing at all at the start of the dance. By the time couple A had completed all the figures of the contredanse, it had moved down to position 2 in the column, while couple B had advanced to position 1. (Although couple B was now at the top of the set, it was not yet active: see below.) Couple A then repeated all the dance's figures a second time, this time displacing couple C, who advanced from position 3 to position 2. Couple A repeated the entire sequence of figures as many times as it took to move to the end position in the column (in this case to position

4), at which point it became *in*active. In fact, it would never again be an active couple during the contredanse, but it would be advanced up the set again, one position at a time, as new active couples moved down it. Feuillet insisted that each couple must have the opportunity of moving from the top to the bottom position in the set.[113] That effectively meant that the contredanse could not conclude until couple A once more reached position 1, at the top of the column, and all the other couples had returned to their original starting positions.

What of the other couples? The partners in each couple of a longways contredanse, since they advanced a position every time an active couple moved down the set, eventually found themselves moved to position 1. It was only *after* this position was reached that a couple became an active one, and then had its opportunity to work down the column, just as the original couple had done. Feuillet makes it clear, however, that there was no need for one active couple to move all the way from the top to the bottom of the set before a second active couple could begin. He advised:

> A couple that has arrived at the top position [in the set] must not begin to dance until the couple that has preceded it has first completed two repetitions [of the complete sequence of figures], as from A to C [that is, from position 1 to position 3].[114]

By the third occurrence of a complete sequence of the figures in a contredanse performed by eight persons, in other words, there were *two* active couples: couple A, now dancing in position 3, and couple B, dancing in position 1. By the fourth occurrence there was just one active couple again (couple B, now dancing in position 2), because couple A had reached position 4, and had become inactive. In a set made up of just four couples there could never be more than two active couples at a time. In a set of six, however, there could be a maximum of three of them, and in one of eight, as many as four active couples were possible.

Because it is one of the dances mentioned in the *Mercure*'s account of 1727, and because it is a rather straightforward longways contredanse, I reproduce below Feuillet's 1706 rendering of 'La bonne amitié.' The dance has just four figures, and is accompanied by an

---

[113]ibid., [p.xxii]: 'quand un couple a commence à danser, il ne discontinüe point qu'il ne soit déscendu jusque au 1er [sic] rang, comme depuis A jusque à D.'

[114]ibid.: 'Qu'un couple qui a ateint le 1er rang ne doit point commencer à danser jusqu'à ce que celui qui le précède n'aye fait auparavant deux répétitions comme depuis A jusqu'à C.'

attractive gavotte-like tune in G major, set out in the following way: a four bar opening phrase that is repeated (for figures 1 and 2 of the contredanse), and an eight bar phrase that is played only once (to accompany figures 3 and 4). In the first figure the gentleman and lady (couple A of my general scheme, above) offer right hands to each other in measure one, left hands in measure two. They then circle each other in a clockwise direction for two measures, holding both hands, and finish on the opposite side of the column to which they began. This entire pattern is repeated in figure two, but the hand taking and circling by couple A are now done with the gentleman and lady of couple B. By the end of the second figure, as a result, couple A has already moved to position 2, and couple B has advanced to position 1. In figure three the gentlemen and ladies of both couples A and B (once more facing across the column) advance towards each other for two measures, and then retreat for two measures. Curiously, at the end of this figure there is an indication for the two couples (gentleman A and lady B, lady A and gentleman B) to release hands. I believe this properly belongs to the end of figure 2 (or the start of figure 3), because the two-handed circling of figure 2 needs to be concluded with the same dropping of hands and ninety degree turn in direction that completed figure 1. In the fourth figure, finally, the gentleman and lady of couple A take four measures to make a crossing pattern that moves them around the outside of the lady and gentleman respectively of couple B. This figure returns them not only to position 2 but also to the 'correct' side of the column, preparing them to begin their second complete set of the dance's four figures.

Even when danced by just four couples a longways contredanse (such as 'La bonne amitié') was repetitious: it took nine occurences of the complete sequence of figures for the dance to run its course.[115] If performed by a set of six couples it took fifteen iterations, or if by eight, fully twenty-one! The accompanying music was even more repetitive, because it almost always had its own internal repeat schemes that were compounded by repetitions of the entire tune (one for every occurrence of a complete set of the dance's figures). The repetitive nature of the longways contredanse seems not to have been regarded as a liability by practioners of the earlier eighteenth century. By 1762, on the other hand, de La Cuisse expressed a preference for the

[115]Although couple A returns to position 1 by the end of the seventh repetition, and couple B to position 2 by the end of the eighth, still one more repetition is required to return couples C and D to their original starting positions. During these repetitions couples A and B presumably remain still (as couples C and D at the beginning of the dance), although Feuillet offers no clarification on this point. Appendix 5 represents graphically the progress of all couples in contredanse sets of four, six, and eight couples. This progression remains the same no matter how many figures are involved.

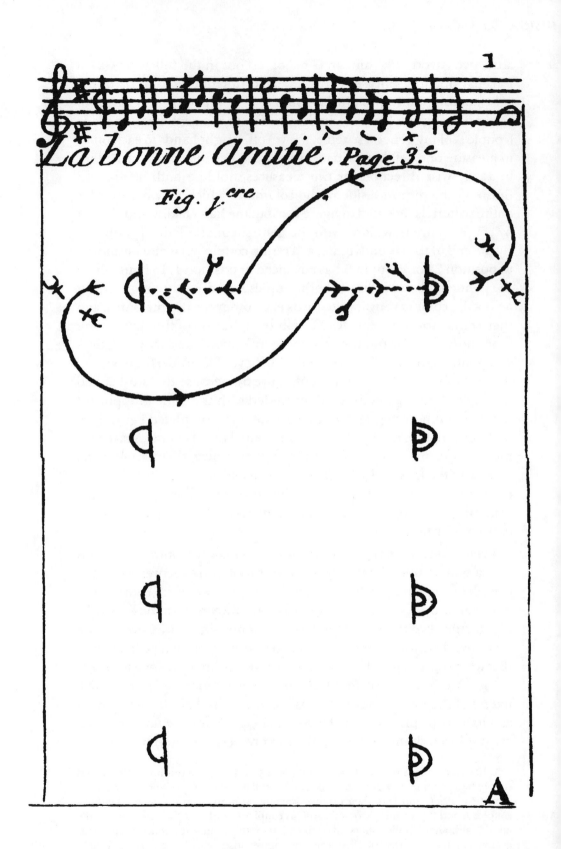

Illustration 6, 4 plates: 'La bonne amitié' from Feuillet's *Recueil de contredanses*, (Paris, 1706).]

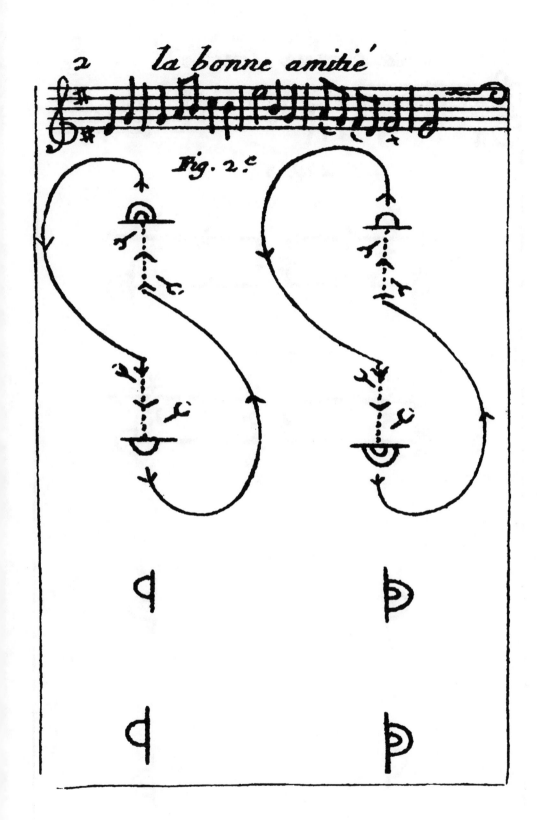

la bonne amitié

Fig. 2.ᵉ

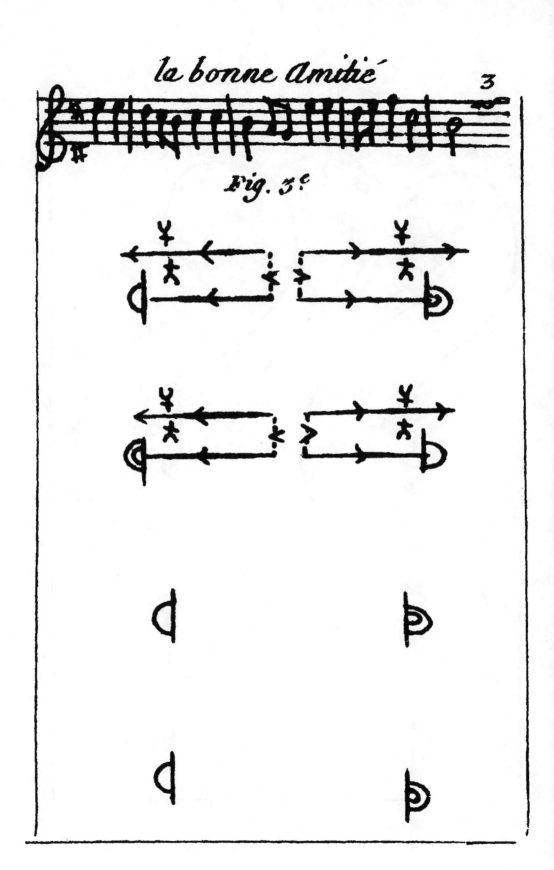

Fig. 3.ᵉ

la bonne Amitié.

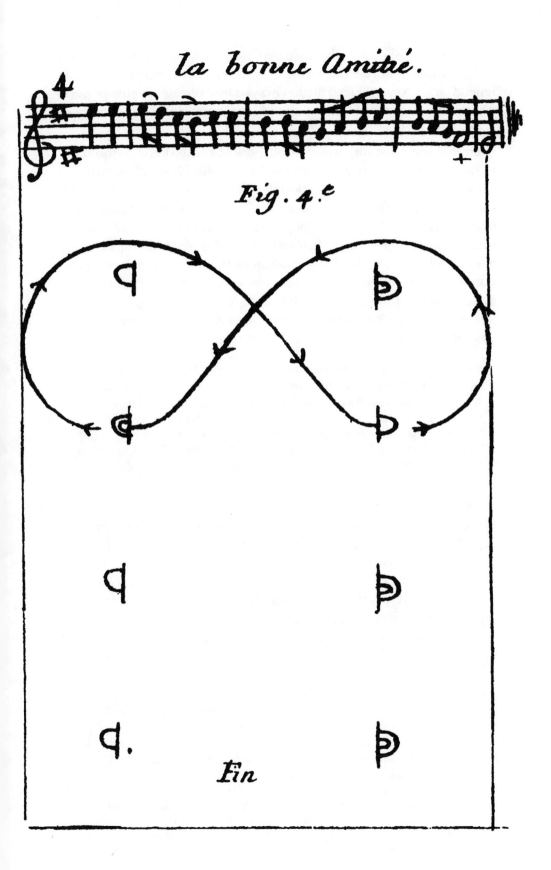

Fig. 4.ᵉ

Fin

contredanse à la française (to be discussed presently), because the longways variety, 'while good, becomes boring in the end, as a result of too much repetition.'[116] Nevertheless, the longways dance remained quite popular (though it was certainly less frequently encountered) even in the later eighteenth century.

One of the most important publishers of contredanse anthologies in Paris in this later period, Monsieur Landrin (fl. 1760-1785), included among his many works a collection devoted exclusively to the longways contredanse, by that time typically referred to as the 'anglaise.' His undated *Receuil Danglaise*[117] [sic] contains nine of them, for each of which a tune, a set of verbal instructions on the steps and figures to be made, and a schematic representation of those figures are provided. Landrin also found it useful to provide a very brief description of the general conduct of this type of dance, suggesting, perhaps, that it was not as generally well known as it had been earlier in the century. The 'Avertisement pour danser les Anglaise' relates:

> All Anglaises are danced the same way. At the start the first couple begins a figure, and continues to the end of the set, which can have as many persons as desired, provided they are all in couples. And as soon as two couples have been passed, those who have reached first position begin the same figures as the others [before them had done], until the last couple [also has danced these figures]. The Anglaise is finished when the first couple has returned to its [original] position.[118]

Landrin's prescriptions are entirely consistent with those offered by Feuillet in 1706, except on one significant detail. While Feuillet expected *everyone* to return to her or his original position before the contredanse was complete, Landrin regarded it as concluded once the first couple had returned to the top of the set. This modification, of course, resulted in a (not inconsiderable) reduction in the number of repetitions required to finish the dance. In a set of four couples, for example, just seven iterations (instead of the nine required by Feuillet) sufficed; in a set of six couples, eleven instead of fifteen; and in a set of

---

[116]*Le répertoire des bals*, Préface, 5: '...anciennes Contredanses, qui quoique bonnes ennuyent à la fin par une trop frequente repetition...'

[117]*Receuil DANGLAISE arrangees avec leurs traits. telle quels se danse ché la Reine. Mis au jour par M' Landrin, M^{tre} de danse et compositeur des traits des Contre-danse* (Paris, nd).

[118]ibid., [2]-3: 'Toutes les anglaises se dansent de même. Dabord le premier Couple commence la figure et continue jusquau bout de la danse, qui peut être autant de personnes que lon le desire pourvu que les Couple soit Complet, et sitot quil y a deux Couple depassez, ceux qui tienent la place des premiers commencent de même la Figures que les autres, ce qui continue jus quau dernier. Langlaise est finie lors que les premiers sont a leurs Place.'

eight couples, fifteen instead of twenty-one. (Because the number of required repetitions is far from self-evident, readers may find the 'progression' charts of longways sets offered in Appendix 5 useful to consult.) This economy of process, however, also significantly diminished the participation of couples at the bottom end of the set as *active* members in the contredanse. The bottom couple in any sized contredanse set, in fact, would have just one opportunity to perform a single, complete set of the figures before the contredanse was deemed by Landrin to have concluded.

But even though Landrin (and others, as well) regarded the modified longways contredanse as still viable in the second half of the eighteenth century, the *contredanse à la française* was most certainly the dominant type in Paris by that time. Just when the *à la française* variety assumed this dominant position has been addressed competently by Jean-Michel Guilcher.[119] Guilcher argued that many features characteristic of this type of contredanse were already in place in the *cotillon* of the early eighteenth century and, moreover, that by the second half of the century the two terms (*contredanse à la française* and *cotillon*) were used interchangeably.[120] He made a strong case that the two terms may well have been synonymous earlier in the century, as well, although he was forced to admit that there are no surviving choreographic sources that make this association explicit. On the whole I am inclined to agree with Guilcher's arguments, but I believe that one need not restrict a search for examples of an earlier eighteenth century *contredanse à la française* (or at least a prototype of one) to dances of the *cotillon* family. Indeed, I am convinced that the rather sharp distinction regularly made after c1760 between the longways contredanse (the *anglaise*) and the *à la française* variety was not possible earlier in the century, *except* in the case of the *cotillon*. The latter, in other words, was but one of several possibilities of a contredanse that was regarded as *à la française*. Before exploring the evidence for my viewpoint, however, I will briefly summarize the chief characteristics of the *cotillon* and the vast majority of later eighteenth century *contredanses à la française*.

These dances, first of all, were for a fixed number of performers— either two or four couples earlier in the century, and almost always four couples later in the century—rather than for the variable number of couples the longways dance permitted. When for eight performers, the four couples were usually organized in a square formation. Both the music and the choreography of the *cotillon* and *à la française* were

---

[119]*La Contredanse*, see especially the sections titled 'De la danse grave à la contredanse française,' 57- 86, and 'l'Apogée de la contredanse française,' 87-146.

[120]ibid., 82.

set out in a refrain structure: an opening figure and its accompanying music (the refrain) alternated with a series of *couplets*. Earlier in the century the couplets offered a series of new figures, each of which was followed by the refrain, while in the later century the couplets, frequently referred to as 'changes' (*entrées* or *syncopes*), became a fixed number (usually nine) of standardized figures. Guilcher has provided an excellent analysis of the conventional figures of this later type,[121] so it is unnecessary to go into greater detail here. In terms of their musical layout the earlier *cotillon* and the later *contredanse à la française* were identical (except that the number of couplets in the former was variable, while that of the latter was fixed). The earlier *cotillon*, though, was invariably in duple meter with the half measure anacrusis of the gavotte,[122] and the *contredanse à la française* was almost always in either 6/8 or 2/4. In their choreographic structures, however, the two dance types were slightly different. The refrain figure of the *cotillon* behaved very much like a principal theme, from which the intervening couplets departed, and to which they invariably returned. The couplets, in other words, provided variety and contrast. The refrain figure of the *contredanse à la française*, on the other hand, was the *only* unique element of the entire dance (one that nevertheless was repeated several times): it was the *refrain* in this dance type that provided variety to a standard sequence of couplets—the 'changes.'[123]

I am not convinced that in the first three decades or so of the eighteenth century a contredanse had to exhibit all these features (or even just some of them) to qualify as *à la française*. In their printed collections of contredanses, issued respectively in 1706 and 1712, Feuillet and Dezais allude to their inclusion of both *contredanses anglaises* and *françaises*. Guilcher believed that these claims were nothing more than a reference to a repertoire composed by both English and French dancing masters, but he otherwise regarded the dances transmitted in these two collections as exclusively of the longways type.[124] I do not believe the claims of Feuillet and Dezais, however equivocal they may appear to be, should be dismissed so quickly. The Dance Collection of the New York Public Library includes a little known manuscript source with the following title: *Recueil de contredanses francois et anglois Mis au jours Par Monsieur feuillet Maitre compositeur de Danses a Paris, se vend 4*

---

[121]ibid., 135-139. A useful, but much shorter English language description may be found in the *International Encyclopedia of Dance*, s.v. 'Cotillon' by Desmond F. Stroebel.

[122]See Semmens, 'Branles, Gavottes, and Contredanses,' passim.

[123]In some ways, therefore, the later type was rather easier to learn, since one only had to memorize the opening figure to master the dance.

[124]*La Contredanse*, 79.

florin et 12 Sols, che[z] lauteur Rue de Bussy faubourg St. germain a la cour imperiale, avec privilege du Roÿ en 1716.[125] There is not space here to consider the numerous difficult questions this title raises, such as why Feuillet, who had relinquished his printing privilege to Dezais shortly before his death in June, 1710, is named as author of a collection with a 'privilege' dated 1716? What is important for my present purposes, however, is to consider the repertoire the source transmits, and the title under which it is offered.[126]

There are forty-five contredanses in the collection, the first thirty-two of which are drawn directly from (and in exactly the same sequence as) Feuillet's 1706 publication: the collection is reproduced in its entirety. The remaining thirteen dances are all drawn from a selection of the Dezais collection of 1712, but in no particular order. Although the repertoire transmitted in this source consists entirely of dances issued previously,[127] the title of the compilation is new, and without equivocation it describes the contredanses it introduces as *francois et anglois*. Whoever the compiler was, even if it wasn't Feuillet, certainly seems to have recognized both French and English varieties of contredanse in the collection. Which are the *contredanses françaises*?

In the introductory material to his 1706 publication Feuillet distinguished two procedural models—he called them *desseins*—for the contredanse. The first model is that of the longways variety already described in the preceding paragraphs. The second is one in which 'the gentlemen finish all their repetitions on the ladies' side, and the ladies on the side of the gentlemen.'[128] Additional features of this second design are that couples may begin dancing without first having reached the top of the set, and all the couples eventually find themselves dancing at the same time.[129] Is this second model one he regarded as French? I am not able to answer the question. But it is curious, indeed,

---

[125]Shelf number *MGRN-Res.

[126]I am grateful to Patricia W. Rader, Cataloguer and Reference Librarian of the Dance Division, New York Public Library, for providing me with a complete inventory and detailed description of the source.

[127]Although 'complete' in all other respects, the source contains no music for the choreographies. This omission is all the more conspicuous because a hand-drawn border around each page of dance notation leaves no room for entering music.

[128]*Recüeil de contredances*, unpaginated preliminary matter [p.xxii]: 'Le 2.me dessein est celui ou les hommes terminent toûtes leurs repetitions à la place des femmes, et les femmes en la place des hommes.'

[129]ibid., [p.xxiv]: 'quand un couple commence à danser de quelque endroit qu'il parte, il ne doit point discontinuer qu'il ne soit arrivé... à la même place ou il a commencé... A mesure que chaque répetition recommence, elle augmente toûjours d'un couple... enfin jusque à ce que tout le monde soit en mouvem[en]t.'

that Feuillet's collection contains *no* dances that follow precisely this second design. There is one dance, however, that behaves very much like a *contredanse à la française*, or like a *cotillon* for four couples. 'La Chaîne'—the penultimate dance of the collection—begins with a refrain danced by all eight dancers. When it recurs as the third figure of the dance, Feuillet offers the following instruction: 'Cette figure doit être toûjours répetée à la fin de chacune des autres Figures.'[130] The intervening figures, like the couplets of a *cotillon*, are of a contrasting nature, often featuring patterns introduced by one or more of the couples that are then repeated by the others. Because it is in 6/8, however, 'La Chaîne' is not properly a *cotillon*, and because the four couples are arranged in a column (longways style), it is not really a *contredanse à la française* of the kind that was popular later in the century.

Several other dances in the 1706 collection are laid out in a couplet format, as well, but never in the design employed in 'La Chaîne,' or in the manner typical of the *cotillon* more generally. Instead of a refrain structure, the other couplet dances of Feuillet's 1706 *Recüeil* feature one or more repetitions of the *entire* tune with a completely new set of figures for each. Each repetition, with its new figures, is labelled 1ᵉʳ, 2ᵉ, 3ᵉ, etc. 'couplet' in the imprint. The dances set out in this way are: 'Le Prince George' (33-38), 'Les Galeries d'Amour' (39-44), 'La Buffecotte' (45-48), 'La Liboulaire' (70-75), 'Le Menuet de la Reine' (89-93), 'La Bourée de Basque' (107-112), 'La Pantomime' (129-132), and 'La Fanatique' (161-165). These eight dances—a sizeable proportion (25%) of the collection overall—share a number of features beyond their couplet design. All but 'La Bourée de Basque' (which has six dancers in its notation) are notated with just two couples. It is unclear, however, if this is an indication that Feuillet intended just two couples to take part in the dance. It may be that just two couples are shown because Feuillet found it difficult to find space to include any more.[131] Yet, two of the couplet dances—'Le Prince George' and 'La Fanatique'—have a final figure that is probelmatic. In the former the first couple does not progress to the second position, so even if additional couples were intended (though not indicated), they would never be moved up the set to participate in the dance. And in the final figure of 'La Fanatique' a progression is made 'correctly', but the new first couple ends with the gentleman and woman on the wrong side of the set. Perhaps he

---

[130]ibid., 181.

[131]The page layout in all eight couplet dances has the figures for each couplet notated one above the other, such that the choreography is to be read in the following way. The top panel on each page is read from the first to the last figure. Then the panel below that on each page is read for all the figures of the second couplet, and so on. In those dances with three couplets (three dances of the eight) it would have been almost impossible for the engraver to fit in more than two couples in each panel.

expected these dances to be performed in sets of two couples arranged in a column, as if they were of the longways type, but otherwise operating in two-couple units.

Another feature shared by most of the eight couplet dances in the collection is that both couples (in at least some of the figures) are equally engaged in the dance, especially in the opening couplet.[132] Such a feature is only sometimes encountered in the normal longways contredanse which, more often than not, assigns the principal activity to just the active couple(s). In some respects the couplet dances of the 1706 collection behave very much like the *quadrille*, a four couple dance that became very popular by the end of the eighteenth century. The quadrille was nothing more than a *contredanse à la française* (or 'cotillon') from which the nine standard 'changes' had been removed. The tune of a quadrille was played several times over, and with each repetition a new set of figures was introduced.[133] This is exactly the procedure of Feuillet's couplet style contredanses first anthologized in 1706, except that the later dance always engaged a square formation of eight dancers who shared equally in most of the figures.

Along with Feuillet's 'La Chaîne,' in summary, I believe that the eight couplet dances of Feuillet's 1706 collection might legitimately be regarded as early varieties of the *contredanse à la française*. These nine dances were very likely those that the compiler of the manuscript now preserved in the New York Public Library had in mind when he gave the collection the title, *Recueil de contredanses francois et anglois*.

I have indulged in this brief excursion for two principal reasons. First, I believe it is an over-simplification to conclude that in the Parisian ballroom of the eighteenth century (including the public one at the opera house), the longways contredanse was predominant in the earlier years of the century, while the *contredanse à la française* or *cotillon* was popular only later. The two types both enjoyed currency throughout much of the period. That being said, I believe, nevertheless, that at the opera ball—and perhaps in private ones as well—the longways contredanse must have presented some logistical difficulties for both dancers and musicians, and this leads me to my second reason for the excursion of the previous few paragraphs. I think it must have been easier to implement performances of contredanses at the opera ball when the dance to be performed could be undertaken by a fixed number of participants, and when the musicans knew beforehand the

---

[132]A notable exception among these eight couplet dances is 'La Bourée de Basque', in which there is only one truly active couple in both couplets of the dance.

[133]See further Guilcher, *La Contredanse*, 147-167. A brief, but useful summary of the development of the quadrille may be found in the *International Encyclopedia of Dance*, s.v. 'Cotillon' by Desmond F. Strobel.

precise repeat schemes that would be required to bring the dance to its conclusion. In dances like 'La Chaîne,' or in ones organized in couplets (especially those in which dancers clearly do not progress down a set) these two criteria are met. And even in couplet dances that *do* progress, it seems a perfectly reasonable suggestion that they were normally performed with only four dancers (precisely as in Feuillet's notations). In a dance with two couplets, that likely would have meant four repetitions of the entire tune (with whatever internal repeats the figures required): two for the original top couple, and two more for the second couple. In a dance with three couplets, six repetitions would be required, and so on. Indeed, I think that the couplet design dances such as found in the 1706 *Receüil* were only rarely performed in a standard longways manner, if only in the name of expediency. A typical four-couple set (typical, at least, in the printed anthologies that have survived) performing a contredanse with three couplets would have required twenty-seven repetitions of the entire tune for the routine to run its course!

Once begun, contredanses of the French variety could be accompanied by the opera ball orchestras with a predictable set of repeat schemes. In a longways dance, in contrast, the players would have to know how many dancing couples were involved before such a determination could be made. When required, such determinations *were* made, however, as the 1727 account of the *Mercure*, makes clear. The account certainly implies that longways dances of a variable number of couples were performed at the opera ball that season, likely to the exclusion of dances of the French variety.[134] Perhaps because it was more predictable, musically, the *contredanse à la française* was to be featured more conspicuously in later eighteenth century printed anthologies of opera ball music. These dances presented musicians with a consistent set of directions for repeat schemes in performance. In short, the players knew, once started, when the contredanse was to be concluded.

But how did a contredanse *begin*? How did those in attendance at the *bal public* know when and in what way they should organize themselves for a contredanse of any variety (or even a menuet, for that matter)? If the late eighteenth century play, *Le Bal de l'Opera* (1777), considered briefly near the end of the last chapter can be believed, somehow a group of eight dancers, readying themselves to dance a quadrille, knew precisely when they needed to claim space for their performance (thereby displacing the characters of the play).[135] I believe that dancers at a veritable *bal public* were able to know when to prepare

[134]See above, n92.
[135]See pp.113-114.

themselves because they were following a program that had been prepared in advance by personnel at the opera ball. A program such as this might have been distributed to those in attendance as they entered the opera house, or it might simply have been posted in conspicuous places about the theatre. The latter possibility is confirmed, in fact, by a poster preserved at the Universiteit Gent, Centrale Bibliotheek, mentioned in chapter one.[136]

This document is not a 'program' for a public ball, neither does it have any direct connection to the opera balls of Paris (although it is printed in French). Rather, it is an announcement for subscriptions to an upcoming series of eight public balls ('*redoutes*') to be held in a theatre—very likely in the city of Ghent—in January and February, 1783. The poster announces several procedures that would be followed in the upcoming public balls, procedures that were clearly based in practices of past seasons. The seventh article of the document reads:

> To avoid arguments and disagreements that may arise from many people having conflicting suggestions for the contredanses [to be danced], at each redoute a notice will be posted on the columns [in the room] and in the Orchestra that will indicate the titles and the order of the contredanses [to be performed]. This sequence will be strictly observed, so as not to upset anyone.[137]

Such procedures may well have been in place for most eighteenth century venues for the *bal payant*, including the opera balls of Paris, for they make good practical sense, and would certainly have been less expensive than preparing and distributing programs for everyone in attendance. Program posters like the ones described in the document from Ghent were probably put together rather hastily, to accommodate up-to-date fads in, and recent additions to the contredanse repertoire. If they were ever printed (not particularly likely, it seems to me), I have not been able to discover surviving examples in any of the libraries or archives I have consulted, including those of Paris.

Although I cannot prove that programs were posted in the opera house in Paris on the evenings of public balls, I think it a real likelihood. Even with such posters in place, however, it would certainly have been difficult for those in attendance to know at what stage in the proceedings they found themselves at any given point. Some sort of additional prompting must have been required just before a dance was to begin. The opera balls apparently had a protocol in place for

[136]See chapter one, n117. A complete transcription of this document is given as Appendix 2.

[137]The original is given in Appendix 2.

such prompting. A payment ledger for the 1780-1781 season indicates that three *avertisseurs* were hired for each ball that year, and were paid at the rate of three pounds per service.[138] Because they were stationed on the ballroom floor—two of them on the king's side, and one on the queen's—they were ideally located to call out the titles of dances, and to work in coordination with the two orchestras.[139]

On especially crowded evenings at the opera ball it still must have been very difficult to organize a set of dancers, and to get a contredanse successfully underway. But this does not mean, as some have suggested,[140] that dancing was, for all intents and purposes, an impossibility in these circumstances. A revealing case in point is a dance entitled 'La Folie ou le Goût du Siècle,' issued in de la Cuisse's third collection of contredanses in 1765.[141] The title page of the dance informs us that it was first performed at the opera ball held on 14 February 1765. That ball was the fourth to last of the season (the second season in which balls had moved into the Tuilleries palace, while a new facility in the *Palais-Royal* was being planned and constructed), and took place on the Thursday before *mardi gras*. That particular night of a typical opera ball season, as we saw in chapter three, was always well attended. As it turns out, the gate receipts for the ball of 14 February 1765 have survived. Ten thousand, four hundred and twent-eight pounds were taken in that evening, so I estimate that there were one thousand, seven hundred and thirty-eight in attendance—a very large gathering indeed (but only the second largest of that season). And yet a contredanse with a brand new choreography (by 'Sr Carel') was performed at this ball.[142]

---

[138]See *Archives Nationales*, AJ[13]-23, dossier 8. These avertisseurs were mentioned on p. 64.

[139]*Archives Nationales*, AJ[13]-23-dossier 8. The ledger specifically locates the three individuals—their names were Boucauls, de Ferend, and Gallet—in the 'fond du Théâtre, côté du roy,' or 'côté de la reine.'

[140]For example, Naïk Raviart, 'Le bal français, du début du règne de Louis XIV à l'aube de la Révolution,' in *Histoires de bal*, 45.

[141]*Suite du Répertoire des bals, ou 3.e volume du recueil des airs et figures des meilleures et plus nouvelles contredanses* (Paris, 1765), cahier 17, feuille 89 [4 pages]. For online access to this souce see the general information provided above in n87. The dance 'La Folie, ou le Goût du Siècle' is transmitted in four pages, and may be accessed as follows:

title page = http://memory.loc.gov/musdi/213/0407.tif;

verbal description of the figures = http://memory.loc.gov/musdi/213/0408.tif;

graphic presentation of the figures = http://memory.loc.gov/musdi/213/0409.tif;

and the music = http://memory.loc.gov/musdi/213/0410.tif.

[142]The title page of this dance (for the url of an online reproduction see n141, above) reveals a number of interesting facts. The choreography was made to a tune that had been used several times before, and was known as 'La Strasbourgeoise.' (cont.)

I believe with ballroom prompters in place—with or without the additional aid of posted programs—that those in attendance at the Parisian opera ball were able to take their places in either of the two dancing areas, and to begin their dances in a reasonably orderly way. It may well be, in fact, that on this count the public balls at the opera house were better organized than many others in the city. De la Cuisse expressed concern about the lack of order frequently encountered at balls in the 1762 preface of his *Répertoire des bals*. His concerns were directed, in part, towards beginning a contredanse:

> From this [results] the multitude of balls, public as well as private, that one sees mounted at the onset of winter. But why are these sorts of gatherings, at which the young should find only useful exercise and honest leisure, so often filled with trouble and disorder? This confusion is almost always born of the difficulty experienced in convening a contredanse, or in executing it once it has begun.[143]

As de la Cuisse points out, getting a contredanse started in an orderly fashion—something those in attendance at an opera ball at least had a decent chance of achieving[144]—was no guarantee that the performance would subsequently go smoothly.

In most respects, in fact, the dancing and music of the Parisian opera ball must have seemed rather chaotic to the uninitiated. I base this assessment on the offhand remark made by Cahusac in the article he prepared on the contredanse for the *Encyclopédie* in 1754. He observed, 'at the opera ball different contredanses are danced at the two ends of the room.'[145] Are we to take this remark literally, and conclude that

---

The choreographer, Sr Carel, entered into a debate in the pages of the *Mercure galant* with another dancing master—a Mr DesHayes—concerning authorship of the dance, and page references are given. DesHayes claimed that Carel had made use of some of his material, while Carel responded that he had simply reused the tune. See *Mercure galant*, août (1764), 177-179, for the charge of DesHayes, and octobre (1764), 197-204, for Carel's response. The title page is reproduced in the frontispiece of this book.

[143]*Répertoire des bals*, [5]: 'De là cette multitude de Bals tant publics que particuliers que l'on voit se former à l'entrée de l'Hyver. Mais pourquoi ces sortes de Sociétés où la Jeunesse devroit trouver qu'un exercise utile et un délassement honête sont-elles si souvent remplies de trouble et de désordre. Cette confusion naît presque toujours de la difficulté que l'on a, ou à convenir d'une Contredanse, ou à l'éxécuter lors que l'on en est convenu.'

[144]Their chances for success were quite good, because the opening figure of the *contredanse à la française* was always the same: all eight dancers, holding hands, danced in a circle to the opening eight measures of the music in what was known as *le grand rond*.

[145]*Encyclopédie*, s.v. 'Contredanse' by Louis de Cahusac: 'Au bal de l'Opera on danse dans les deux bouts de la salle des *contredanses* différentes.'

different contredanses were performed *simultaneously*? I was initially unwilling to accept that this was a possibility (precisely because it seemed too chaotic), and tried to consider other options that nevertheless remained consistent with Cahusac's observation. The first option I entertained was that the two orchestras played the same dances together, accompanying two groups of dancers, and that what Cahusac really meant was: 'at the opera ball *various* contredanses are danced at the two ends of the room.' It must be remembered, though, that the opera house ballroom occupied a sizeable space. In chapter two I argued that the two orchestras were spaced apart by at a distance of roughly 17 to 18 meters. If the center of the room (the *salon quarré*) were kept reasonably clear of people, I believe the two orchestras might have been able to manage coordinated playing, although it would have been challenging, since the two groups of dancers would have been placed between them. But, as we have seen, there were often throngs of people moving about in the centre of the room at well-attended balls. In these circumstances it would have been almost impossible for members of the orchestras to have maintained any visual, let alone reliable aural contact.

A second possibility is that the two orchestras played in alternation, one group spelling the other for several dances. Such an arrangement would have done much to alleviate the fatigue that the musicians surely must have endured, and it is consistent, moreover, with the procedure adopted at a royal ball held at the Tuilleries in 1722.[146] On the surface this second suggestion seems quite plausible. At the opera ball, however, alternating the two orchestras must have meant that the two dancing spaces were used in alternation as well. If that were the case, then I can see no reason why Cahusac—who was, after all, offering information about contredanses here—would have gone to the trouble of writing that they were *danced at both ends of the room*: while this information tells us something about dancing in general at the opera ball, it contributes nothing to our understanding of the contredanse in particular. On the other hand, if he meant that they really were danced simultaneously at two ends of the room, the information contributes significantly to Cahusac's point (one made strongly in his short article) that the contredanse had become overwhelmingly popular.

I have come to believe that a literal reading of Cahusac's remarks is the only viable one, and that different contredanses were indeed performed simultaneously at the opera ball in Paris, however chaotic the results might have been. The practice immediately calls to mind the famous banquet scene in Mozart's *Don Giovanni* of 1787. Although

---

[146]See above, n6.

this banquet takes place in a private residence, and is hosted by the Don (who is, in principle, a noble character), it is anything but a formal affair. In this scene (which is accompanied by hilarious stage antics) Mozart, with deft contrapuntal control, successively introduces a menuet, a contredanse, and finally a Teutscher (a German dance) into the musical texture, all in their characteristic meters, and accompanied by their own band. Eventually all three dances are playing simultaneously. Daniel Heartz has given this scene a most thoughtful treatment and analysis,[147] concluding, 'Mozart did not invent the idea of contrasting dances…[danced] in combination with each other simultaneously. He had observed such phenomena in the world about him.'[148] Three different dances performed simultaneously in a single room, as occurs in *Don Giovanni*, was probably not really an observable phenomenon of Mozart's world, of course. But as part of a buffa style finale, the dancing of the banquet scene was fashioned to contribute to the crescendo of comic activity that typically attended such scenes. Just as too many characters, each with her or his own views to express, join into an ever growing complex of ensemble singing, too many couples take to the dance floor at the same time, each with its own dance to perform. Though slightly exaggerated, the simultaneous dancing depicted here, as Heartz suggests, was something that really *did* occur at social gatherings of the time. The practice might well have originated at the opera ball in Paris, where as early as the 1750s it seems not to have been viewed as any particular novelty (at least not by Cahusac). Indeed, it might have first been introduced in 1727, when the two-orchestra layout was put into place.

The performance of different dances simultaneously at the Parisian opera ball lends additional support to my arguments, put forward in chapter four, that dancing could only rarely be a focus of attention there. Not only was it marginalized—removed from the centre of the room, and relocated at the two ends—it was rendered rather unexceptional, as well, through its very plurality. Although dancing at the *bal public* was not something to be observed by attentive onlookers, it was, nevertheless, something to be enjoyed by those on the dance floor.

Ironically, because it did not very often command the attention of an interested audience, dancing at the opera ball was rendered rather less public than it was in the private ballroom. While it seems unlikely that this circumstance had any direct effect on the general quality of

---

[147]'An Iconography of the Dances in the Ballroom Scene of *Don Giovanni*,' in Daniel Heartz, *Mozart's Operas* (Berkeley, 1990), 179-193.

[148]ibid., 193.

dancing at the *bal public*, it nevertheless must have lent emphasis to the idea that dancing was a means of individual expression as well as a social activity. Performing a dance well at the opera ball, in other words, was not driven by some social imperative, by a quest for approbation from the group, as it often was at a private ball. A skilfull performance, rather, was more a matter of pride and personal gratification. In this way, as I have already suggested, dancing at the *bal public* really did celebrate the individual.

Bibliography of Cited Sources

A considerable number of short documents (typically less than three pages in length), as well as posters, engravings, financial statements, and personnel lists preserved in various archives and libraries have not been given individual entries in this bibliography, although they have been referenced frequently in this study. Complete documentation for these sources is given in footnotes throughout the investigation. An extremely valuable inventory of many of the documents relating to the Paris opera preserved in the *Archives Nationales* is:

Labat-Poussin, Brigitte. *Archives du Théâtre national de l'Opéra :* (AJ[13] 1 à 1466). *Inventaire*. Paris: 1977.

(Musical and choreographic sources are given in a separate listing.)

1. Sources before 1900

Almanach historique et chronologique de tous les Spectacles. Paris: 1752.

Anecdotes historiques de l'Opéra de Paris depuis 1672 jusqu'en 1749. Paris: *Bibliothèque-Musée de l'Opéra*, Ms., C.989, [c1749].

Boislisle, Jean Georges Léon Michel de, ed. *Mémoires de Saint-Simon*. 25 vols. Paris: 1879-1928.

Bonnet, Jacques. *Histoire générale de la danse sacrée et profane*. Paris: 1724.

Burney, Charles. *The Present State of Music in France and Italy*. London: 1773. Modern ed. by Percy A. Scholes, *An Eighteenth-Century Musical Tour in France and Italy*. Oxford: 1959.

Cahusac, Louis de. *La danse ancienne et moderne, ou Traité historique de la danse*. 3 vols. [in one]. La Haye: 1754.

Catalogue général des ouvrages publiés par Boivin. Paris: 1742.

'Collection Rondel.' Paris: *Bibilothèque de l'Arsenal*, R°13033.

The Daily Courant. London: 1702-1735.

Diderot, Denis, and Alembert, Jean Le Rond d', eds. *Encyclopédie ou dictionnaire raisonné des sciences, des arts, et des métiers*. Paris: 1751-1780.

DuCoudray, Le Chevalier. *Le Bal de l'Opéra, Comédie en un acte, en prose, ornée de Chants et de Danses*. [Bound with idem.]. *Essai sur la comédie, la farce et la parodie*. Paris: 1777.

Dulaure, Jacques Antoine. *Histoire physique, civile et morale de Paris depuis les premiers temps historiques jusqu'à nos jours*, 2nd ed., 10 vols. Paris: 1824.

[Durey de Noinville, Jean-Baptiste]. *Histoire du théâtre de l'Académie Royale de Musique en France depuis son établissement jusqu'à présent*. 2nd ed. Paris: 1757.

Fétis, François-Joseph. *Biographie universelle des musiciens*. 2nd ed. 8 vols. Paris: 1874.

Furetière, Antoine. *Dictionnaire universel, contenant generalement tous les mots francois*. Den Haag: 1690. Modern ed. by Pierre Bayle. Paris: 1978.

_____. *Dictionnaire universel, contenant generalement tous les mots francois*. Rev. 2nd ed. by Jean-Baptiste Brutel de la Riviere. Den Haag: 1727. Reprint ed. Hildesheim: 1972.

Ganeau, Étienne. *Histoire journalière de Paris*. Paris: 1716.

Lajarte, Théodore de. *Bibliothèque musicale du théâtre de l'Opéra. Catalogue historique, chronologique, anecdotique*. 2 vols. Paris: 1878.

Lasalle, Albert de. *Les treize salles de l'Opéra*. Paris: 1875.

Lescure, M[athurin] de, ed. *Journal et Mémoires de Mathieu Marais, avocat au parlement de Paris, sur la Régence et le règne de Louis XV (1715-1737)*. 4 vols. Paris: 1863.

Lettres historiques sur tous les spectacles de Paris. Paris: 1719.

Memoire concernant la Regie de l'Opera, & sa situation au premier avril 1721. Paris: *Archives Nationales*, AJ^{13}-1, dossier 3.

Memoires pour servir a l'histoire de l'Academie Royale de Musique, vulgairement l'Opéra, depuis son établissement en 1669 jusqu'en l'année 1758. Paris: *Bibliothèque-Musée de l'Opéra*, Rés. 516.

Mercier, Louis-Sébastien. *Parallèle de Paris et de Londres*. Paris: *Bibliothèque de l'Arsenal*, fonds Mercier 15 079 (3), [1781].

Mercure galant. [*Mercure de France*]. Paris: 1672-1832.

Mulsane (pseud.). 'Les bals de l'Opéra.' *La Chronique musicale. Revue bi-mensuelle de l'art ancien et moderne* 2/10 (1873): [198]-203.

Parfaict, Claude. *Histoire du théâtre françois*. 15 vols. Paris: 1734-1749. Reprint ed. Genève: 1967.

Prévost, Antoine-François [l'Abbé]. *Mémoires et aventures d'un homme de qualité qui s'est retiré du monde*. Tome V, 'Séjour en Angleterre.' Paris: 1739. Modern ed. by Mysie E. I. Robertson. Paris: 1934.

Rameau, Pierre. *Le Maître à danser*. Paris: 1725.

Réponse d'une artitste a un homme de letters, qui lui avoit écrit sur les Wauxhalls. Amsterdam: 1769.

Report on the Manuscripts of his Grace the Duke of Portland, preserved at Welbeck Abbey. Vol. 5. Norwich: 1899.

Rousseau, Jean-Jacques. *Dictionnaire de Musique*. Paris: 1768. Reprint ed. Hildesheim: 1969.

Rozier, Victor. *Les bals publics à Paris*. Paris: 1855.

Soulié, E[udoxe], *et al*, eds. *Journal du Marquis de Dangeau*. 19 vols. Paris: 1854-1860.

Les Spectacles de Paris, ou calendrier historique & chronologique des théâtres. Pt.22. Paris: 1773.

The Spectator. London: 1711-1714. Modern ed. by Donald F. Bond. 5 vols. Oxford: 1965.

Tomlinson, Kellom. *The Art of Dancing Explained by Reading and Figures*. London: 1735. Reprint ed. London: 1970.

Villegille, Paul Arthur Nouail de la, ed. *Journal historique et anecdotique du règne de Louis XV par E.-J.-F. Barbier*, 4 vols. Paris: 1849.

2. Sources after 1900

Alm, Irene. 'Operatic Ballroom Scenes and the Arrival of French Social Dance in Venice.' *Studi musicali* 25 (1996): 345-371.

Amiel, Olivier, ed. *Lettres de Madame, Duchesse d'Orléans, née Princesse Palatine, 1672-1722*. Le Temps retrouvé, vol. xxxii. Paris: 1981.

Anthony, James R. *French Baroque Music from Beaujoyeulx to Rameau*. Rev. ed. New York: 1978.

Antoine, Michel. *Le conseil du roi sous le règne de Louis XV*. Geneva: 1970.

Avery, Emmett L., ed. *The London Stage. Part 2: 1700-1729*. 2. vols. Carbondale, Illinois: 1960.

Benoit, Marcelle. *Musiques de Cour. Chapelle, Chambre, Écurie, 1661-1733*. Paris: 1971.

Bachmann, Werner, general ed. *Musikgeschichte in Bildern*. Bd. IV/4. Salmen, Walter, ed. *Tanz im 17. und 18. Jarhundert*. Leipzig: 1988.

Besseler, Heinrich, and Schneider, Max, general eds. *Musikgeschichte in Bildern*, Bd. IV/1. Wolff, Hellmuth Christian, ed. *Oper. Szene und Darstellung von 1600 bis 1900*. Leipzig: n.d.

Bouvet, Charles. 'L'Académie royale de musique et les deux salles de spectacle du Palais Royal.' In *La Merveilleuse vie du Palais-Royal*, 31-44. Paris: 1929-30.

Bruneteau, Claude, and Cottret, Bernard, eds. *Parallèle de Paris et de Londres*. By Louis-Sébastien Mercier. Paris: 1982.

Campbell, Peter R. *Power and Politics in Old Regime France, 1720-1745*. London: 1996.

Chuquet, Arthur, ed. *Souvenirs du baron de Frénilly, pair de France (1768-1828)*. Paris: 1908. English trans. by Frederic Lees, *Recollections of Baron de Frénilly, Peer of France (1768-1828)*. London: 1909.

Coeyman, Barbara. 'Social Dance in the 1668 *Feste de Versailles*: Architecture and Performance Context.' *Early Music* 26/2 (1998): 264-82.

_____. 'Theatres for Opera and Ballet during the Reigns of Louis XIV and Louis XV.' *Early Music* 18/1 (1990): 41-49.

Cohen, Selma Jeanne, *et al* ed. *International Encyclopedia of Dance*. 6 vols. New York, Oxford: 1998.

Cyr, Mary. '*Basses* and *basse continue* in the Orchestra of the Paris Opera 1700-1764.' *Early Music* 10/2 (1982): 155-170.

Demuth, Norman. *French Opera. Its Development to the Revolution*. Sussex: 1963.

Devriès, Anik. *Édition et commerce de la musique gravée à Paris dans la première moitié du XVIIIe siècle*. Genève: 1976.

Duchêne, Roger, ed. *Correspondance / Madame de Sévigné*. 3 vols. Paris: 1972.

Ducrot, Ariane. 'Les représentations de l'Académie Royale de Musique à Paris au temps de Louis XIV (1671-1715).' *Recherches sur la musique française classique* 10 (1970): 19-55.

Dufourcq, Norbert, ed. *La musique à la cour de Louis XIV et de Louis XV d'après les Mémoires de Sourches et Luynes*. Paris: 1970.

Duindam, Jeroen. *Myths of Power. Nobert Elias and the Early Modern European Court*. English trans. by Lorri S. Granger and Gerald T. Moran. Amsterdam: n.d. [c1994].

Elias, Norbert. *The Court Society*. English trans. by Edmund Jephcott. London: 1983.

Gourret, Jean. *Ces hommes qui ont fait l'Opéra*. Paris: 1984.

Guilcher, Jean-Michel. *La contredanse et les renouvellements de la danse française*. Paris: 1969.

Hardy, James Daniel Jr. *Judicial Politics in the Old Regime: The Parlement of Paris during the Regency*: Baton Rouge, La.: 1967.

Harris-Warrick, Rebecca. 'Ballroom Dancing at the Court of Louis XIV.' *Early Music* 14/1 (1986): 41-49.

_____. '*La Mariée*: The History of a French Court Dance.' In *Jean-Baptiste Lully and the Music of the French Baroque: Essays in Honor of James R. Anthony*, ed. John Hajdu Heyer, 239-257. Cambridge: 1989.

_____ , and Marsh, Carol G. *Musical Theatre at the Court of Louis XIV. Le Marriage de la Grosse Cathos*. Cambridge: 1994.

Heartz, Daniel. 'An Iconography of the Dances in the Ballroom Scene of *Don Giovanni*.' In *Mozart's Operas*, 179-193. Berkeley: 1990.

Hilton, Wendy. *Dance and Music of Court and Theatre. Selected Writings of Wendy Hilton*. New York: 1997.

Hyde, H. Montgomery. *John Law: The History of an Honest Adventure*. Rev. ed. London: 1969.

Isherwood, Robert M. *Farce and Fantasy. Popular Entertainment in Eighteenth-Century Paris*. Oxford: 1986.

Kettering, Sharon. 'Friendship and Clientage in Early Modern France.' *French History* 6 (1992): 139-158.

_____. 'Gift giving and Patronage in Early Modern France.' *French History* 2 (1988): 131-151.

_____. 'The Patronage Power of Early Modern French Noblewomen.' *Historical Journal* 32 (1989): 139-158.

_____. *Patrons, Brokers and Clients in Seventeenth-century France*. New York: 1986.

LaGorce, Jérôme de. *L'Opéra à Paris au temps de Louis XIV*. Paris: 1992.

_____. 'L'orchestre de l'Opéra et son évolution de Campra à Rameau.' *Revue de Musicologie* 76/1 (1990): 23-43.

LaGrave, Henri. *Le Théâtre et le public à Paris de 1715 à 1750*. Paris: 1972.

Lesure, François. *Catalogue de la musique imprimée avant 1800 conservée dans les bibliothèques publiques de Paris*. Paris: 1981.

Little, Meredith Ellis, and Marsh, Carol G. *La Danse Noble. An Inventory of Dances and Sources*. New York: 1992.

Marsh, Carol G. 'French Court Dance in England, 1706-1740. A Study of the Sources.' PhD dissertation, The City University of New York: 1985.

Milhous, Judith, and Hume, Robert D. 'Heidegger and the Management of the Haymarket Opera, 1713-17.' *Early Music* 27/1 (1999): 65-84.

Mongrédien, Georges. *Daily Life in the French Theatre at the Time of Molière*. London: 1969.

Mortier, Roland, and Hasquin, Hervé, eds. *Topographie du plaisir sous la Régence. Études sur le XVIIIe siècle*. Vol. 24. Bruxelles: 1998.

Mousnier, R. 'The Development of Monarchical Institutions and Society in France.' In *Louis XIV and Absolutism*, ed. Ragnhild Marie Hatton, 37-54. London: 1976.

Pagès, Georges. *La monarchie d'ancien régime en France*. Paris: 1928.

Pitou, Spire. *The Paris Opera. An Encyclopedia of Operas, Ballets, Composers and Performers*. Vol. 1. *Genesis and Glory*. London: 1983.

Proschwitz, Gunnar von, ed. *Tableaux de Paris et de la Cour de France, 1739-1742. Lettres inédites de Carl Gustaf, comte de Tessin*. Paris: 1983.

Raunie, Emile, ed. *Chansonnier historique du XVIIIe siècle. Recueil de chansons, vaudevilles, sonnets, épigrammes, épitaphes, et autres vers satiriques et historiques*. Osnabrück: 1972.

Raviart, Naïk. 'Le bal français du début du règne de Louis XIV à l'aube de la Révolution.' In *Histoires de bal*, ed. Claire Rousier, 19-54. Paris: 1998.

RISM [*Recueil International des Sources Musicales*]. *Recueils imprimés. XVIIIe siècle*. Munich: 1964.

Rosow, Lois. 'Lallemand and Durand: Two Eighteenth-Century Music Copyists at the Paris Opéra.' *Journal of the American Musicological Society* 23/1 (1980): 142-163.

Sadie, Stanley, ed. *The New Grove Dictionary of Music and Musicians*. 20 vols. London: 1980.

_____. *The New Grove Dictionary of Music and Musicians*, 2nd ed. Executive ed., John Tyrrell. 29 vols. London: 2001.

_____. *The New Grove Dictionary of Opera*. 4 vols. London: 1992.

Sadler, Graham. 'Rameau's Singers and Players at the Paris Opéra. A little-known inventory of 1738.' *Early Music* 11/4 (1983): 453-467.

_____. 'The Role of the Keyboard Continuo in French Opera, 1673-1776.' *Early Music* 8/2 (1980): 148-157.

'Saint Cloud: résidence princière, royale et impériale.' In *L'Histoire de Saint Cloud* © 2000. Available from: http://saintcloud.histoire.free.fr. Internet. Accessed 22 July 2001.

Semmens, Richard. 'Branles, Gavottes and Contredanses in the Late Seventeenth and Early Eighteenth Centuries.' *Dance Journal* 15/2 (1997): 35-62.

Shennan, J. H. *Philippe, Duke of Orléans, Regent of France, 1715-1723.* London: 1979.

Skeaping, Mary. 'Ballet under the Three Crowns.' *Dance Perspectives* 32 (1967): 1-62.

Survey of London, vol. xxx, *The Parish of St. James Westminster, South of Piccadilly.* Part 1. London: 1960.

Swartz, David. *Culture & Power. The Sociology of Pierre Bourdieu.* Chicago: 1997.

Terrier, Agnès. *Le billet d'Opéra.* Paris: 2000.

Wood, Caroline, and Sadler, Graham, eds. *French Baroque Opera. A Reader.* Aldershot: 2000.

Zaslaw, Neal. 'At the Paris Opera in 1747.' *Early Music* 11/4 (1983): 515-17.

3. Choreographic Sources

Dezais, Jacques. *Recüeil de nouvelles contredanses mises en Choregraphie.* Paris: 1712.

Feuillet, Raoul-Auger. *Recüeil de contredances mises en Choregraphie.* Paris: 1706.

_____. *Vme Recüeil de danses de bal pour l'année 1707.* Paris: 1706

_____. *VIme Recüeil de danses et de contredanses pour l'année 1708.* Paris: 1707.

Gaudrau, M. *Nouveau Recüeil de dance de bal et celle de ballet contenant un tres grand nombres des meilleures Entrées de Ballet de la composition de Mr Pecour.* Paris: c1713.

La Cuisse, M. de. *Le répertoire des bals, ou Théorie-pratique des contredanses, décrites d'une manière aisée avec des figures demonstratives pour les pouvoir danser facilement, auxquelles on a ajouté les airs notés. Par sr. de La Cuisse.* Paris: 1762-1765.

Landrin, M. *Receuil DANGLAISE arrangees avec leurs traits. telle quels se danse ché la Reine. Mis au jour par Mr Landrin, M^{tre} de danse et compositeur des traits des Contre-danse.* Paris: nd. [after c1760].

Pemberton, E. *An Essay for the further Improvement of Dancing: Being a Collection of Figure Dances, Of Several Numbers, Compos'd by the most Eminent Masters*. London: 1711.

Recueil de contredanses francois et anglois Mis au jours Par Monsieur feuillet Maitre compositeur de Danses a Paris, se vend 4 florin et 12 Sols, che[z] lauteur Rue de Bussy faubourg St. germain a la cour imperiale, avec privilege du Roÿ en 1716. Ms. Dance Division, New York Public Library: *MGRN-Res.

4. Musical Sources

Cinquieme Recüeil de Contredanses Telles quelles ont etées Dansées au Bal de l'Opera. Pour les Violons Flutes et Haut-bois. Paris: nd.

Deuxieme Recueil de Contredanses Telles quelles ont etées Dansées au Bal de l'Opera. Pour les Violons, Flûtes, et Hautbois. Paris: nd.

Douzieme Recueil de Contredanses Telles quelles ont étées Dansées aux Bals de St Cloud et de l'Opera. Pour les Violons, Flutes et Hautbois. Paris: nd.

Huitieme Recueil de Contredanses Telles quelles ont eteés Dansées au Bal de Versailles et au Bal de l'Opera. Pour les Violons, Flutes, et Hautbois. Paris: nd.

Dixieme Recueil de Contredanses Telles quelles ont étées Dansées aux Bals de St Cloud et de l'Opera. Pour les Violons, Flutes et Hautbois. Paris: nd.

'Livre du Bal. Dessus de violon.' Paris: Bibliothèque-Musée de l'Opéra, Ms. fr. Rés. 1187.

[Maupetit, Jean-Baptiste Edmonde]. *Contredanses Nouvelles Tel quils ont etés Dansés au Bal du Roy et au Bal de l'Opera. Pour les Violons flutes et Hautbois et autres instruments. 1e Recueil*. Paris: nd. [series begins c1745]

_____. *Dixieme Recueil de Contredanses Telles qu'elles ont étés Dansés aux Bals de St Cloud et de l'Opera. Pour les Violons, Flûtes et Hautbois*. Paris: nd.

_____. *Douzieme Recueil de Contredanses Telles qu'elles ont étés Dansées aux Bals de l'Opera Pour les Violons, Flûtes et Hautbois*. Gravée par Mlle Bertin, Paris, Lyon: nd.

_____. *Huitieme Recueil de Contredanses telles qu'elles ont étés Dansés aux Bals de versailles et de l'Opera*. Paris: nd.

_____. *Neuvieme Recueil de Contredanses telles qu'elles ont étés Dansés aux Bals de versailles et de l'Opera*. Paris: nd.

_____. *Onzieme Recueil de Contredanses Telles qu'elles ont étés Dansées aux Bals de St Cloud et de l'Opera. Pour les Violons, Flûtes et Hautbois.* Gravée par Mlle Bertin. Paris, Lyon: nd.

_____. *Septieme Recueil de Contredanses telles qu'elles ont étés Dansés aux Bals de versailles et de l'Opera.* Paris: nd.

Minuetti diversi. Ve [-IXe] recueil de menuets nouveaux français et italiens tels qu'ils se dansent aux bals de l'Opéra. Paris: [c1745].

Montéclair, Michel Pinolet de. *Contre-dances et Branles qui se dancent aux bals de l'Opera. Pour les violons, flûtes, et haubois, avec la basse.* Paris: nd. [c1730].

_____. *Menuets, tant anciens que nouveaux, qui se dansent aux bals de l'Opéra. 1er recueil contenant cent et un menuets disposés en dix suittes par Mr Montéclair.* Paris: nd. [before 1725]

_____. *Menuets, tant anciens que nouveaux, qui se dansent aux bals de l'Opéra. Deuxième recueil, contenant cent & un menuets...mis en ordre avec la basse chiffrée par Mr Montéclair.* Paris: 1725.

Neuvieme Recueil de Contredanses Telles quelles ont étées Dansées aux Bals de St Cloud et de l'Opera. Pour les Violons, Flutes et Hautbois. Paris: nd.

Les Nouvelles Contre-danses qui se dansent aux Bals de l'Opera Pour le Violon, Flûte, Hautbois avec la Basse chiffrée. Paris, nd.

Nouvelles Contredanses Telles quelles ont etées Dansées au Bal de l'Opera et au Bal de son Excellence l'Ambassadeur d'Espagne. Pour les Violons Flutes Hautbois et autres Instruments. IIIe Recueil. Paris: nd.

Onzieme Recueil de Contredanses Telles quelles ont étées Dansées aux Bals de St Cloud et de l'Opera. Pour les Violons, Flutes et Hautbois. Paris: nd.

Philidor, André Danican (l'aîné). *Suite de dances pour les violons et hautbois qui se joüent ordinairement à tous les bals chez le Roy.* Paris: Bibliothèque Nationale (Musique) Ms. fr. Vm^{7}3555. [c1712]

_____. *Suite de danses pour les violons et haubois qui se jouent aux bals chez le roy.* Paris: 1699.

Premier recueil de contredanses telles quelles ont été dansées au bal de l'Opéra. Pour les violons, flûtes et hautbois. Paris: nd. [series begins c1754]

Quatrieme Recueil de Contredanses telles quelles ont etées Dansées au Bal de l'Opera. Pour les Violons Flutes et Hault-bois. Paris: nd.

IXme Recueil de Contredanses avec la Basse Chiffrée; et la Table par Lettres Alphabetiques. Qui se dansent au bal de l'Opera, et de St Cloud. Paris: nd. [?first 8 volumes lost].

Xe Recueil de Contredanses avec la Basse Chiffrée; et la Table par Lettres Alphabetiques. Qui se dansent au bal de l'Opera, et de St Cloud. Paris: nd.

Recueil des Contredanses à la Mode dansées au bal de l'Opera & de St Cloud. Paris: nd.

IIᵉ Recueil des Contredanses à la Mode Dansées aux bals de l'Opera, de St Cloud, et de Vincennes. Paris: nd.

IIIᵉ Recueil des Contredanses à la Mode Dansées aux bals de l'Opera, de St Cloud, et de Vincennes. Paris: nd.

Septieme Recueil de Contredanses Telles quelles ont eteés Dansées au Bal de Versailles et au Bal de l'Opera. Pour les Violons, Flutes, et Hautbois. Paris: nd.

Sixieme Recueil de Contredanses Telles quelles ont eteés Dansées au Bal de Versailles et au Bal de l'Opera. Pour les Violons, Flutes, et Hautbois. Paris: nd.

Suite de menuets pour les violons, flûtes, hautbois avec l'accompagnement de basse ou de basson tels qu'ils s'exécutent au Bal de l'Opéra. Mis en ordre par M. d'Avesne. Paris: [c1763].

[1er] *Suitte de Contredances pour les Violons Flutes Haubois et avec l'Accompagnement de Basse telles qu'elles s'executent au Bal de l'Opera. Recueillies avec soin*. Paris: nd. [series begins after 1752]

[5e] *Suitte de Contredances Pour les Violons Flutes Hautbois et avec l'Accompagnement de Basse telles qu'elles Sexecutent au Bal de l'Opera. Recueillies avec soin*. Paris: nd. [?volumes 2 - 4 lost]

[6e] *Suitte de Contredances Pour les Violons Flutes Hautbois et avec l'Accompagnement de Basse telles qu'elles Sexecutent au Bal de l'Opera. Recueillies avec soin*. Paris: nd.

Treizieme Recueil de Contredanses Telles quelles ont étées Dansées aux Bals de St Cloud et de l'Opera. Pour les Violons, Flutes et Hautbois. Paris: nd.

Appendix 1

Transcription of the *Reglement concernant la permission accordée à l'Académie Royale de Musique de donner des bals publics.* From Durey de Noinville, *Histoire du théâtre de l'Académie Royale de Musique en France depuis son établissement jusqu'à présent.* 2nd ed. (Paris, 1757), 148-150.

REGLEMENT

Concernant la Permission accordée à l'Académie Royale de Musique, de donner des BALS publics.

A Paris, le 30 Décembre 1715.

DE PAR LE ROY.

Sa Majesté ayant trouvé bon que l'Académie Royale de Musique donnât un Bal public, en conséquence du Privilége à elle accordé par Lettres Patentes du 8 Janvier 1713, & confirmées par celles du 2 Décembre 1715, de l'avis de Monsieur le Duc d'Orléans son Oncle, Régent du Royaume, a ordonné & ordonne ce qui ensuit.

ARTICLE PREMIER

Aucunes personnes, de quelque qualité & condition qu'elles soient, même les Officiers de Sa Maison, ne pourront entrer dans le Bal sans payer, & n'y pourront rentrer après en être sortis, sans payer de nouveau, ainsi qu'à la premiere fois.

II.

Fait Sa Majesté très-expresses inhibitions & défenses à toutes personnes, de quelque qualité & condition qu'elles soient, d'entrer dans ledit Bal sans être masquées; comme aussi d'y porter des épées, ou autres armes.

III.

Il n'y aura de porte d'entrée audit Bal, que celle qui donne sur la Place du Palais Royal; avec défenses à toutes personnes d'entrer par celle du Cul-de-sac, qui pour éviter la confusion sera uniquement réservée pour la sortie.

IV.

Défend pareillement Sa Majesté à toutes personnes de commettre, soit aux Portes, soit dans la Salle dudit Bal, aucune violence, insulte ni indécence.

V.

Veut Sa Majesté, que les Contrevenans à la présente Ordonnance soient punis de prison, & de plus grandes peines, s'il y échet.

VI.

Ordonne Sa Majesté que la présente Ordonnance sera lüe, publiée & affichée par tout où besoin sera. Fait à Paris, le 30 Décembre 1715. *Signé* LOUIS, & plus bas PHILIPPEAUX.

Appendix 2

Transcription of a poster announcing a subscription series of *redoutes* in 1783. From the copy preserved at the Universiteit Gent, Centrale Bibliotheek, FVB I R 7.

PROJET D'ABONNEMENT

Les Directeurs du Spectacle ont l'honneur de
Proposer à Messieurs & Dames ce Projet
D'Abonnement pour la Redoute

I.

Il y aura huit Redoutes, à commencer dès Lundi, 13 Janvier 1783. & se succèderont tous les Lundis.

II.

Elles commenceront comme d'ordinaire à quatre heures, & fineront à la volonté des Abonnés.

III.

Les Directeurs fourniront Tables, Cartes, & Bougies à ceux qui voudront jouer,
moïennant la rétribution ordinaire.

IV.

l'On païera comme de coûtume 20. Escalins de change pour l'Abonnement de huit
Redoutes.

V.

l'On ne pourra s'Abonner que pour le nombre de huit Redoutes.

IV. [sic]

Les non-Abonnés païeront pour chaque Redoute quatre Escalins de change par personne.

VII.

Pour éviter les contestations & les désagrémens qui resultent de la préference qu'exigent les Personnes qui proposent en même-tems différentes contredanses, on affichera, chaque Redoute, aux colonnes, ainsi qu'à l'Orchestre, une Note qui indiquera les noms & l'Ordre des Contredanses: Cet arrangement sera suivi exactement, pour ne pas mécontenter Personne.

VIII.

Les Personnes qui souhaiteront de faire danser des Contredanses nouvelles ou anciennes sont prier de vouloir confier (tout au moins huit jours d'avance) l'Air & les Figures au Maître de Danse Sr. Fisse, afin qu'il en prenne l'intelligence pour les montrer avec plus de facilité, & qu'on ait le tems de faire arranger l'accompagnement complet des Airs & doubler les Parties.

IX.

Les Personnes qui souhaiteront de s'abonne sont priées de signer le Présent Projet d'Abonnement, & de le faire remettre à la Dlle St. Flour, Buraliste du Théâtre.

Appendix 3

Transcription of the description of the Paris opera house ballroom from the *Mercure galant*, November (1727), 2512-2519.

BAL DE L'OPERA.

Description de la nouvelle Salle.

Le 11. de ce mois, Fête de S. Martin, il y eut à l'Opera le Bal public qu'on donne tous les ans à pareil jour, & qui continue tous les Dimanches jusqu'aux Avents. On le reprend ordinairement à la Fête des Rois, & on le donne pendant le Carnaval deux ou trois fois la semaine jusqu'au Carême. Il commence à onze heures du soir, & finit à six heures du matin. On a payé six livres à l'entrée de ce premier Bal. La Salle étoit parée d'une nouvelle décoration faite par M. Servandoni, habile Peintre Florentin, Auteur du superbe Palais de Ninus dans l'Opera de *Pirame & Thisbé*, dont on trouvera la description détaillée dans le Mercure d'Octobre de l'année derniere. Cette nouvelle décoration est ornée de glaces, dont quelques-unes sont très ingenieusement employées pour l'effet qu'elles doivent faire: & pour cela on les a élevées hors de vûë, afin qu'on ne puisse pas s'y mirer, & que les yeux puissent être trompez par leur moyen, en faisant paroître la Salle une fois aussi grande qu'elle est, par les objets opposez qui s'y repetent, soit en faisant paroître des lieux percez ou des enfoncemens & ouvertures en tous sens, où l'on ne croit voir que le vague de l'air; mais avant de décrire cette Salle, disons un mot de l'ancienne.

On sçait qu'on éleve le Parterre de l'Opera au niveau du Théâtre & de l'Amphit[h]éatre pour composer le plein-pied de la Salle du bal, qui avoit 86. pieds de long sur 23. de large. Elle se terminoit en ovale du côté des Loges; c'est encore de même aujourd'hui. Elle formoit un quarré étroit du côté du Théâtre, avec une alcove dans le fond, ou la Symphonie étoit placée. Sur les côtez on avoit peint des Loges avec des Masques & autres figures, pour imiter les Loges réelles qui se trouvoient sur la même ligne: cet endroit n'étoit point plafoné.

Dans la nouvelle disposition, M. Servandoni a trouvé le moyen de gagner 7. pieds sur la largeur & 12. sur la longueur, y compris le Salon demi-octogone qu'il a placé avec ménagement dans un espace de 24. pieds de large que lui laissoit le mur du fond.

La nouvelle Salle forme une espece de Galerie de 98. pieds de long, compris le demi-octogone, lequel par le moyen des glaces dont il est crusté, devient aux yeux un Salon octogone parfait. Tous les lustres, les bras & les girandoles se repetent dans ces glaces, ainsi que toute la Sale dont la longueur par ce moyen paroît doublée, de même que le nombre des Spectateurs.

Les glaces des côtés & vûës de profil, sont placées avec art & symétrie, selon l'ordre d'une Architecture composite, enrichie de differentes sortes de marbres, dont tous les ornemens sont de bronze doré.

La Sale ou Galerie peut être divisée en trois parties; la premiere contient le lieu que les Loges occupent; la seconde un Salon quarré, & la troisiéme le Salon demi-octogone, dont on vient de parler. Les Loges sont ornées de balustres avec des tapis des plus riches étoffes & des plus belles couleurs sur les appuis, en conservant l'accord necessaire entre ces ornemens & la peinture de l'ancien plafond qui regne au-dessus des Loges.

Deux buffets, un de chaque côté, séparent par le bas des Loges du Salon qui a 30. pieds en quarré sur 22. d'elevation, & terminé par un plafond ingenieux, orné de roses dorées, enfermées dans des lozanges, & entourées d'oves qui font une spece de bordure.

Deux Pilastres de relief sur leurs piédestaux, marquent l'entrée du Salon. On y vort [sic] un rideau réel d'une riche étoffe à frange d'or, relevée en feston. Ces Pilastres s'accouplent dans les angles, de même que dix-huit autres Pilastres canellés, peints sur les trois autres faces du Salon. Ils imitent la couleur du marbre de breche violete, ainsi que la frise. Leur dimension est de 13. pieds & demi, compris la base & le chapiteau. Leurs Piédestaux ont cinq pieds, compris les Socles; l'Architrave, Frise & Corniche [ont] trois pieds & demi. La grande corniche qui regne autour du Salon est de relief. Les Entrepilastres du côté des grandes arcades ont 12. pieds, & ceux du côté des petites arcades, quatre pieds & demi. Aux trois côtés du Salon il y a une grande arcade & deux petites. Celles qui sont à droite & à gauche, ont 14. pieds de haut, compris les balustres, sur 7. pieds & demi de large; elles sont soutenües par des colonnes couplées. Leurs arriere-pilastres qui soutiennent une corniche, ont 18. pouces; cette corniche sert d'imposte aux grandes arcades, & regne également sur les Salons quarré & octogone. Au-dessus s'éleve une Archivolte, ou l'on voit deux figures soutenant un Cartel. Au milieu de ces grandes arcades, il y a un groupe de quatre figures jouant de differens instrumens. Ces arcades où paroissent des glaces, sont ouvertes par des rideaux de velours cramoisi, brodés d'or & relevés avec des cordons qui en tombant servent à cacher le joint des glaces; ensorte qu'elle paroissent être d'une seule piece. Des festons de guirlandes, & d'autres ornemens produisent le même effet.

Le Salon quarré & le Salon octogone sont encore enrichis de 20. colonnes avec leurs arriere-pilastres de marbre bleu jaspé, ainsi que les 4. Pilastres du Salon demi-octogone. Six Satues dans le gout antique, representent Mercure & Momus dans le fond, & aux autres côtés quatre Muses peintes en marbre blanc & de grandeur naturelle, ainsi que les autres. Ces ouvrages sont de M. Charles Vanlo, & peints de très-bon goût.

Au milieu des grands pilastres couplés, excepté dans ceux des angles, est une Statuë qui pose sur un cul de lampe de bronze doré, placé sur le piédestal, des Pilastres; & au-dessus de la Statuë, il y a une girandole réelle de metal doré à cinq branches. Des festons de fleurs colorées sont attachés à ces piédestaux.

Les petites arcades sont aussi ouvertes, & ont 3. pieds huit pouces de large sur huit pieds de haut, compris les balustres qui portent un vase de bronze doré rempli de fleurs.

Au milieu de l'Archivolte il y a un Mascaron de bronze doré, avec un anneau dans la bouche, pour soutenir deux festons qui viennent s'attacher ensuite aux deux côtés de l'Imposte, & servent encore à cacher le joint des glaces. Au-dessus de la corniche qui sert d'Imposte aux grandes arcades, il y a des Génies de marbre blanc, appuyés sur une coquille de bronze, au-dessus de laquelle il y a un paneau de marbre bleu jaspé, avec des bordures d'ornemens de bronze doré; les deux côtéz à droit & à gauche sont semblables.

La grande Arcade au fond, où commence la troisiéme partie de la Galerie, a 16. pieds de haut sur 10. de large: deux Renommées y soutiennent les Armes du Roy en relief. Cette arcade sert d'entrée au Salon demi-octogone, dans lequel on monte par trois marches, & dont le plan est de niveau au bas des balustres, pour marquer la possibilité d'aller derriere les Arcades des côtés.

Dans le fond du demi-octogone on voit une pareille Arcade, excepté
que les arriere pilastres des colomnes [sic] qui soutiennent la corniche
servant d'Imposte, sont éloignés jusqu'au mur, & laissent ainsi un grand
vuide de chaque côté. Au-dessus de la corniche se trouve une ouverture
ovale. Dans les Angles du demi-octogone, il y a quatre Pilastres qui
soûtiennent un plafond très-orné. Entre ces Pilastres on a placé deux
portes, sur la corniche desquelles on voit deux enfans & un buste au
milieu, avec des festons de fleurs. Ces portes communiquent dans les
lieux que les glaces suspposent.

Vingt-deux lustres de crystaux, garnis chacun de 12. bougies,
descendent des trois plafons par des cordons & des houpes d'or & de
soye. 32. Bras portant des doubles bougies, sont placez dans l'entre-
deux des Pilastres qui soutiennent les Loges. Dix Girandoles de cinq
bougies chacune, sont placées sur les Pilastres couples du grand Salon;
& dans le Salon octogone, il y a sur chacun des Pilastres, une Girandole
à trois branches.

Trente Instrumens placez, quinze à chaque extrémité de la Sale,
composent la Symphonie pour le Bal; mais pendant une demie heure,
avant qu'il commence, ces Instrumens s'assemblent dans le Salon demi-
octogone, avec des Timbales & des Trompettes, & donnent un Concert
composé de grands Morceaux de Symphonie des meilleurs Maîtres.

Appendix 4

Daily attendance at the opera ball for complete seasons with surviving records.

The data from which the attendance figures have been calculated in each season has been compiled from the sources given after the year.

1756-57. *Bibliothèque-Musée de l'Opéra*, CO 5.

1. Thursday, 11 November	data lacking
2. Sunday, 14 November	133
3. Sunday, 21 November	279
4. Sunday, 9 January	98
5. Sunday, 16 January	189
6. Sunady, 23 January	326
7. Sunday, 30 January	492
8. Thursday, 3 February	98
9. Sunday, 6 February	587
10. Thursday, 10 February	210
11. Sunday, 13 February	992
12. Thursday, 17 February	1,462
13. Sunday, 20 February	569
14. Monday, 21 February	1,477
15. Mardi gras, 22 February	811

1757-58. *Archives Nationales*, AJ[13]-9, pièce 141.

1. Sunday, 13 November	219
2. Sunday, 20 November	236
3. Friday, 6 January	405
4. Sunday, 8 January	279
5. Thursday, 12 January	205
6. Sunday, 15 January	508
7. Thursday, 19 January	245
8. Sunday, 22 January	558
9. Thursday, 26 January	411
10. Sunday, 29 January	1,006
11. Thursday, 2 February	1,346
12. Sunday, 5 February	759
13. Monday, 6 February	1,649
14. Mardi gras, 7 February	940

1758-59. (as above)

1. Sunday, 12 November	288
2. Sunday, 19 November	272
3. Sunday, 26 November	367
4. Thursday, 30 November	300
5. Sunday, 7 January	416
6. Sunday, 14 January	343
7. Sunday, 21 January	337
8. Thursday, 25 January	66
9. Sunday, 28 January	433
10. Sunday, 4 February	487
11. Thursday, 8 February	147
[Sunday, 11 February—no ball: 'Mort de Mad. la Duchesse d'Orléans']	
12. Thursday, 15 February	204
13. Sunday, 18 February	863
14. Thursday, 22 February	1,309
15. Sunday, 25 February	453
16. Monday, 26 February	2,148
17. Mardi gras, 27 February	591

1759-60. (as above)

1. Sunday, 11 November	191
2. Sunday, 18 November	124
3. Sunday, 25 November	190
4. Sunday, 6 January	284
5. Sunday, 13 January	184
6. Sunday, 20 January	232
7. Sunday, 27 January	425
8. Sunday, 3 February	712
9. Thursday, 7 February	242
10. Sunday, 10 February	1,065
11. Thursday, 14 February	1,225
12. Sunday, 17 February	520
13. Monday, 18 February	1,477
14. Mardi gras, 19 February	765

1760-61. (as above)

1. Tuesday, 11 November	152
2. Sunday, 16 November	140
3. Sunday, 23 November	194
4. Tuesday, 6 January	269
5. Sunday, 11 January	318
6. Thursday, 15 January	155

7. Sunday, 18 January	545
8. Thursday, 22 January	225
9. Sunday, 25 January	782
10. Thursday, 29 January	1,215
11. Sunday, 1 February	data lacking
11. Monday, 2 February	1,389
12. Mardi gras, 3 February	890

1761-62. (as above)

1. Wednesday, 11 November	183
2. Sunday, 15 November	126
3. Sunday, 22 November	208
4. Wednesday, 6 January	249
5. Sunday, 10 January	230
6. Sunday, 17 January	308
7. Sunday, 24 January	426
8. Sunday, 31 January	468
9. Thursday, 4 February	107
10. Sunday, 7 February	453
11. Thursday, 11 February	148
12. Sunday, 14 February	672
13. Thursday, 18 February	834
14. Sunday, 21 February	390
15. Monday, 22 February	1,387
16. Mardi gras, 23 February	659

1762-63. (as above)

1. Thursday, 11 November	136
2. Sunday, 14 November	95
3. Sunday, 21 November	137
4. Friday, 6 January	202
5. Sunday, 9 January	148
6. Sunday, 16 January	232
7. Sunday, 23 January	370
8. Sunday, 30 January	496
9. Thursday, 3 February	285
10. Sunday, 6 February	775
11. Thursday, 10 February	1,194
12. Sunday, 13 February	585
13. Monday, 14 February	1,576
14. Mardi gras, 15 February	901

1764. (as above)

1. Thursday, 2 February	723
2. Sunday, 5 February	469
3. Thursday, 9 February	326
4. Sunday, 12 February	521
5. Thursday, 16 February	319
6. Sunday, 19 February	648
7. Thursday, 23 February	410
8. Sunday, 26 February	861
9. Thursday, 1 March	1,406
10. Sunday, 4 March	662
11. Monday, 5 March	2,070
12. Mardi gras, 6 March	949

1764-65. (as above)

1. Sunday, 11 November	224
2. Sunday, 18 November	211
3. Sunday, 25 November	324
4. Friday, 30 November	297
5. Sunday, 6 January	304
6. Sunday, 13 January	320
7. Sunday, 20 January	516
8. Sunday, 27 January	702
9. Thursday, 31 January	169
10. Sunday, 3 February	724
11. Thursday, 7 February	352
12. Sunday, 10 February	1,154
13. Thursday, 14 February	1,738
14. Sunday, 17 February	700
15. Monday gras, 18 February	1,973
16. Mardi gras, 19 February	867

1765-66. (as above)

1. Monday, 11 November	253
2. Sunday, 17 November	254
3. Sunday, 24 November	287
[Monday, 6 January—no ball: 'mort de M le Dauphin']	
4. Sunday, 12 January	112
5. Sunday, 19 January	283
6. Thursday, 23 January	95
7. Sunday, 26 January	402

9. Sunday, 2 February   668
10. Thursday, 6 February   1,249
11. Sunday, 9 February   559
12. Monday, 10 February   2,077
13. Mardi gras, 11 February   985

1766-67. (as above)
1. Tuesday, 11 November   278
2. Sunday, 16 November   251
3. Sunday, 23 November   354
4. Tuesday, 6 January   275
5. Sunday, 11 January   215
6. Sunday, 18 January   351
7. Sunday, 25 January   510
8. Monday, 2 February   628
9. Sunday, 8 February   762
10. Thursday, 12 February   308
11. Sunday, 15 February   895
12. Thursday, 19 February   432
13. Sunday, 22 February   1,256
14. Thursday, 26 February   1,842
15. Sunday, 1 March   938
16. Monday, 2 March   1,944
17. Mardi gras, 3 March   1,183

1769-70. (as above)
1. Sunday, 12 November   218
2. Sunday, 19 November   202
3. Sunday, 26 November   276
4. Thursday, 30 November   279
5. Sunday, 7 January   205
6. Sunday, 14 January   340
7. Sunday, 21 January   487
8. Sunday, 28 January   625
9. Sunday, 4 February   669
10. Thursday, 8 February   208
11. Sunday, 11 February   850
12. Thursday, 15 February   425
13. Sunday, 18 February   1,049
14. Thursday, 22 February   1,594
15. Sunday, 25 February   688
16. Monday, 26 February   1,913

17. Mardi gras, 27 February   927

1770-71. *Bibliothèque-Musée de l'Opéra*, CO 10
1. Sunday, 11 November   711
2. Sunday, 18 November   470
3. Sunday, 25 November   574
4. Friday, 30 November   551
5. Sunday, 6 January   470
6. Sunday, 13 January   376
7. Thursday, 17 January   174
8. Sunday, 20 January   514
9. Thursday, 24 January   295
10. Sunday, 27 January   771
11. Thursday, 31 January   541
12. Sunday, 3 February   1,111
13. Thursday, 7 February   1,890
14. Sunday, 10 February   714
15. Monday, 11 February   1,755
16. Mardi gras, 12 February   1,019

1775-76. *Archives Nationales*, AJ^{13}-9, pièce 2
1. Sunday, 12 November   250
2. Sunday, 19 November   309
3. Sunday, 26 November   375
4. Thursday, 30 November   360
5. Sunday, 7 January   345
6. Sunday, 14 January   338
7. Sunday, 21 January   359
8. Thursday, 25 January   123
9. Sunday, 28 January   281
10. Sunday, 4 February   693
11. Thursday, 8 February   535
12. Sunday, 11 February   1,263
13. Thursday, 15 February   3,252
14. Sunday, 18 February   924
15. Monday, 19 February   2,437
16. Mardi gras, 20 February   1,499

1785-86. *Archives Nationales*, O^{1}624-pièce 209
1. Sunday, 13 December   56
2. Sunday, 20 December   64
3. Friday, 6 January   134
4. Sunday, 8 January   98

5. Sunday, 15 January	172
6. Sunday, 22 January	174
7. Sunday, 29 January	202
8. Thursday, 2 February	78
9. Sunday, 5 February	197
10. Thursday, 9 February	104
11. Sunday, 12 February	330
12. Thursday, 16 February	189
13. Sunday, 19 February	584
14. Thursday, 23 February	97
15. Sunday, 26 February	831
16. Monday, 27 February	839
17. Mardi gras, 28 February	1,294

1786-1787. (as above)

1. Sunday, 12 December	41
2. Sunday, 19 December	61
3. Sunday, 26 December	34
4. Sunday, 7 January	79
5. Sunday, 14 January	66
6. Sunday, 21 January	94
7. Sunday, 28 January	94
8. Sunday, 4 February	215
9. Thursday, 8 February	97
10. Sunday, 11 February	422
11. Thursday, 15 February	1,173
12. Sunday, 18 February	875
13. Monday, 19 February	924
14. Mardi gras, 20 February	1,588

Appendix 5

Progression charts for the longways contredanse for sets of four, six, and eight couples.

These charts map the progression of couples in a longways contredanse. Each stage in this progression represents the performance of a complete set of the dance's figures and its accompanying music. The charts show how many iterations of the figures and music are required to allow the dance to run its course for both the 'standard procedure' outlined by Feuillet in 1706, and the abbreviated one permitted by Landrin after c1760. In the case of the latter, the contredanse is completed once couple A is once more at the top of the set.

Each couple is represented by a single letter. Each iteration of the dance's figures and accompanying music is indicated by a number. Every stage is graphically represented at two moments: its beginning (the lefthand column), and its conclusion (the righthand column). Downward and upward arrows along the lefthand columns indicate the repositioning a couple must make with each iteration. Downward arrows represent 'active' couples, upward arrows 'inactive.' Letters with no arrows indicate couples that do nothing at that stage in the dance.

Longways for 4 couples

1			2			3	
↘A	B		B	B		↘B	C
B↗	A		↘A	C		C↗	B
C	C		C↗	A		↘A	D
D	D		D	D		D↗	A

4			5			6	
C	C		↘C	D		D	D
↘B	D		D↗	C		↘C	A
D↗	B		↘B	A		A↗	C
A	A		A↗	B		B	B

7			8			9	
↘D	A		A	A		A	A
A↗	D		↘D	B		B	B
↘C	B		B↗	D		↘D	C
B↗	C		C	C		C↗	D

Longways for 6 couples

1			2			3	
↘A	B		B	B		↘B	C
B↗	A		↘A	C		C↗	B
C	C		C↗	A		↘A	D
D	D		D	D		D↗	A
E	E		E	E		E	E
F	F		F	F		F	F

4			5			6	
C	C		↘C	D		D	D
↘B	D		D↗	C		↘C	E
D↗	B		↘B	E		E↗	C
↘A	E		E↗	B		↘B	F
E↗	A		↘A	F		F↗	B
F	F		F↗	A		A	A

7			8			9	
↘D	E		E	E		↘E	F
E↗	D		↘D	F		F↗	E
↘C	F		F↗	D		↘D	A
F↗	C		↘C	A		A↗	D
↘B	A		A↗	C		↘C	B
A↗	B		B	B		B↗	C

10			11			12	
F	F		↘F	A		A	A
↘E	A		A↗	F		↘F	B
A↗	E		↘E	B		B↗	F
↘D	B		B↗	E		↘E	C
B↗	D		↘D	C		C↗	E
C	C		C↗	D		D	D

13			14			15	
A	A		A	A		A	A
B	B		B	B		B	B
↘F	C		C	C		C	C
C↗	F		↘F	D		D	D
↘E	D		D↗	F		↘F	E
D↗	E		E	E		E↗	F

Longways for 8 couples

	1			2			3	
↘A	B		B	B		↘B	C	
B↗	A		↘A	C		C↗	B	
C	C		C↗	A		↘A	D	
D	D		D	D		D↗	A	
E	E		E	E		E	E	
F	F		F	F		F	F	
G	G		G	G		G	G	
H	H		H	H		H	H	

	4			5			6	
C	C		↘C	D		D	D	
↘B	D		D↗	C		↘C	E	
D↗	B		↘B	E		E↗	C	
↘A	E		E↗	B		↘B	F	
E↗	A		↘A	F		F↗	B	
F	F		F↗	A		↘A	G	
G	G		G	G		G↗	A	
H	H		H	H		H	H	

	7			8			9	
↘D	E		E	E		↘E	F	
E↗	D		↘D	F		F↗	E	
↘C	F		F↗	D		↘D	G	
F↗	C		↘C	G		G↗	D	
↘B	G		G↗	C		↘C	H	
G↗	B		↘B	H		H↗	C	
↘A	H		H↗	B		↘B	A	
H↗	A		A	A		A↗	B	

	10			11			12	
F	F		↘F	G		G	G	
↘E	G		G↗	F		↘F	H	
G↗	E		↘E	H		H↗	F	
↘D	H		H↗	E		↘E	A	
H↗	D		↘D	A		A↗	E	
↘C	A		A↗	D		↘D	B	
A↗	C		↘C	B		B↗	D	
B	B		B↗	C		C	C	

Lonways for 8 couples (cont.)

13		14		15	
↘G	H	H	H	↘H	A
H↗	G	↘G	A	A↗	H
↘F	A	A↗	G	↘G	B
A↗	F	↘F	B	B↗	G
↘E	B	B↗	F	↘F	C
B↗	E	↘E	C	C↗	F
↘D	C	C↗	E	↘E	D
C↗	D	D	D	D↗	E

16		17		18	
A	A	A	A	A	A
↘H	B	B	B	B	B
B↗	H	↘H	C	C	C
↘G	C	C↗	H	↘H	D
C↗	G	↘G	D	D↗	H
↘F	D	D↗	G	↘G	E
D↗	F	↘F	E	E↗	G
E	E	E↗	F	F	F

19		20		21	
A	A	A	A	A	A
B	B	B	B	B	B
C	C	C	C	C	C
D	D	D	D	D	D
↘H	E	E	E	E	E
E↗	H	↘H	F	F	F
↘G	F	F↗	H	↘H	G
F↗	G	G	G	G↗	H

INDEX